THE LEADING WOMEN

Stories of the First Women Bishops
of The United Methodist Church

THE LEADING WOMEN

STORIES OF THE FIRST WOMEN BISHOPS
OF THE UNITED METHODIST CHURCH

—————— COMPILED BY ——————

JUDITH CRAIG

ABINGDON PRESS
Nashville

THE LEADING WOMEN
Stories of the First Women Bishops of The United Methodist Church

Copyright © 2004 by Abingdon Press

This book is printed on recycled, acid-free, elemental-chlorine–free paper.

Library of Congress Cataloging-in-Publication Data

The leading women: stories of the first women bishops of The United Methodist Church / compiled by Judith Craig.
    p.   cm.
ISBN 0-687-08838-0 (bdg. : pbk. : alk. paper)
1. Methodist Church—Bishops—Biography.   2. Women clergy—Biography.   I. Craig, Judith, 1937-

BX8493.L43 2004
287'.6'0922—dc22

2004002413

06 07 08 09 10 11 12 13—10 9 8 7 6 5
MANUFACTURED IN THE UNITED STATES OF AMERICA

CONTENTS

ACKNOWLEDGMENTS

No project like this book can be done by one person. Encouragement, instruction, and great improvement on my original submissions came from many directions and persons. How do I thank people such as my friends, Judy and Bill McCartney, who listened to me mutter and stew by the hour as I sat at a computer in our mutual lakeside home? How about my colleagues at Methodist Theological School in Ohio, who kept asking and urging, knowing themselves the work of publishing? President Ned DeWire of the seminary was determined this work should come to fruition and found ways to support me financially and emotionally. Through him, many individuals, whose names I do not know, made substantial contributions toward providing a stipend for me in these months. How do I say thank you?

Of course, this is really a gift of trust on the part of the women bishops of The United Methodist Church. Their gracious hospitality, both in terms of hosting me in their homes and trusting me to tell their stories, is the bedrock foundation of this, their offering. Our male colleagues in the Council of Bishops have also been eager and supportive inquirers after the progress of the work.

In addition, there was support from the coffers and staffs of The General Board of Higher Education and Ministry, The General Commission on the Status and Role of Women, and The General Commission on Archives and History. God's grace has been in all of these people.

I am thankful for my sister Jeanette who transcribed almost seventy-five hours of taped interviews. But most of all, I am thankful to have been born the child of Ray and Edna Craig, whose home and love have never failed to make me think I could do almost anything and have been the heritage paving the roadway of my life. To them I offer a private dedication and for them I thank God.

DEDICATION

*This book is dedicated
to Marjorie Swank Matthews, 1916–1985*

July 1980, Dayton, Ohio: In the waning hours of the North Central Jurisdictional Conference, the presiding officer received a motion from the floor: "I move Marjorie Swank Matthews and Emerson Colaw be elected to the episcopacy." A second, the vote, and the announcement, "Motion carries."

With those words, United Methodist church history changed forever. For the first time in postreformation history, a woman was elected to the office of Bishop in a major Protestant church. Diminutive Marjorie Swank Matthews, barely five feet tall, was almost carried by two escorting bishops to the platform of the North Central Jurisdictional Conference. It was late on Thursday afternoon, just hours before the Service of Consecration was to take place. Hearts pounded and huge sounds of elation soared. She stood before us, so small in stature, yet so huge in presence. The moment was like the gushing up of a new spring that would stream out into a great river of history.

Bishop Matthews served four years as Resident Bishop of the Wisconsin Area. She retired in 1984 and taught for a few months before suffering a recurrence of cancer and becoming ill. Brought back home to her native state of Michigan, she spent her last months in Clark Home, a United Methodist Retirement Center in Grand Rapids. There, she died on July 30, 1985. A great celebration of her life crowded her home church at Alma, Michigan. There were former parishioners from her years as a pastor beginning in 1959, those who had served under her leadership as District Superintendent from 1976 to 1980, and those across The United Methodist Church who experienced her as Bishop. Her son and grandson and those who knew her in years before her fame were there. More than a dozen bishops attended. They shared tears of thanksgiving for this tiny pioneer who had changed the course of Church history.

So many images of Bishop Matthews crowd the minds of those who knew her well. She was a scholar of the Bible, deeply schooled in the Wisdom literature, the field she taught at Florida Southern College in Lakeland, Florida, upon retirement. Some remember the moment that the Episcopal stole was placed around her neck at the Service of Consecration, and it was so long it curled up at her feet. Her height led her to quip: "Don't give me a crozier. It will make me look like Little Bo Peep." When introduced to the Clergywomen's Consultation in 1979 as a potential candidate, someone shouted, "Stand up, Marjorie!" "I am standing!" she replied. Though small in stature, she had an expansive mind and spirit. Her capabilities as church leader were never questioned. She was strong and firm when necessary, gentle and patient when appropriate, and always searching for the just and right.

To be the first is to carry unique and heavy burdens along with the thrill and wonder of making history. Marjorie was pulled in many directions; her presence was desired everywhere at once. Every move she made was under scrutiny by those who had doubts about women in the episcopacy. What she said was quoted and twisted, which is the case for most in leadership roles, but she was subject to extraordinary pressure from the press, from doubters in the Church, and from general naysayers. I hope she also knew the strong web of those who thanked God for her and held her in high esteem and deep prayer. An unnumbered community of spirit-sisters and spirit-brothers accompanied her unseen from place to place and throughout her life as Bishop. We continue to carry her with us as a mother, a forerunner, and a sign of encouragement.

So it is that the thirteen of us who are her legacy dedicate our stories to her and thank her for her courage and faithfulness that became the doorway through which we have been privileged to walk into the service she began as a woman who is a Bishop.

INTRODUCTION

SCENE I

The ten of us—all women bishops of The United Methodist Church—sat on the floor of a bed-and-breakfast living room in San Francisco in 1998. The stories were flowing freely, the laughter raucous, the tears frequent, and the sense of being sisters almost palpable. Somewhere in the midst of all that joy, an idea emerged: We are a set of significant stories. How could they be told in a way that others could hear or read them? Perhaps a writer could come and sit in our midst and listen to us. No, someone who has not lived this journey cannot hear us into being the same way as someone who has. Then came the fatal moment when someone turned toward me and said, "You're retiring. You do it."

In 2000, The United Methodist Church elected three more women to the office of Bishop. Now the number of living stories would be thirteen, having become larger than I ever imagined. During my first year of retirement, I thought about how crazy it was to accept that challenge. Somewhere in the midst of the second year, I thought again about how crazy it was. And by the middle of the third year, I was sure it was crazy. I was having a wonderful time, but the work was harder and more frightening than I had imagined it would be. I was dealing with stories of children and families that were appealing, but the trust of those stories was sometimes a burden. I was making headway, but the deadline was a fast-moving train pointed at my desk chair!

SCENE II

An explosion of applause rocked the room. Nothing slow and mounting—just sudden and sustained applause. Wave after wave it came, loud and long. After several minutes, the shouts started rising above the applause, loud and haunting in soprano and alto and high tenor. Then the whistles broke through the teeth of those who can make that wonderful piercing sound. And next came the tongues clapping out the high African sound of exultation and joy.

No bank of television cameras caught the mayhem of excitement. There was no bank of microphones and no pushy reporters with their pads squeezing in upon those who were the recipients of this spontaneous eruption of amazing excitement. It had not even been planned. Rather, it was one of those moments that just happened. We were all there—thirteen women bearing the title United Methodist Bishop and over a thousand women ordained to the ministry in The United Methodist Church.

Women laughed and women cried. Women put their hands together until they were red and stinging. We waved back, and we cried and looked at one another in wonder. The shouts, the whistles, the chants—it was a huge wave of emotion born of waiting a long time and hoping steadily set loose at the sight of thirteen women in robes standing across the stage. What mystery! What joy! What satisfaction! What humility! We felt all of that—and more.

That scene took place in 2001 on the opening night of the International Clergy Women's Consultation in San Diego. It was reminiscent of another scene in 1983, this time in New Mexico, where only about five hundred clergywomen gathered but raised the roof again with applause and shouting. This time, the focus of celebration was one diminutive woman named Marjorie Matthews, the first and only woman bishop of The United Methodist Church in 1983. Those of us who had been in New Mexico felt the connection in our bones and marveled that we now stood in her wake and felt her presence with us in the great cloud of witnesses surrounding the San Diego moment. She was our foremother, and we daughters were mindful of her pioneering as we received the welcome and affirmation of those clergywomen.

There had been other Consultations, and each time the number of women who wear the title Bishop increased. But this time—this time—thirteen! It was a picture not yet imagined. There we were—tall and short, black and white, young and not so young, active and retired—thirteen! I looked up and down the line and thought, *Where did we come from? Who are we? What kinds of little girls were we, and when did the stirrings start that led us to be found and claimed by the church for such a moment?*

BEGINNING

Once I had accepted the gift of compiling some parts of our life stories, the need to focus presented itself. I am not a historian or a skilled researcher and have never undertaken such a project before. Yet I was intrigued. The question that kept coming to me had to do with the formative influences in our childhoods and teen and young adult years. What happened to us? What kind of ethos formed us, made us emerge as leaders, be noticed by others, and have the courage to allow the Church to claim us?

Friends began to offer suggestions and good advice. Others undertook raising funds to underwrite some of the costs and pay a modest stipend through the time of writing. It was not long before I was so obligated to all of them that backing out was impossible. So I set out to uncover our stories.

From east to west, south to north, from city to country, from leisure village to working ranch, I visited the women of United Methodist episcopacy. I carried a tape recorder and started the conversation—Tell me about your family of origin—and sat back. No two oral histories were taken with the same specific set of questions, a procedure I have sometimes rued. However, the stories do carry the flavor of the respondents' memory patterns, and the stories are genuine and not forced. Some questions always emerged—about home and play and church and grandparents, about grade school and high school, about college and the first sense of call. But each woman had some particular story to tell that either transcended or cut across any categories I might have created.

The interviews netted pages and pages of transcript, conversational in tone and grammar, and full of the reports of laughter and asides. As I reread them, I could put myself back in the living room or the kitchen or the porch where the tapings took place. It was and is delicious material.

Then came the task of organizing and editing. I had in my possession personal stories. They were told in unguarded and trusting ways. How could I justify that trust and still do the work of a writer? Moments of deep personal sharing occurred during the times together and have not been brought forward to this book. They were gifts to me, and I am thankful for them. But I sense they are not essential to the stories and not ready to be told to a wider public. They remain hidden on the diskettes on which this material and its many stages of shaping now reside.

A great deal of editing was required to turn conversational sentence fragments and asides and turns and twists into coherent sentences and paragraphs that would read smoothly. That required the alteration of the exact words of the storytellers, the deletion of unnecessary words that violate written grammatical rules, and the reordering of the material so it flows in some semblance of progressive timelines. These are, then, more semi-quotes than exact quotations. They are the words of the women, but their words are filled out with bridge phrases and antecedent nouns that were not there in the oral flow.

When I had finally created a story that each woman had told, I thought I was beginning to get somewhere. Then a fatal decision: Let each sister see her transcript reformed and reshaped, and allow her to (1) correct any factual errors; (2) delete anything she absolutely did not want in print; and (3) add stories she thought were important but had not emerged in our conversations. The reactions were varied and put me back on my heels in some cases. Some accepted what I had produced with gratitude, a few minor corrections, and comfort. Others rewrote some sections and deleted a few things. But a few were not at all happy with what they saw. They offered major rewrites, which came back sounding like something written, not spoken. Major deletions of stories I thought important and illustrative puzzled me. Some asked for more time to do a complete rewrite. I was stunned. Seeing the narratives was apparently disquieting. But when I talked with some who had made major changes and secured agreement for reverting to the original in some cases, putting it all back in conversational language, the stories were again what I had heard.

These are not autobiographies in any sense of the word. What is contained here is a set of memories provoked by questions and conversation at a particular point in time. Each woman merits a full book and a longer story. The choice to stop at the point of finally reaching ordination is arbitrary. I am interested in our early years. These early stories are only a short foray into the rich mines of memory of formative events that helped us become who we are. There are other stories to be told of our experience as clergy, of the ordeal of being elected to the episcopacy, and, of course, the stories of our service and what this life work has brought into our lives—both joyful and not so joyful.

While I did reorder the material to make the stories flow better, there are times when they will seem disjointed, for the harkening back is part of the memory flow. I cannot overstate the importance of approaching these stories as partial memories. Each woman has mentioned to me wonderment about whether or not she remembered to tell this or that. It doesn't matter. The stories are placed in the frame of those lovely hours when they ushered me into their recollections. I never thought they would be "complete," but I knew they would be revelations of a larger story when read with any kind of intuition.

So I offer these stories with a hope for several outcomes. First, I want to make human and accessible some of the life stories of this extraordinary community of women who emerged in a specific role in the late-twentieth century for the first time in the history of The United Methodist Church. They are real people who grew up mostly in middle-class America in the middle of the twentieth century. Seeing them in their strength and poise as Bishops, it is not always easy to see behind them the families, the friends, the experiences of the girls they were, and are.

Second, I hope young women might find here encouragement for seeing their supposedly ordinary lives as capable of becoming extraordinary. To be sure, the limitations on women are much less prescribed now than they were in the decades when we were growing up. Yet, some reservations about what women should desire and aspire to still linger among both women and men. I hope that is less and less a truth. But if a young woman finds here the courage to aspire to something not yet thought to be within reach because she is a woman, the book will have been worthwhile.

Perhaps my most important hope is that those who have opportunity to nurture and encourage and provide opportunity for young women will recognize the power and possibility they may have to offer them. All of us can quickly name persons whose comments or encouragement or questions made all of the difference in the unfolding of our lives. I hope those who read this book will recognize with fresh clarity the importance of being a mentor. None of us would be telling this story without our mentors.

SOME THREADS TO TRACE

There is a commonality among the majority of this company of thirteen that merits further exploration. We are women who were finding our way during a very activist time in United States history. The Civil Rights Movement, the Vietnam War and its provocation of social consciousness, and the emergence of the Women's Movement all form the backdrop for our "coming of age." I continue to wonder if we would have become women with such keen social consciousness, such tenacity regarding matters of justice and rights for all people, or found our voice as leaders to carry the tone of those convictions so clearly had we not been invited into those rivers of turmoil and change. It is a truism that we are shaped by the history through which we live. This company lived through times of extraordinary social change, and we have become change agents extraordinaire.

To be sure, the older four or five of us knew teen years in a much quieter culture—that comfortable time of the 1950s when life was pretty secure. We were already beginning to play young adult roles by the time the strong currents of social reformation swept across the streams of our lives. Yet we were in places and circumstances that caught the edge of our garments, began to seep into our beings, and pulled us from the edges into the swirling waters. We have some memory of World War II, which lingers with us, as well as some of the Depression-era consciousness of our parents.

Yet, despite the age differences—some teens and college students in the 1940s and 1950s, the others teens and college students in the 1960s—we are a generation in the life of the Church. We are those who followed the pioneer woman who broke open the episcopacy in The United Methodist Church with her election in 1980. We are, in truth, fourteen. This book is built around oral histories and

16

memories of the living. But all through our stories as Episcopal leaders runs the thread of our foremother, Marjorie Matthews.

The original thought was to include the stories of the women elected to the episcopacy from the generation between 1980 and 1996. Those elected in 2000 would seem to have been formed in a church changed by the previous twenty years. Though true, the stunning gift of the election of three women of color to the episcopacy in one summer made their inclusion an offering not to be refused. Hence, the stories included here number thirteen—that of the living women bishops. The memory of our sister, Bishop Marjorie Matthews, cheers us on from the Great Cloud of Witnesses.

FLASHBACK

I keep seeing the ten of us in San Francisco, amazed at our individuality and bound so tightly by our common experience as bishops. We were all incredulous to some degree of the office we hold, to which we had been elected and for which consecrated. How did the Church find us? Who shaped us? Those questions and our musings have continued to shape this writing.

I keep hearing that thundering demonstration of joy in San Diego, and the questions rush to my mind again: *Why us? How did we arrive here? Who made this happen?*

Of course, we can all say the Holy Spirit is a significant actor. No quarrels there. But who were the instruments of that Spirit's employment, and what were the circumstances under which that Spirit offered guidance or a twist or turn in the journey?

Every woman is a great story (whether she is a bishop or not!), but all of those stories cannot be told in their entirety in one book. So here are some images, some peeks, some teasers from the early years of life up through the times of calls and ordinations. The years beyond ordination and the years since consecration await some other soul to undertake. This book seeks to answer: who were these little girls, these young women, whom the Church claimed as bishops in the late-twentieth century?

Sharon Ann Brown Christopher

Meeting Sharon in her home is to meet Sharon in her sacred space. The walls are free of pictures and painted a soft white. The furniture is modest and muted. There is a sense of calm and order all around—her monastic side evidenced in the space Charles and she created for her to come home to after the hectic days of episcopacy.

I am the first child, the eldest of the three children of Mavis and Fred Brown. I was born in the middle of World War II. Seventeen months after I was born, my brother, Fred, was born, and then five and a half years after I was born, Jana was born.

My dad was a chemist at a petrol-chemical refinery in Corpus Christi, Texas, that converted oil to gasoline for use in warplanes. My mom was a schoolteacher but stopped teaching for a while to tend to her children until they were school age. When the youngest of the three of us started school, my mom started back to school, too, as a teacher. She was an English teacher in the junior high I attended. Then she became Language Arts Consultant for the seventh through twelfth grades in the Corpus Christi Independent School District. She retired from that position when she reached retirement age.

Both sets of grandparents were highly involved in Sharon's early life. Though she claims not to know much about their history, their presence was evident, and she remembers them fondly.

My grandfather, my mom's dad, Leo Kreuger, whom we called Paw Paw, came by boat from Germany when he was two years old. We suspect he was one of the Germans who landed on the Texas coast at Galveston. It was supposedly a dangerous place to come ashore. My mom's mother, Mamie Pearl Weaver, whom we called Toppie, came to Texas from North Carolina. My dad's family migrated across the South. I have been told that my great, great-grandfather, Franklin Brown, was a medical doctor and a minister and my great-uncle, Pressley Brown, was also a minister. I did not learn of them until after I was ordained.

My mom's father farmed for a while. In the middle of the Depression, when my mom graduated from high school, her dad left the farm and moved his family to San Marcos, Texas, so that my mom and my aunt, Alice, could go to college. His taking care of his daughters in that way exhibited a commitment to the education of women that wasn't common at that particular point in history. My mom finished her college education in three years and then worked so she could also help her sister complete her college education. I don't have the slightest idea where Paw Paw got his vision about education for women. He himself was not college educated. Neither was my grandmother. But they were adventurous people. They eloped when they got married.

We visited Toppie and Paw Paw often during our growing-up years. In fact, my first night away from home was spent at their house. They would take us fishing, play games with us, and load us up in the car for Sunday afternoon drives and picnics.

Toppie always fixed our favorite foods when we visited her. That's one way she demonstrated her love for me. She knew I loved gumbo, and so when I'd visit, she'd make it. For a while, Paw Paw worked in a hardware store, and he'd let us come down to the store and play in the bins of nails and with the other little gadgets sold there. They lived next to a lumberyard. So we played in the lumberyard, too.

My dad's parents farmed in Mathis, Texas. We'd visit there often. I grew up playing on the farm. I'd pick cotton when the cotton was ripe. I remember one time I filled a gunny sack full, about twelve or thirteen pounds of cotton, and really thought I'd accomplished something. I gathered eggs, learned to milk cows, and played in the grain after Granddaddy had harvested it.

Granddaddy had a wry sense of humor. He was always teasing us. I didn't know Grandmama as well. She developed dementia when I was in high school. Consequently, she was not with us mentally for a long time. As a young child, I remember her as a warm, loving presence. I still have an image of her churning milk to make butter and wringing chickens' necks.

She attributes to her grandmother the arranging of the great feasts at the family table. The valuing of that table is still central in the Brown family and on into the Christopher household.

Grandmama was the keeper of the Brown table. She was the one, when the family got together, who would put us around the family table. When the whole family was there for high holy days, she would attach a card table so that the children could eat with the adults. That table time was really important. A lot of family storytelling took place around the dinner table. We laughed a lot at that table.

Listening to Sharon speak of her childhood, one senses a tremendous sense of appreciation and comfort with the memories. She speaks of security rising out of those family relationships.

All of my family members were loving, caring people, and I had a real sense of being surrounded by a whole host of people who really cared about me. I don't know if I realized it at the time, but when I look back on it, home was a place where I knew I was loved and accepted. I knew that. I was taught that the universe was a trustworthy place. I was taught this not by words, but by the fact that home was stable and secure. It wasn't idealistic. We had our arguments, spats, and disagreements. My brother was only seventeen months younger than I was, so though he and I had a wonderful childhood relationship, we also were sibling rivals. All in all, home was a very caring place.

From the beginning, church was a place of involvement for all of the family. It was a place for worship and learning and became the place where music was central.

Church was really the fulcrum for our family. My dad sang tenor in the church choir, so when we sat in church, he never sat with us. We built a new church building when I was in the sixth or seventh grade. But the first building was one of those old buildings with a balcony in the sanctuary. My mom, brother, sister, and I sat in the balcony. My dad was in the choir loft, down on the main floor of the sanctuary.

My dad, through his singing in the choir, gave me the gift of the psalms. We would learn his tenor parts with him at home, where he would practice. He often sang solos, so we learned the solo parts and would threaten to stand up and sing them with him at church. We knew all of the tenor solos he sang.

We were formed as a family in church. We were formed not only through worship participation, but also through participation in potluck meals and Sunday school. As we got older, we participated in Methodist Youth Fellowship on Sunday afternoons. My family would worship together again on Sunday evenings. During the evening services, the lights would be turned down and we were invited to pray at the altar. Our family prayed together at the altar at those Sunday night services.

The world in which the Browns lived was not confined to south Texas. It was in church that Sharon's boundaries and awareness began to stretch.

I think it was when I was in junior high that our vacation church school class collected money for the migrant workers who worked in the fields of south Texas. I was chosen to deliver the things we bought with the money. That's when I first saw housing with dirt floors, no running water, and no electricity. I began to be aware that some people lived in a world quite different from my own.

My home church supported a couple who were missionaries to Cochabamba, Bolivia, and I tithed part of my allowance to their mission. They would come to our church when they were on furlough, and we'd go hear them. That couple expanded my boundaries. About that time, I read about Albert Schweitzer, the missionary in Africa. I admired him so much and wanted to be like him.

In high school, our conference took a group of youth to Bolivia. I wanted to go so badly, but I wasn't chosen. Oh, I cried and cried because I wanted to go to South America as a missionary. I was so disappointed.

There is an interesting side story about the missionary couple. One year in the 1980s, when I was on the General Board of Global

Ministries, I was sitting in a Greenwich Village restaurant with some Global Ministries people. A staff member was sitting next to me. As we talked about her childhood, I learned that she grew up in Cochabamba, Bolivia. I asked if by any chance she knew this missionary couple. And she said, "They saved my life. I was literally in the gutter of the street one day when they walked by, saw me, and got me help. I probably have my life today because of them." And I said, "My tithe on my allowance as a child [ten cents out of my dollar] went to their mission work." Isn't that a wonderful story? My tithe as a child in south Texas was contributing to the life of a woman who eventually became a staff person with the General Board of Global Ministries and who is now serving as a missionary in Cochabamba, Bolivia. It demonstrates the power of our Christian and United Methodist connection.

And again, the table—the all-important table.

We came together as a family not only at church, but also at the meal table. We ate breakfast and supper together almost every day. The meal table still integrates our family. Our mom still feeds us our favorite foods when we go home. To this day, she'll buy shrimp for me and make noodles with beef tips for Fred and Mexican food for all of us.

Our mom and dad fed us in many ways. My family formed me in faith. My parents exhibited faithfulness in ways that weren't necessarily talked about. We were not a pious family, and we didn't talk much about faith. We said grace at meals and participated in the life of the Christian community. But we didn't talk about our faith much. It was something we did and were rather than something we talked about.

The Brown family laughs a lot when we get together. June, our aunt, often initiated the funny business. She lived with us for the first five years of my life. She has a great sense of humor and was always up to something prankish. Jana, my sister, now plays that role. We're always laughing when we're together. My dad's brother was funny. And my mom's sister has a great sense of humor.

When Sharon tells her story, it almost always includes "the tree."

There was a sycamore tree in the front yard of the house where I grew up. It was an excellent climbing tree. It had low branches that we could swing on, but we could also pull ourselves up into the

23

tree and climb almost to the top. At some time in my childhood, the top of that tree became a retreat place. I would crawl up to the top of the tree where I could hide from everybody. The leaves would cover me up.

I took an old belt of my dad's up the tree with me. I tied it around the trunk of the tree and put pencils between the trunk and belt. Then I took an old autograph book, and I wrapped it in waxed paper. That was before aluminum foil or baggies. So I wrapped it in waxed paper and attached it between belt and the trunk. I would climb up in the top of that tree and think about my life and write in that little autograph book. It was my first journal. I'd think about what I was going to be when I grew up. I wrote about being a missionary. In fact, I still have that old autograph book. Of course, I never thought about being a pastor. I'd just reflect on my life and take a few notes. It was my monk cell.

This is not an indication that Sharon was a loner. She was appreciative of silence and space, however.

I don't remember spending a lot of time alone as a child. I shared a room with my sister, so I didn't have any personal space that was just my own, except my bed. But there were places like the tree. There would be silent times in worship and retreat times at church camp. Both the conference and our congregation's camp really honored silence and time alone. I would go off in those settings and have time by myself. I liked it a lot.

One place I was alone was on the organ bench and at the piano. I'd go into the sanctuary and practice. I'd be there all by myself. Practicing the piano at home was another time alone although there were other people around. Reading also created a quiet, alone space for me.

Sharon has a deep and abiding gratitude for the way congregational life in First United Methodist Church in Corpus Christi shaped her.

I really appreciate the role my home congregation played in forming me in faith. It was a loving community; the members cared about me. We were not focused on matters about the church or about the faith as much as we were focused on relationships and the practices of the faith. In that Christian community I learned John Wesley's spiritual disciplines without ever knowing they were Wesley's general rules. I learned to pray, contemplate scripture, worship, and participate in Christian conversation. The Lord's Supper was very important. I was formed in faith by hymnody—both singing the hymns and playing them on the piano. One hymn we sang in our youth group was "Dare to Be Brave." It went like this: "Dare to be brave; dare to be true. Strive for the right, for the Lord is with you." We sang it as if our lives depended on it. They probably did. I developed a real sense that I was on a journey of living with God and that it was radical, countercultural, and life giving. I learned that I could stand strong in the midst of whatever might come my way.

Worship was an important part of life. As I have said, we went to worship every Sunday morning and evening. In that worship was a lot of singing. I loved the singing. And in that worship was prayer. Worship provided a quiet place for the whole community.

Several years ago, on behalf of the Council of Bishops, I attended the Oxford Institute in Oxford, England. Once every five years Wesleyan scholars and others from around the world gather to examine aspects of Wesley's life and theology. After I had been immersed in Wesley for several days, I realized that all that was being talked about described who I am. I realized that without its being named Wesleyan, I have been formed in my home church by the Wesleyan ethos.

It is interesting that I haven't talked much about pastors in my formation. Part of it was because my root congregation was a large church, and I didn't have personal relationships with the senior pastors. However, I was strongly shaped by preaching. I knew some of the associate pastors personally. I was shaped significantly by a woman who spent one year at our church as a youth director. In her I saw for the first time a woman engaged in a full-time ministry within the church. She became a role model for me.

School was a place of high achievement and good relationships—once she got going!

I had no memory of this, but my mom recently told me that when I was in the first grade, I didn't want to go to school. She investigated and found out that I was bored because I already knew how to do what was being taught. I learned to read before I went to school. But school soon became an enjoyable place. I remember my first- and second-grade teacher was a warm and caring person. I remember school as a good place. Throughout my schooling, I participated in a lot of extracurricular activities.

Trustworthy adults surrounded Sharon, giving her a sense of security even in her introversion.

I had adults in my life who were trustworthy. And they deemed me trustworthy. They had confidence in me and believed I could do whatever they put before me. They helped me understand that the unknown was not threatening, but simply the open door to my next step. I had adults always placing before me the next step of what I needed to do in order to grow. They invited me to come out, to come forward. I was a shy child. In my kindergarten class photograph, I was the only child looking down at the ground. I was too shy to look at the camera. When my parents asked me what I was looking at with my eyes cast to the ground, my reply was, "Ants." I was also very quiet. I didn't speak much in group discussions. I listened. I heard. I processed. I learned. I was very much present.

Scholarship was important, but friends were always present.

I had a close-knit group of friends, and we did lots of things together. Most of them were girls, though there were some boys I considered friends. We were a group of five girls who hung out together and moved around to one another's houses. While we had a good time together, we were serious about learning. We studied together.

I had two sets of friends in high school—my school friends and my church friends. The people I went to church with went to Ray High School. I went to Miller High School. Earlier, in junior high, I decided I wasn't going to MYF, because I didn't have a place there. I felt left out. There were several junior high schools represented in our youth group, and I was the only one from my junior high. One Sunday afternoon, because I felt left out, I decided I wasn't going to MYF anymore. However, my mom decided I was going. We argued about it. I cried and cried. I must admit that knowing I couldn't go to MYF with puffy, red eyes, I cried all the more. I was tenacious. Although I did not attend MYF the day of the argument, in a few weeks I was back in the youth group and made lasting friendships. My mom lost the battle but won the war. Having two sets of friends was a blessing.

Having her mother as a teacher was a treat for Sharon, though there were moments of dismay.

I had my mom as a teacher all three years of junior high. Before I began seventh grade, she sat me down at the kitchen table and she said, "Sharon, we have a decision to make." All the students who already knew how to read music were in band together and were taught English by my mother. The students who didn't know how to read music were taught English by another teacher. I had studied music many years so my mom and I worked it out. She would teach me English.

For the first nine weeks or so, I was anonymous in my mom's English class. One day, however, I was so excited about the topic being discussed, I shouted out, "Mama!" as I raised my hand. Everybody turned around and stared. I had blown my cover. When others asked me what grades she gave me, I replied, "She gives me the same grade all my other teachers give me."

As my English teacher, my mom gave me the gifts of poetry and literature—especially Edgar Allan Poe and Robert Frost—and helped me discover the joy of learning. She also taught me how to edit a school newspaper. Oh, it was wonderful!

My family took learning seriously. I took learning seriously. To this day, my mom is a learner, and so am I. I trust I will be until the day I die. The Brown family enjoyed learning together. I loved most of my classes. Music was important, and I had other loves. I loved English literature and read voraciously. I also enjoyed history and biology.

Not all academic pursuits were equally pleasurable. There were struggles.

I hated eighth-grade algebra. I couldn't understand algebra. My dad would work with me at the kitchen table. He'd try to help me understand. But I couldn't get it and would be frustrated and start to cry. He'd say, "Now, Sharon, if you'd just quit crying, maybe you can understand this." I made an A in algebra, but it was only because of the patience of my dad. *He* made the A in algebra. He deserved it. It was terrible. My dad saved me.

I also struggled with chemistry in college. Since my dad was a chemist, I was a bit embarrassed by my "chemical imbalance." We were assigned many experiments, and we'd go to the lab on our own time to do them. In their carelessness, the students would contaminate the reagent bottles, so it was hard to get accurate results. In addition, I just was not fascinated by chemical equations and anything connected with chemistry. When mid-term came around, I was averaging a C in chemistry. I was not accustomed to Cs.

Trying to figure out how to solve the dilemma, I thought, "I don't know chemistry, but I do have a good memory." When my chemistry professor gave us a practice exam and told us the final exam would be the same test with different numbers, I was relieved. I memorized how to do each problem. I didn't understand the problems, but I memorized how to do them. True to his word, the professor gave us a final exam that paralleled the sample test. I made an A+ on the final. I came out of that class with a B+. I enjoyed most of my classes—except algebra.

Music was very important in high school. It became a major outlet and involvement.

I played clarinet in the band all three years of junior high. I played first chair. I worked hard. I was the second-chair clarinet in the All-City Band. We were a marching band and performed at our junior high football games and in the parades of Corpus Christi. Our band director took us to a contest every spring and expected us to get the top score. We always did. In high school, I gave up band and accompanied the high school choir.

During my first year in high school I played on the school tennis team. Lois Rhea, who was the choir director, came to the tennis court one day and said, "Sharon, I want you to come to the choir room and audition to accompany the choir." Well, I knew I couldn't play well enough to do that. So, I said, "Okay," and returned to my tennis game. The next week, Mrs. Rhea returned to the tennis court since I had never shown up at the choir room. She said, "I really want you to come audition." I didn't. I knew I didn't have the ability to do what she expected. She came back the next week and said, "You're coming with me right now, and you're going to audition to accompany the high school choir." I laid down my tennis racquet and went with her to the choir room where I played a few things at her request. She then said, "I want you to accompany the choir next year."

Every time I thought I couldn't play something, she showed me I could. In front of the whole choir, she would put new music on the piano and ask me to play it. I would look at it for a second and then play it, sight unseen. In addition to accompanying the choir, I also accompanied forty or so classmates for solos at all of the spring contests.

Mrs. Rhea wasn't through with Sharon Brown. The pushing continued.

She just pushed me and pushed me. And I kept measuring up—most of the time. Since she was our church organist, she also taught me to play the pipe organ. Once when I was a junior in high school, I played the organ for the primary worship service for First United Methodist Church in Corpus Christi, my home church. The church had more than three thousand members . We had a huge sanctuary and big pipe organ.

What an empowering event this was in my life! I knew I didn't have the ability to play for such a service, and yet I did it. I'll never forget the moment. I played the prelude and survived. As I started playing the first hymn, the congregation stood up and the choir started moving down the center aisle—in rhythm with the music! The choir kept coming down the aisle, and the congregation kept standing and singing. In that moment, I discovered a personal power I didn't know I had. Mrs. Rhea asked more of me than I had previously done and more than I thought I could do, and, in so doing I was empowered.

This busy, happy, talented teenager was blessed with a mother full of lessons. What's more, she can draw straight-line applications of those lessons.

In the seventh grade, I was elected "most likely to succeed." Even my classmates recognized my firstborn inclinations. I have come to believe that class favorites are too big of a burden for such an age. But through the class-favorite process, my mom taught me an important lesson. She happened to be one of the faculty members responsible for counting the votes, so she knew who had won. The school policy was to announce the favorites at a school dance in front of the whole school. Rather than telling me the results, my mom prepared me both to win and to lose. She helped me think through what I would do if I won and what I would do if I lost. It was a big responsibility for a seventh grader to handle, but my mom prepared me to handle it. What a gift she gave me.

In that process I learned about graciousness. I also learned about faithfulness. This experience helped me learn that the source of my significance lies not in winning or losing, but ultimately in something bigger—my relationship with God. This was my first lesson that the meaning of life is not lodged in achievement.

I remember the morning I woke up at the North Central Jurisdictional Conference, the day on which I was elected a bishop. I knew that by the end of that day, I would either be returning to Wisconsin to serve as assistant to the bishop, or be elected to serve as a bishop and assigned to live somewhere I had never lived before. As I lay in bed that morning, I thought, "Either one's fine." I remembered my mom's class-favorite lesson. I knew my significance wasn't tied up in the election process or in being a bishop. I knew either option before me would be filled with new life. I carried peace in my heart throughout that turbulent day.

Sharon had some other heroes and heroines who inspired her.

Althea Gibson was a heroine. She played tennis and came to Corpus Christi to play an exhibition match. I wanted to be like her. Then there was Shirley Chisholm, a member of the House of Representatives of the United States Congress. A woman! I had a poster of her with the words "Unbought and unbossed" on it. Albert Schweitzer was a hero as were Clara Barton and Abraham Lincoln.

Being such an achiever and so well accomplished in many ways, it is not surprising that vocational musings were important, also. She thought about it a great deal—what should she be and do?

All of my childhood, as I thought about what I was going to be when I grew up, I focused on music—church organist or a teacher of music. Given my discomfort with recitals, I did not entertain the notion of performance. Then in high school, as I thought about a college major, I sensed a tug toward the church. Remember, I had encountered that Christian education earlier, and I had been a part of a lifelong faith-forming process in the church. When I was a senior, I decided to major in religion. I announced it first to Mrs. Rhea when she and I were sitting at the organ console at the church. She had been grooming me to be a musician for several years. She slammed the books closed and stomped out of the room. One of my mentors had rejected my decision. It was painful. We continued to work together, however. A number of years later, I got a letter from her affirming my decision.

I had gone to the conference camp, Mount Wesley, every summer since the seventh grade. Those camp experiences were key to my spiritual and vocational formation. At camp, we were asked the vocation question frequently. It was at Mount Wesley that I gave my life to God as revealed in Jesus. And it was at Mount Wesley that I chose a Christian vocation. I signed a commitment card and took it to the altar as an offering to God. I indicated on the card that God was calling me to Christian vocation. I wasn't specific. I think I checked missionary, Christian education director, and organist. (Ordination wasn't a viable option for women at that time.) This commitment came after an evening of silence, which began at vesper point and a morning hike up the hill.

At Mount Wesley I continued to learn Wesley's spiritual disciplines. The observance of vespers and morning watch were part of the discipline. Bible study was a camp discipline. And then there was prayer. Prayer was really real at Mount Wesley. God seemed so close. And Communion, oh, the Eucharist. It was incredible!

That experience was major. But it had turned her from what had been her assumed direction—music. Her parents were the probing, supportive instruments of being tested about her decision.

Because I had done so many musical things as a child and youth, I think my parents assumed music would form my vocation. And my dad always said, "A teaching certificate is insurance." However, I lived in a parental environment that was open to surprise. I could count on my parents asking me important, clarifying questions and ultimately supporting me in whatever vocation I chose. After I had decided to walk the path of Christian education, my dad told me, "You know, when I was in MYF as a youth, I thought about being a minister." When he learned of my ordination decision, he reminded me of his youthful thoughts about ministry and said, "Now, my daughter's going to be a minister." My parents, brother, and sister were present for my episcopal consecration. It was a dramatic act of love and support since my dad was seriously ill at the time.

Many people fingerprinted young Sharon Brown, and she is quick to give credit and express gratitude.

There was a community of adults in that congregation—too many to name individually but whose names I do remember—who cared for its children and youth and brought us to new depths of faithfulness. After I was elected to the episcopacy, I returned to preach at my home church. As I walked up into the pulpit, I looked down, and there on the first two rows were many of the adults who had formed me—Sunday school teachers, youth counselors, vacation Bible school leaders. My first response was surprise. At the time they taught me, when I was a child and youth, I thought they were, well, old, and here they were! After the worship service, one of them cornered me in the hall, pointed her finger in my face, and said, "Sharon, you may have left us, but we have never left you. We pray for you every day."

Corpus Christi was a segregated town with a large Hispanic population, a large Anglo population, and a smaller population of African Americans. Sharon's attendance at the more integrated high school was, in her mind, of crucial importance in terms of forming sensitivity to racial issues. It was at school, not at church, that she learned these lessons.

There was racial diversity and racial tension in my high school. At football pep rallies, the Anglo kids sat on one side of the gym and the Latino kids sat on the other. However, the school choir was a setting where we all came together. We sang together. But we not only sang together, we also were a number-one rated choir. There was an esprit de corps, a sense of team. We worked for a common goal that transcended our differences.

The firstborn achiever reached the end of high school fifth in her class of 456. Now it was off to college to major in religion.

I went to Southwestern University in Georgetown, Texas, where I worked toward a B.A. in religion with a minor in psychology. The small campus provided me a setting in which I could focus on academics and form close friendships. In my senior year, I felt nudged to go to seminary for a master's degree in Christian education.

While there were several professors at Southwestern who significantly shaped my life, there are two who stand out in my memory. Dr. Douglas Hooker, my psychology professor, opened me to myself, setting me on a path of growing self-awareness. Dr.

Norman Spellmann, my religion professor, deepened and broadened my knowledge of the church and faith formation methodologies.

Gender bias was a part of the culture at that time in history and on the Southwestern campus. One of my history professors called me into his office one day to discourage me from pursuing a major in religion. He indicated such pursuit was a waste of my time. Another professor discouraged me from attending seminary, indicating that I would probably marry soon, have children, and therefore not be able to use such a degree.

I was on the college campus during the Vietnam War. My male classmates were making decisions about the draft. There was the Cuban missile crisis. President Kennedy was assassinated during my sophomore year. This out-of-the-mainstream, small campus provided a place of stability for me during those rocky times.

She did not work for a church while in school, but did spend some summers in work related to her chosen vocation.

During the summers of my college and seminary days, I worked in church-related situations. While in college, I worked as a youth director for two summers in the Methodist church in a little town called Kennedy, Texas. I received more from the youth, the congregation, and the pastor than I could have possibly given them.

During a summer while I was in seminary, I was the song director at the Southwest Texas Conference camp, Mount Wesley, where I had been a camper as a youth. Those were the days when campers sang camp songs. And every camp song you have ever heard I knew and led. Although I couldn't sing very well, I could carry a tune. I remember one week of camp when I had to vie for the attention of the campers with the crickets that had arrived by the droves and were jumping all around and over the campers. What trials and tribulations—and what fun!

Ever the student, she was beckoned by seminary.

Despite the discouraging words from some of my college professors, I decided that I did feel beckoned to seminary. I applied at Garrett Evangelical, Union, and Perkins. I chose Perkins, in part because of the attractive scholarship they offered, but mainly for their offerings and faculty. During my second year there, I decided to stay a third year for what was then a Bachelor of Divinity degree.

But during that time, I never considered ordination. It was completely off my radar screen and off the radar screen of our culture and even the Church. I had not met an ordained woman.

Seminary was a stimulating time for me. While I was in seminary, Martin Luther King Jr. and Senator Robert Kennedy were assassinated. The Southern Methodist University African American students took over the law building. We seminary students were integrating lunch counters and driving poor African Americans to pay their poll tax and vote. The seminary curriculum was open, allowing us to select almost all of the courses we took. All kinds of experimentation in worship took place. Even though we single women students were not provided housing on campus, we found our voice. (A faculty comment written at the bottom of the first paper I wrote in my Kierkegaard class was, "You *can* think intelligently!)"

At Perkins I had Dr. Bill Power in Old Testament, and he opened the Hebrew scriptures for me. I went to seminary thinking I didn't have much use for Old Testament. Then I studied the Pentateuch with Dr. Power, and the scriptures were transformed before my eyes. I would leave class crying tears of joy on some days. I studied the epistles with Dr. Victor Furnish and John Wesley with Dr. Albert Outler. Oh, I wish I had appreciated Dr. Outler then the way I now do. Dr. Schubert Ogden and Dr. John Deschner taught systematic theology together. Their point/counterpoint methodology created a great context for the writing of my own credo. I was stretched and pushed and challenged. Seminary was a rich experience that led me to grow in incredible ways.

I took very few Christian education courses even though I intended to get a degree in Christian education. My decision to stay a third year was not oriented toward ordination. Rather, I simply wanted a full seminary experience that a third year could provide.

Reflecting on her call, Sharon sees a series of turning points that issued out in finally recognizing what God desires of her.

Looking back, I realize my call to ordained ministry evolved through a series of decision points—a decision to major in religion rather than in music, a decision to go to seminary, a decision to seek a B.D. degree rather than an M.R.E., a decision to stay in seminary for a third year. I was being led in a countercultural direction that required, I guess, a journey in stages.

It was only after I got to Appleton, Wisconsin, and was working as a director of Christian education, that I began to hear a call to ordained ministry. It was in 1969. Our country was divided into Hawks and Doves. Racial integration was controversial. Women were waking up. Betty Friedan, Germaine Greer, Gloria Steinem were angry and were writing, and I was reading.

I loaded up my car with all of my worldly possessions and drove by myself to Appleton for my first job after seminary. Being a director of Christian education felt so safe, so expected of me by others. Ordination? Controversial! Bucking the norm! Stepping outside the box! Tampering with the sacred symbols of the Church! I wasn't sure I wanted to be a member of this men's club called the order of Elder. I preached my first sermon that year. I was the first woman I had ever heard preach.

I talked and prayed with the male pastors on the staff of the church I served and with those in other churches in Appleton. They became a supporting network that helped me open my ears to the voice of God and keep them open when those around me were encouraging me to live within the cultural expectations. They stood by me when church members spoke against a license to preach for me because Paul told women to keep silent in church. They supported me when a district superintendent neglected to call together the District Committee on Ordained Ministry on the day he had given me to meet with them. They were the ones who spoke on my behalf when the Board of Ordained Ministry, composed of men in black suits, white shirts, and skinny black ties, asked me no theological questions but rather wanted to know how I could possibly be a pastor when I got married and had children and had to live where my husband's work required. This supporting network of pastors heard God's voice with me, would not allow it to be silenced, and invited others to calm down just enough to hear it too.

When trying to capture the essence of Sharon Brown Christopher, there is always a sense of her gratitude for formative influences in her life. It is reflected in a story about returning to her home church after becoming a bishop and continues in other ruminations.

When I went back to preach at my home church for the first time, I was given a stole. The Sunday school children had made it. The children had put their hands in finger paint—red, green, purple, blue—and then placed their hands on the white stole, leaving their differently sized handprints on it. When it was given to me in worship in front of the whole congregation, the presenter said, "This is a reminder of all of the people who touched you and laid their hands on you in your spiritual formation process."

I think the stole says it—all of those people who have touched my life. But the forming process continues. I get to sit with a conference cabinet. In their own way, sometimes subtly and sometimes directly, the cabinets with whom I have worked have touched me over and over again with amazing grace and empowered me to step out in faith when I didn't think I had the courage to do so.

The journey tests people, and Sharon felt that testing in the uprooting from friends and community.

When I left the Minnesota cabinet, I grieved. I thought, "I will never be able to love a cabinet the way I have loved this one." They had laid their hands on me and, in so doing, blessed me. Then, about a year into my Illinois Great Rivers Conference ministry, I was sitting in cabinet one day. I looked around the room and almost laughed out loud. I realized that I had fallen in love with this cabinet, too. They, too, were laying their hands on me, blessing me, and evoking ministry from me in ways I didn't think possible. God works in amazing ways!

And the Council of Bishops. Gosh! I sat in the midst of our North Central College of Bishops meeting recently, and I thought, "God! How did I ever get to sit among these people?" As I glanced around the circle, I saw spiritual giants sitting around this table, and somehow I get to sit among them! What an honor it is to sit in their midst.

Sharon wishes to conclude with specific words of gratitude.

Although this project is not intended to include our adulthood, I cannot quit without identifying my Christopher journey as a key formative presence in my life. When Charles and I married, we each added "Christopher" to our names. We each then had our baptized names, Sharon Ann and Charles Edmond, our family names, Brown and Logsdon, and our new covenant name,

Christopher. Charles's companionship has held me, nudged me, challenged me, pushed me, protected me, loved me, formed me, and kept me sane!

I've been shaped by family, college, seminary, congregations, and the people with whom I have worked. An ongoing source of growth for me is the *daily examen*, an ancient practice of the people of God. Every night I think back through the day, and I ask myself a series of questions. Where have I noticed the presence of God today? What do I need to confess? Whom do I need to forgive? For what do I give thanks? I ask, "What have I learned today?" Then I name the day, identify the gifts needed for the following day, and offer my life back to God. I am learning and growing day by day. What a wonderful journey I have been given and claim. I *am* grateful.

The church should be grateful for the gift of Sharon Brown Christopher. I have long admired her focus, her sense of being formed by and giving back to the community of faith, and her deliberative and wise way of leading. Not only is she tall in stature, but also she "stands tall" in the annals of our stories. The Council of Bishops made a wise choice in selecting her as President for a term—the first woman to hold that office. She brought her dignity, grace, and welcoming way of leading to the office and to her colleagues. The year that she and Sharon Zimmerman Rader (then Secretary of the Council) held the two highest offices of the Council was a signal year. Upon the end of that term, many colleagues spoke with appreciation about the way they had conducted themselves and the business of the Council. It was a year to remember with a woman to remember.

Judith Craig

My story comes in written form, rather than in a taped interview. Having listened to all of the other stories, I had a sense of what would have been provoked by such an interview.

On June 5, 1937, Ray and Edna Craig welcomed a fifth child. The four others ranged in age from six to twelve. The home birth brought me into a family filled with promise and trauma. Joe, six years old at the time, suffered from grand mal epilepsy, a disease that lived with us all of our lives until his death in 1994. Jeanette, then eight years old, had been through a terrible time of burns and surgeries. Corky and Bibby, nine and twelve, were busy with their emerging teen years.

My mother always said I raised myself, and the siblings agree that I was a pleasant and happy child. Truth is, I fastened myself to my father, following him around all of the time and, according to reports of others, talking a blue streak. He never told me I couldn't do something because I was a girl, and, in fact, throughout my life, I don't remember ever being told that by my parents or siblings. If I could do it and wanted to do it, and it wasn't something that would be wrong, I could try.

Mother was by no means inattentive. She was busy. We didn't have much money. She made all of our clothes, and we raised almost everything we ate—including meat. I can remember the washing machine with the hand wringer and the lines and lines of clothes flapping in the wind—in the summer and winter. In fact, in her late years of retirement on a farm in southwest Missouri, she reverted to hanging clothes outdoors. I would do my laundry on my last day at home on a visit and pack them straight off the line. When I opened the suitcase back home—wherever that was—that smell jumped out at me.

Mom's hands were busy with the next oldest brother, Joe. He was six when I was born and had already developed grand mal epilepsy. It was a lifelong struggle for him, managed to some degree by drugs, but leaving him slowed down so much that he was always a bit on the fringe of things. But in those early years, he was very sick, and they had not yet managed the illness. It took a lot from Mother. In addition, she had been through a terrible time with Jeanette, then eight. Jeanette had suffered burns from her waist down when she was three and had almost died. By the time she was six, she had developed scar tissue that was going to cripple her. The Shriners took her under their wing, and she went to St. Louis to one of their hospitals for skin grafts. But as soon as she got there, the hospital was put on quarantine because of a measles outbreak. She was there for several months and underwent several surgeries by herself, and Mom and Dad were clear across the state wondering about her. She was doing fine by the time I was born, but all that was in Mom's background. I doubt she was totally thrilled when she first found herself to be pregnant in the fall of 1936!

My memories of those first years in Lexington, Missouri, may be as much from stories told to me as they are mine. Sometime in those years, Grandma and Grandpa Forsha moved in with us. I remember a time when Mom was ill with a floating kidney and had to be in bed upstairs. Grandma and Grandpa couldn't carry a tray up the stairs, so I was dispatched with mother's meals during the day. I must have been three or four, but I can remember Grandma standing at the foot of the back stairs, saying, "Careful, Baby. Don't fall, Baby. Careful, Baby." I never did drop a tray. But there was one thing that worried them. Mom needed lots of water, and I would be sent to fill her pitcher. It dawned on her that I couldn't reach the sink, and she began to worry about where I was getting that water. She asked dad to follow me one night. I went to the bathroom, put the pitcher down in the tub, filled it, climbed back out, and picked it up. Pretty resourceful!

The Forsha grandparents lived with us until their deaths, moving with us to Liberty in 1942. I have some pretty good memories of them. Actually they lived in a little one-bedroom house about a city block down the road from our house in Liberty. It was my safe haven. If I could get there, no matter what I had done, I was safe! I loved Grandpa Forsha. He had been a sheriff for a long time, and he used to tell me outrageous stories. Mom would scold him, and he would say, "Oh, Babe, it won't hurt her. Leave us be." So I would spend hours listening to him and begging for more.

When Grandma died, Grandpa moved into our house on the condition that dad dig him a privy. He never trusted indoor toilets. Dad did that. I'll never know why, but one hot summer day I locked Grandpa in that outhouse and sat down on the back porch and listened to him holler. Mom ran by me and said she wondered why I was just sitting there. When she found him, he told her I had done it. He scolded me really hard, but when he went around the corner of the house, I saw his shoulders shake. I loved that man. He died when I was seven.

I didn't know my Craig grandparents as well. They lived in Joplin, about 150 miles south of us. Dad had a whole passel of brothers and sisters; I think about twelve survived out of fourteen births. Grandma Craig was a tiny little woman who cooked on a wood-burning stove. I can still see that kitchen when I smell oak smoke. We went there a couple of times a year, I suppose. I remember rowdy gatherings with hard-livin' men, most of whom were miners. Dad was the only one to get out of that world, and I don't know how he did that. Grandma and the women would cook up a storm, but the men always ate first, then the kids, and then the women. Both those grandparents died by the time I was six, but we kept going to Joplin to visit uncles for a long, long time.

In 1942, we moved from my birth town of Lexington to Liberty, across the Missouri River about forty miles. There was a college in Liberty, and Dad chose the town partly because he wanted to have higher education available, but was not sure he would be able to provide room and board as well as tuition. So it was that three of us went to college at William Jewell, no questions asked. It was just a natural progression.

We moved in the summer, and everyone went off to school that fall, leaving me at home alone with Mother, as had been the case all of my life. All of my preschool years were spent at home with Mother while the others were away for the day. I loved it. I was not at a loss for entertainment, for my imagination was vivid. Across the road, and back behind trees, was another house where an invalid woman lived. Early one September, she called Mother and asked how many children she had at home. Mother replied, of course, that there was only Judy. The woman protested and said she heard the voices of several children playing in the yard. Mom replied, "Oh, that's just Judy with her imaginary football team. Each has a name and a distinctive voice—but it is really just Judy!" At least I never took "them" anywhere with me!

The thirty acres on which we lived provided a lot of our sustenance. We had huge gardens and berry patches and lots of room to raise cattle both for meat and milk. It was a good life, but my folks worked hard. Yet I can recall Mother taking time for the little wonders of life. I especially recall the afternoon she took me to the garden where we sat for an hour and watched the beans come up. It is really visible! The earth moves a little, then a crack, and suddenly a little bean sprout jumps up, pushing a piece of dirt aside. That memory is so indicative of my mother.

Dad owned a laundry route. He picked up laundry in the mornings, drove it into Kansas City, about twenty-five miles away, got the clean laundry, and brought it back for delivery in the afternoon. I loved that laundry route. Now and then I would go along. I learned to break string around my hand and to tie sheets in bundles. I loved a pocket full of change and taking the laundry to someone's door. Dad said he loved that job because he was his own boss, was out of doors, and interacted with lots of people. I loved going along because it was great time with Dad. We talked and talked as we rode along. No telling how much I learned that way.

The paneled laundry truck was our only car for several years. We would pile into it to go to church or town or school—and sit on laundry bundles. When Jeanette was in college, she sang in operas, and the first night she went for her makeup call, sitting on a bundle of laundry, she said wistfully, "I always thought I'd be taken to my first performance in a fine carriage behind white horses."

Our house was "kid central." Though we lived in the country, a mile from the square of a town of seven thousand, we were within walking distance of almost everyone. A mile was nothing to us and our friends. We had an acre of yard, half of it open enough for baseball, and half of it populated with large trees, many of them pine trees. In that yard, late into the evening dusk, grand games of hide-and-seek caught up anybody who was there. It didn't matter how old you were; if you could run, you could play. Mom and Dad played right along with us.

The big brick house, built right after the Civil War, had huge rooms and high ceilings. In the two big rooms at the front we didn't have furniture. In one room was a table for table tennis and in the other the grand piano. Our lives revolved around them. I learned to play table tennis as soon as I could see over the table. And we all played the piano to varying degrees of expertise. I used to play the golden oldies with dad and his saxophone, hour after hour. Music was really big stuff for us.

When it was time to start first grade, everything at school seemed okay to me, but somehow, about the second or third week, I became disturbed and wanted to go home. When the teacher denied my request, I began to cry, and she locked me in the empty kindergarten room. Then appeared my deliverance in the form of the much-loved custodian. He took authority to take me out of that room and dry my tears and take me home. For the next week, I resisted going to school. I cried and trembled; I made a scene at home and a scene at school. After carrying me down the school hall screaming at the top of my lungs for two or three days, Mom decided it was all right if I ended up delayed a year. It wasn't worth my pain. So I stayed home.

I sat on the steps watching what had taken place at the time I started school. Mom had started a preschool. I watched mothers bringing their preschool kids. I watched and I watched. It took me six weeks to decide whatever it was I needed to decide before I announced I was ready to go back to school. Mom made a game of it, "fooling the older kids," until I could stand up at dinner on Friday night and make the grand speech: "I've been going to school all week." There were huzzahs and celebration—and a pair of leather chaps as a reward. I've been going to school ever since without a hint of regret or caution.

After that, elementary grade school was pretty normal for me, I think. I did well, save for art. In the second grade, the teacher laughed at one of my drawings, and I have been tied up in knots about drawing to this day. I was a classic tomboy and still am, I think. I had lots of friends and played hard with them. A bunch of us walked to school together, picking up friends along the way. It was a good life. I was athletic and loved softball and other games.

My eighth birthday was a great moment. I had been fussing about wanting to do something when a truck pulled up and out of it came this saddle mare. Dad said she was mine! I completely forgot everything else. She was six or seven years old, five-gaited, and, I thought, the most perfect horse in the world. I named her Twinkle, and we were inseparable for the rest of my school years until she got too old to ride. There would be whole days when I would roam the country roads, go into town and visit the guy at the ice company while he made ice, and generally entertain myself and all whom I met on that wonderful horse. It was so safe to do that all by myself!

In my late-elementary years, I began my 4-H career. A neighboring farmer gave me a newborn piglet—the runt and extra of the litter. I took her home, fed her with a spoon and then a bottle, and raised her to be a huge sow that had several litters of pigs, which I sold and then saved the money for college. Pigs were my first 4-H project. Mom had me sign up for sewing, too. After all, she made all of my clothes and had a "red hot needle and a burning thread." It was natural that she encouraged her children to learn to sew. About four weeks into the project time, the leader called mother and said, "Edna, let her raise pigs." Thus ended my sewing career.

But the pig career went on for several years, including the time I took a market-sized white pig to the pet show. We transported him in dad's laundry truck—the vehicle out of which he made our living. All went well until on the way home, the quart of milk he had consumed at the show created the next event—and that truck smelled to high heaven! We worked all night trying to clean it so dad could put clean laundry in the truck. However, Pedro the Pig and I won first prize at the pet show—$10, which I gave to the church for the new chimes!

All of those years and all of my life, really, my brother Joe's presence was a mixture of tenderness and what probably would be embarrassment. His seizures were violent. He often fell. He often screamed. He would finally pass out. That happened in public places—in school, at church, with friends. The drugs he took slowed him down so much that it was sometimes hard to talk with him. Yet he had a sweet demeanor, and a voice—what a voice he had. He took voice lessons as a young adult, and I spent many an evening during my high school and college years—and then when I visited later after I moved from home—accompanying him as he sang. We had a huge repertoire, and when he sang it was magnificent. He was always in demand as a soloist and always found a choir to sing in—right to the time of his death in 1994. I don't know what effect Joe's presence really had on me. I know he would have loved to be a minister, but he just couldn't do it academically. Our family is marked with the pathos of this brother. I grew up in the shadow of his illness and bore my parents' pain without knowing it. Some have speculated that when I was born, I had a sense that my mom's hands were full and that part of my being a really easy child had to do with that inner sense. I don't know if that's true or not. But I do know that I have always been the one who tries to make peace and keep things light. I believe part of that is tied to Joe.

Church was already pretty central in our life. My older siblings sang in the choir, and we went every Sunday. Strange, in my mind, is my lack of memory of Sunday school before junior high. I know I was there. But I remember better being in church and going to sleep during the sermon with my head on Dad's lap. My earliest memory of church is just that—and that warm, secure feeling still is my primary sense of church. I know Mom was heavily involved in the Women's Society of Christian Service, predecessor to United Methodist Women. I think she taught Sunday school.

All of my teen life I was actively involved in church. I sang in the choir as soon as my voice developed enough. I was active in the Methodist Youth Fellowship, holding all kinds of offices across the years. I got active in district affairs and even conference stuff.

Sometime in my teen years I met Bishop Ivan Lee Holt. He was a tall man with a shock of white hair. The conference youth officers visited him in his office, which was very imposing. I thought he must be like God!

My senior high Sunday school teacher is memorable for many reasons, including being the one to whom I ran when mother was "dumb." But what she taught me, and the rest of my friends, was how to pray in public with no warning. Every week she called on one of us to pray at the end of class. If you hadn't done it for a while, you would spend the hour wondering if this was going to be your time. But we learned! We got comfortable with praying in public in front of our peers. Great gift.

Those teen years were mixed up in some ways. I was very popular in some circles—sports, music, and church. But I was not in the dating circle, and I was still such a tomboy. Along about the ninth grade there was a candid shot of me in the school yearbook, and the caption was "Judy's wearing lipstick!!" It was something to note, but that picture hurt me. I didn't feel pretty, didn't feel socially adept. The guys were my buddies. We played football and basketball together, but instead of dating me, they told me their dating woes. It was rough!

Miss Rust, the music teacher for grades seven through twelve, was one of the most significant adults in my life in those years. She offered an outstanding music program, and I was in it up to my ears. I was in choirs, glee clubs, quartets, and sextets. We went to regional and state competitions every year and almost always took the top place. What a good ride! And along with that came some public poise, even though I still felt awkward.

It was with Miss Rust that I first experienced death personally. There was a quartet of girls who sang together for six years, and we were Miss Rust's personal favorites, I know. Everyone knew. Miss Rust's mother was very ill and one of our parents took us to see her in the hospital. She was comatose, and Miss Rust and her father were very tired, so two of us said we'd sit by the bed for a while so they could get a cup of coffee or something. As we sat there, suddenly Mrs. Rust stopped breathing. It was so scary! Everything was so silent. We ran to the nurse who was really good with us. She calmed us down, showed us how relaxed Mrs. Rust's face was, and sent us to get the family. Everyone in that scene made that moment precious instead of terrible. They took the body home for viewing, and we went. Then we sang at the funeral. I treasure that relationship with and those learnings from Miss Rust.

All of this time our house was still kid-central. When my siblings went to college, those gangs of young adults would come to the house. My friends all gathered there, too. And my parents continued to be our playmates and our friends' advisors. Not mine, of course. They were my parents. I had to go somewhere else to get good advice. They got smart again when I was in my midtwenties. We had a good relationship, but it had its stormy moments. I pushed the edges—stayed out a little too late—went to the movies with boys they didn't like and tried to keep it from them. Innocent but ornery, I suppose.

Our house was also a "safe house" for all of the pastors who served us in those years. Mom and Dad always welcomed the new pastors and their families into our home, and they took advantage of that. The pastors would come for a late afternoon cup of coffee, or the pastor and family would come for Sunday dinner. That continued when my parents retired. Their kitchen table knew many a pastor's elbows, and my parents' hearts held many a pastor's family close and confidentially. That meant I knew those pastors as human beings, fun and silly as well as serious and to be respected.

Liberty was a segregated town. There were two ways to walk downtown, or drive, from our house. We always went one way because the other took us through "Darkie Town." But now and then I would deliberately walk home that way. The people were friendly, if suspicious, and the houses weren't all that bad. But we were segregated!

There was a "colored" school for all grades. There were "colored" churches. One time our choir did an exchange with the choir at St. James African Methodist Episcopal Church. They took up an offering, counted it, said it wasn't enough, and passed the plate again. I about passed out. They did that three times. I thought we ought to try that in our church, but the preacher wasn't much interested.

Dad carried laundry for some of those folks, but he was always cautious about letting me deliver for him there. He would sit in the truck and watch closely. He was a man of his time and place and the "n" word could be heard in our home.

One honored member of the African American community was the custodian at the white elementary school. It was he who rescued me from the locked kindergarten room in first grade and took me home. He was the crossing guard in front of the school, and everyone knew and respected him. The town sort of "exempted" him from his race.

When I was a junior in high school, integration of the schools began. They started with juniors and seniors in high school and then moved down for a series of years. That meant I went to school with African Americans my last two years. It was sometime in that experience that I asked my dad to stop using the "n" word. He worked hard to take it out of his vocabulary. One of my classmates was the African American custodian's daughter. She was beautiful! And my senior year she was the yearbook queen—based on judges who rated beauty. She merited it, sexist as it was. It caused some stir, but most of us in her class were very pleased and proud.

When I was in college at William Jewell, there were some Africans in our classes, but no Black Americans yet. There was a time when some of us were taking a group of visitors into Kansas City for a special meal. There were some Africans in the group. We called to make reservations and indicated we would be bringing some black people, so the restaurant would not be surprised later. The restaurant person hemmed and hawed. We indicated they were from Africa, and all of a sudden it was all right. It made us so mad that we didn't go there.

But there was a parallel life developing, too, that I think is really formative for me. I became a member of the Order of Rainbow for Girls. It seems odd, in some ways, because we dressed in formals and did many ladylike things. I loved the ritual and I was good at it and it was a place I felt comfortable as a young woman. I was so good at it that I became a state officer and, ultimately—the highest office—Grand Worthy Advisor. That was my sophomore year in college, and the duties of the office conflicted with attention to school. My dear mom and I trooped all over Missouri to little towns with grubby Masonic halls and visited every one of the over eighty Rainbow organizations that year. I learned public presence.

I learned public speaking, extempore speaking. I learned organization and administration in some surprising ways. Rainbow was a magnificent training ground for a rough and tumble tomboy who kept on riding her horse and playing sports and singing—but was developing other abilities, too.

I went to summer church camps probably every year of my teens. The important one, though, was when I was fifteen. It was the Girl's School of Missions run by the Women's Division. We "camped" in what was National College in Kansas City, now the site of St. Paul Theological Seminary. There was a hill on which we built a campfire one night and heard the call for Christian vocation. I took one of those cards and looked at the options. Minister wasn't on it, of course, but missionary and doctor and nurse and teacher were all there. I checked medical missionary. Already Albert Schweitzer had become my hero. I was going to be his successor. That night I pledged my life to God in full-time Christian service with that specific way of doing tucked into my being. My folks affirmed it. My church affirmed it. My friends affirmed it. I was launched!

So I went to William Jewell College and declared myself a premed major. I had a good freshman year academically, then slid off when I started that year as Grand Worthy Advisor. In fact, I made ten hours of Cs in chemistry. It was the late 1950s. Girls had a hard time getting into medical school under the best of circumstances, but especially with Cs in chemistry. The jig was up! My promise to God was undone! I felt miserable. I changed my major to English my junior year without a clue about what to do with it.

The crisis was with my faith. I felt I had let God down. I couldn't tell anybody, because I felt so guilty about it. Nobody else told me that, but I felt it. I quit going to church, I was depressed, and I argued with Mother at the slightest provocation. It was a rough year. Sometime in the summer between my junior and senior years, the choir director at the church came to me and asked me to step in for him. His child was very ill and he needed relief. He had been my bandleader in high school, and I would have done anything for him. So, guilty as I felt, and even scared to be near church, I said I would do it. That put me back in the church. Our pastor during my teen years and beyond was a wise old bird. He made no mention of my absence, just welcomed me as his colleague and began to teach me about worship and music. The choir welcomed me and worked with me, and I developed a bit of skill.

But I still didn't know what I was going to do. My folks never put any specific roadmaps or expectations in front of me. I was encouraged to find my way and never was told there were limits. We did have a joke in our family about the kind of women who went to seminary. We said, and I quote, "The women who go to seminary are the ones who can't get married or do anything else, so they tuck their Bible in their bra and march off to serve the Lord." Well, see, being a medical missionary wouldn't have required seminary so I could participate in that joke.

That spring we had the usual Religious Focus Week at William Jewell, and a visiting Baptist missionary freed me from my guilt and told me what I should have been told when I first signed that green card. She sat late into the night on the library steps and helped me see that my promise to let God use my life was still good and that I could keep that promise in lots of other ways. She separated the fifteen-year-old specific vision from the timeless promise, and I felt a huge relief.

Nevertheless, what to do was still a problem. In my senior year, I did practice teaching of ninth grade English but decided I didn't need to be a martyr. So, I applied to graduate schools. Maybe I thought I could learn to write the great American novel, I don't know. I was admitted several places, but nobody offered me money. Two weeks before graduation, I decided to go to St. Louis and enter Washington University where I had been accepted to graduate school for English literature. I called friends made during my Rainbow years and asked them if they would loan me room and board and help me find a choir-directing job to pay for tuition and other costs. (See how the threads began to come together?) Through one of these contacts, I learned that there was a church looking for a youth director. But I thought, "No way!" I had no role models and that awful image of women working in the church that we had created. It was one of the two times I remember my dad being a bit assertive about vocational decisions. He asked me what I had to lose by investigating.

So I went to St. Louis on the train, digging in my heels all of the way. My friends met me and took me to Bellefontaine Methodist Church (it was pre-merger). It was on the edge of greater St. Louis, a pretty little place. But I was not interested. I was just going along. I went in for an interview, frowning and clenching my teeth. I came out an hour later, smiling, laughing, and having agreed to be their youth director part-time and go to Eden Theological Seminary. Seminary! I can't remember anything about that interview except the excitement of the decision. My folks said that when I got off the train back in Kansas City, I was absolutely aglow.

Two weeks later, Dad drove to St. Louis with me to look for housing. We met with the committee again, and they asked him what he and Mom thought about my decision. I shall never forget his answer: "All of our lives we have hoped one of our children would enter some kind of full-time ministry, and we have always prayed and expected that it would be Judy." It blew me away! Had I really made any choices at all? What a surprising gift of grace.

The two years at Eden in Webster Groves, Missouri, and youth ministry at Bellefontaine Church went quickly. I worked part-time at the church, drove across town for classes, and earned a master's degree in religious education. It was a particularly good degree. It was not a lightweight degree and was something I had worked hard to get. I was proud of it. Harold "Hap" Pflug was the main professor of Christian education and was wonderful. At the same time I was becoming a "crackin' good" educator, myself. From 1959 to 1961, we had a whale of a youth ministry at Bellefontaine Church. In addition to the senior pastor was an associate pastor who was straight out of seminary. We made a formidable team. We sparked creativity in each other and in others. What a good time that was!

Dr. Pflug opened the door to the next step of the journey, which took me into another new place. He secured for me a year's internship at the National Council of Churches working with two wonderful women in the Children's Education Division. Off to New York City went this small-town girl. I lived in a small apartment—my bedroom was six-by-nine feet. It was just up the hill from Jewish Theological Seminary. So I walked by that school, by Union

Theological Seminary, and into the Interchurch Center across the street from Riverside Church. Talk about immersion!

That year I met people from all around the world. The Interchurch Center was a beehive of church activity in the early 1960s. My horizons extended farther than my mind could comprehend. It was glorious. I explored New York City. I made friends with all kinds of church leaders. I worshiped at Riverside Church and feasted on the preaching and the music there. Such a strange new world.

At the end of that year, I decided I really wanted to stay on the East Coast for a while. I called the office of the New York Annual Conference to inquire about finding a job as a Director of Christian Education. I found out about a church in Stamford, Connecticut, that had just relocated from downtown to the suburbs and needed a Director of Christian Education. I couldn't believe it. The pastor of that church was Cecil Swackhammer, who had been in St. Louis when I was there, and we had spent two summers in youth camps working together. I went to see him, and he quickly pulled together an interview team. I was offered the job—my first "real" job with a "real" salary! It was 1962, and I was "just a DCE." But I was ready to go!

The Stamford years were delicious. It was a time in the Church when interest in education was high. We had tons of kids—two full shifts of Sunday school and over ninety teachers at work. We had a youth group of anywhere from sixty to seventy high school kids. Kids in confirmation classes numbered in the fifties. Those were also the years in which people were moving a lot. Stamford was a bedroom community, with lots of middle executives in firms with New York headquarters. Folks would be brought in for two years or so and then sent on. We had fifteen hundred members and turned over five hundred every year. Almost every week there was a new teacher in some class. But the energy and interest were high! People quickly joined the activities because they knew they wouldn't be there long. I had a ball—and I was good at my job.

There are folks from those years who are still my good friends. In fact, I lived with a family part of that time, and I am still part of their lives. What a gift! It's always been my habit to adopt a family or two wherever I live. That's how I had kids. I have been effective at helping raise other folks' kids. I was able to be that other significant adult for teenagers who thought their parents are nuts. That has netted for me a handful of kids that are "mine" and now grandchildren that claim me as much as I claim them. These families who have adopted me, and I them, have been the richest bonuses of my life journey—the Milletts and Smiths in Stamford, the Taylors and McCartneys in Ohio. All dear, all formative, all with their fingerprints all over me as I continued to mature over the years. Now they are trying to love me as I get older with them. And they do it well.

After five years in Stamford, I began to wish I had a deeper grounding in theology and ecclesiology than had been required for the M.R.E. So I explored seminaries. Yale was attractive but required residency, and I wanted to do part of this work while still working in Stamford. However, Union Seminary in New York did provide that opportunity. I started the Bachelor of Divinity degree (later converted to Master of Divinity) in 1966 part-time, commuting on the train from Stamford and still working part-time at the church. In 1967, I decided to devote myself full-time to school and resigned my job. In 1968, I was awarded that degree, though my intention was still to work in Christian education, having never heard anyone raise any other alternatives. There were women at Union who were pursuing ordination, I think, but I didn't have much interaction with them.

I was on something of a sidetrack. After finishing my M.Div., I was still recovering from an injury suffered a year earlier that required a number of hand surgeries, and there was more surgery yet to be done. I wasn't sure what to do. I enrolled at Teachers' College in pursuit of a Doctorate in Christian Education of Adults. To stay afloat, I also took a job for the winter in Harlem, working with adults seeking their high school diploma equivalency. That was a wonderful mind- and soul-expanding experience. It was a program funded by the state of New York. Inner city women were teacher aides in elementary classrooms half a day and in my classroom the other half. They were pretty well motivated and streetwise. In exchange for teaching them algebra and literature, they taught me street smarts. It was a great swap!

Then a series of events that are almost a mystery to me unfolded. I often wonder if just one thread had been clipped, what would my life have been like. It's hard to recount them in some ways.

In the Stamford church was a wonderful woman, Helen, who was an active leader in the youth ministry. In the spring of 1969, she died of cancer. It was a blow to all of us, and even though I was not employed at the church by then, I was still living in Stamford and involved in that journey. The family needed to have a car driven to Akron, Ohio. Having no particular plans for Easter, I agreed to drive the car to Akron and then went on to Cleveland to spend Easter with the Briggs, parents of another Stamford church member. It was a fateful visit.

On Easter morning, they took me to church at Epworth Euclid United Methodist Church. I was stunned. I had not experienced worship like that since the year I spent at Riverside Church in New York. That evening the Briggs took me to the pastor's home for dessert, an invitation the pastor himself had extended. The pastor, Bernard Loomis, tried to convince me to take a job at the church as DCE. I was not interested. I still had a year's classes to complete toward my doctorate degree and had discovered there were virtually no children in that congregation. In my mind, this meant the church was in big trouble, and I wondered why they needed a DCE.

I returned to Stamford and to classes without another thought. My dad came for a visit in mid-May and observed that I seemed to be marking time and hiding by going to school—an uncharacteristically direct comment concerning life work. One day, while Dad and I were out, Bernard Loomis called. He wanted me to come for an interview and consider being a consultant for a year while I finished my class work. What a preposterous idea! I asked for time to think about it and then talked it over with Dad. Once more, my dad made a significant comment: "What have you got to lose? He wants to spend his money to fly you up for an interview? Go find out about it."

I did go and ended up taking the job as consultant. I flew back and forth every other weekend for a year. And I did get a youth ministry up and running in that time. I stayed with friends from Cleveland on those weekends. Mom Briggs (they had become

Mom and Pop to me) would pick me up at the rapid transit station with my luggage and take me home. It was great. I would go in on Friday and stir things up until Monday and then leave. It was a good deal. The church paid my travel and a stipend. When I finished all of my class work, I agreed to come on full-time in June of 1970.

Along the way, I began to learn some things about Epworth Euclid and its leadership style with which I was not entirely comfortable. They operated somewhat outside of the United Methodist system. I wondered what would happen when I was a full member of the staff and didn't like the way things were. Also on staff was a wonderful associate pastor. He was a year from retiring and really laid back, but we hit it off very well. Then in July, Bernard Loomis dropped the bomb that he was leaving to become the president of Albion College in Albion, Michigan. Well, the Executive Committee formed itself as a search committee and began to look for their next pastor—which was not United Methodist. But rather than jumping right in, the Bishop wisely gave them some rope. Bernard had been there ten years. I didn't understand it then, but I do now. These folks kept taking names to the bishop, and he kept declining to make the appointment. This went on from September to March. During that time, the associate pastor and I were the staff. He didn't want to preach, and I never preached, you may be sure—I was just the DCE. So we had a string of guest preachers. But I found myself doing lots of pastoral care, administration, and everything but worship and sacraments, it seemed. What a winter!

Then the Sunday after Easter, 1971, Bill McCartney arrived as the new pastor. I held my breath, hoping I would still have a job. I did. And more. Around midsummer, Bill came to my office and said, "Why aren't you ordained? You've been pastoring this church. Everywhere I go people tell me that. You've got the education. Why not be ordained?" It took my breath away. Two seminary degrees, twelve years of professional experience in education, and I had never considered ordination. I was committed to the leadership of the laity. I had a life plan—work in the local church for about ten more years and then teach in seminary. What a preposterous question!

It took me most of the fall to work it through, but I finally went to the District Superintendent in the winter of 1972. He was skeptical and cautious. It was only when I said what I wanted was to be appointed to Epworth Euclid as Minister of Education that he sighed with relief and agreed. The District Committee on Ministry was cursory in their examination—their greatest concern was the possibility of my getting married and having children and how I would manage that.

And so the road took a sharp turn, and my life plan was soundly reformed. My ordination as a deacon in 1972 made me the third woman in connection in the East Ohio Conference. When I was elected to the episcopacy in 1984, that number had grown to over one hundred women. It was an explosive decade for women. My ordination as Elder followed in 1974, and the journey was well under way.

I worked with Bill McCartney for five years before appointment elsewhere. He stayed on at Epworth Euclid for a total of ten years. It is important to note that during those ten years of his ministry, seven women entered ministry. What a mentor.

Like all lives, mine has been a series of twists and turns. Like all lives, it has been filled with significant persons, interruptions, and redirections. But there seems a clear thread through it all, beginning with parents who prayed for a child to spend her life in some form of full-time Christian service. Thank you, Ray and Edna Craig, for your confidence and your faith. I hope you are pleased with how I have lived my life.

Violet Fisher

Violet Fisher comes from a long-standing family on the Eastern Shore of Maryland. As she unfolds her life, her family and its extended manifestation through church and community are always central.

I was born on the Eastern Shore of Maryland, the third of seven children—James, Clementine, Violet, George, Blanche, William, and Tommy. My parents and their parents were also born on the Eastern Shore. My Father, William Fisher, took his responsibility as the head of our family very seriously. Though he finished only the twelfth grade, he worked hard at laborious jobs to care for us and to raise us in the church. Mother, Virginia Fisher, though extremely introverted, was a firm disciplinarian who loved us, cared for us, and guided our spiritual development.

Social life was family and church. The sense of belonging in both places is at the heart of everything Violet says.

Much of our free time was spent visiting relatives, playing with one another, and inventing family games. My childhood was family on top of family. We were very, very close.

Every night, we gathered at the dinner table. My mother and daddy and all of us sat around the table, and our grandmother, too. There was a blessing, and it was done not just by Dad or Mother. We each had to take turns giving the blessing. Then we all had to say a Bible verse before we ate, and we couldn't use the same verse over and over. I so appreciate that family experience.

My mom used to say, "There are enough of you to play with one another." So we did not hang out with others. They came to our house, which was the gathering place. My mother really kept us busy, kept us occupied. We were poor, but we didn't know we were poor since we usually had more than the other children around us.

It was not unusual to come to our home and find extra plates on the table. It seemed there was always another person—young or elderly—living with us. My parents raised four other children whose parents had fallen on hard times and had asked my parents to help out.

We had a good life. We had family, and in the African American culture, the church was the center of everything you did. Even our Girl Scout troop and the 4-H club was at the church. My mom was a Scout leader and, later on, cookie chairman for her grandchildren's troops.

My mother's mother played the piano, and as youngsters, we would gather around her to sing. We organized ourselves into the "Fisher Five." My eldest sister, Clem, was in college, and our youngest brother, Tommy, was not yet born. Mother and Dad transported us from church to church. We traveled all over the Eastern Shore and into parts of the Western Shore. We also sang during talent shows at our local high school.

Sometimes people would throw money on the stage, and my brother would get down on the stage and pick it up. The rest of us who wanted it and needed it were too ashamed and embarrassed to pick it up, but Billy always got down to pick up the money.

The grandparents' farm was another gathering place for family.

At my grandparents' farm, there were always a lot of people around. We had big meals every day. Grandmother's daughters helped her cook.

When we were little, we would go out in the summer to help plant and then pick tomatoes and cucumbers. I'd gather the eggs first thing in the morning and sometimes ride the horses. My grandfather owned a fairly large farm and hired persons to work for him. I remember running up and down the rows, taking ice water to the men who were putting the hay up. Grandma always made sure we had homemade ice cream, potato pies, and fried chicken. There was always a big spread when the workers came up from working.

Hog-killing time was another big time. The laborers would come together at one farm and slaughter all of the hogs there. The women would gather together and work the sausage. I loved listening to the stories. A lot of these people would come to our grandparents' house at night, and we would sit on the stairs and listen.

The father, ah, the father, is held in high reverence and warm memory.

We played with coloring books and jacks on the floor. I appreciate that our dad, not just our mother, got on the floor and played with us. When I was a child it was all of us together, just family. I think it is unusual to have a daddy who plays with all of the kids. Some daddies play only with the boys. But our father played with all of us. So my image of family includes not only the mother hen with all the kids around, but also the rooster.

Everybody always says, "You look just like your father." I was proud to look like my dad. My father showed me special attention, and my mom tried to be the disciplinarian. I think I needed more. So, dad became my heart. My mom would punish me, but I would not cry. I would wait until that magic time—5 o'clock—for Daddy to come home. As soon as he came, I would say, "She beat me. She hit me." And he would go right in the house and say, "Why did you beat this girl?" I tell you, I worked it!

Her parents worked hard to support their extended families.

My father worked for a lumber company as a driver and went from local driving to driving long distance so he could educate us. Truck-driving paid more than many other jobs paid.

My mother's father died when she was five. After mother married and had children, she brought her mother to live with us to help with the family.

We can't trace my father's people back too far, but everybody is from the Eastern Shore of Maryland. All of my grandparents came from Caroline County, Maryland. My maternal grandmother's people are definitely the long line. In fact, I knew my grandmother's mother. She was part of our family gatherings.

Everyone had to work as teens. It took many hands to keep the family going.

When we were young, our mother would take us to the fields to work, to pick cucumbers and string beans. We would crawl up and down the rows. We hung in there with the women.

When I was fifteen years old, I said I was sixteen so I could work in the tomato factory and then the chicken factory. We worked in the factories in the summer to help get our money together for school clothes.

Jobs around the house also kept us busy. Laundry and cutting wood were big jobs. We had to chop the wood when it was brought to us and then had to put it in the wood box for the woodstove. We also had a washing machine with a ringer. I remember my fingers freezing as I hung up frozen clothes on cold days.

I never cooked. I hate cooking. But my sister Blanche enjoyed cooking. I loved cleaning, so I did the cleaning. I would clean the house from top to bottom. I also love to wash clothes. I don't like to iron.

A conversation doesn't go very long without a return to something about the Church.

The Methodist Episcopal Church was a strong movement on the Eastern Shore of Maryland and Delaware. The black church was central to everything that went on in the community. Yes, the community's expectation was that everybody was a part of the church. It was a joy to participate in the life of the church as I took part in plays, oratorical contests, recitations, or special days, and as I served as a junior usher and worship leader. Thank God my parents didn't send us to church, but took us, sometimes twice a week.

I think just about everybody on the Eastern Shore was a part of the Methodist family—either Pan Methodist or Methodist Episcopal. Maryland is the Mother of the Church, the cradle of the Methodist movement in this country.

Family folded into religious experiences, too.

We had church in our house. On Sunday mornings, I don't care if the telephone rang, we could not get up. Everybody had to get on their knees on Sunday morning for family prayer—not around the table, but on our knees. That leadership from Mother and Daddy and our grandmother was so important. It laid the groundwork because all of us are in the church today. And three of us are preachers—my two brothers and me.

This large family was talented, and they put that talent to use.

I was already preaching when the Fisher Five began singing. The two went together. I didn't have a license or anything, but I preached for Youth Day and Children's Day and revivals. My sisters and brothers and family sang, and I would preach.

We sang one song that said, "If the Lord wants somebody, here am I, send me, I will go." I believed that and sang it from the bottom of my heart, never realizing that it was really to be. It was supposed to be.

In addition to the public presence of the Fisher Five were other early experiences that provided Violet with the ability to be a public figure.

The Girl Scouts had oratorical contests where we were given topics on which to speak. When I was twelve, my Girl Scout leader selected me to enter a peninsula-wide competition. But I was shy— I am shy. She helped me prepare, and I won. At twelve years old, I won first place!

Even though I was shy, I was also opinionated and very strong. I was often in trouble for that with my mother. However, I never went to the principal's office. I was a good student. I think the main thing was respect for our elders. Even though the high school teachers were not that much older than we were, we were taught to respect them. I went to an all-black school. These are the same people who worshiped with us on Sunday. They were part of the community, involved in every phase of the community. And our parents respected them and called them "Mr." or "Miss" or "Mrs." The respect was there.

Education was critical.

Clearly we were to finish high school and go to college in order to "get a good job." Though neither my mother nor father went to college, I think my father learned the importance of education from his parents who sent their oldest daughter to Bowie Normal School to be a schoolteacher.

My older sister went to college, became a teacher, and taught for thirty-four years. Daddy said they invested in college for her so she could help the rest of us. We did that in our family. Clementine helped me. Then I helped my brother George, who is now a United Methodist pastor in Delaware. And so it continued. When the baby boy, Tommy, came, he lived with Clementine and her husband. We supported one another—financially, emotionally, and spiritually.

Violet recalls limited contact with whites in her childhood. There was not only the race concern, but also classism to contend with within the black community.

I didn't have much interaction with whites—only those people for whom I baby-sat. I was twelve when I started baby-sitting. We earned our own money. We would baby-sit for white people. There was nothing else we could do. The blacks lived in one particular section, and the whites lived in another.

When my parents moved to the house in Denton, Maryland, I was in the seventh grade. The street right behind us was white territory. There was an alley that separated the streets. Daddy wanted to move to the street that had influential black people—clergy, pastors, doctors. At the same time we moved, the pastor of our church moved there, too. White folks had moved out of the house Daddy bought. But it was the black people on the street who tried to petition to keep our family out. It was a class thing, and we were not middle class.

We earned our way in. When you walked up and down the street and met one of the adults for the fifteenth time that day, we would say, "Good morning, Mrs. So-and-So," each and every time. We made our way in that community.

My parents said, "When you all come in here, come in through the backdoor. Don't make a lot of noise, and don't be running in and out of the front door. We will stay here." We were going to show them that we were good enough. After I went to school and taught in our community while continuing to preach, these same people would celebrate my gifts and exclaim how proud they were of me.

The religious experience is real in Violet's life, both in memory and in practice now.

When I was eleven, I was at a revival meeting at my church. In those days, the invitation was extended to those who wanted to come up and give their hearts to the Lord. I had been going to revival every night with my parents and had already been a part of church. But that night, I felt that it was the time for me to go forward. I asked my sister who was sitting beside me if she was going to go, and she said no. I said, "Well I'm going. I'm going tonight." I went up and knelt down, and the pastor and leaders prayed with me. That night I made my confession of faith that Jesus Christ came into my life.

I just felt, just knew, that I was different. I felt that there was something special for me to do. I didn't know what that would be. Around our community, I saw enough women preachers from the King's Apostle Holiness Church come and go to know that women could be preachers. I was very close to that and watched. I had strong role models. The community helped shape and encourage me. They all would say, "Oh, Violet's different." Of course, our mother and father taught in the Sunday school. My dad was Superintendent. My mom was a teacher and, later on, became Superintendent, young people's leader, and choir president.

Because of my conversion, I began to spend a lot of time reading the Bible and any religious material I could pick up. I learned how to pray. I heard different people talk about fasting and began to fast half a day on Fridays. I just knew that I wanted to be a disciple. I used to look at women preachers and say, "Maybe I can do that." Not in The Methodist Church because black women had no place then, but in the King's Apostle Holiness Church where I was nurtured and my ministry affirmed.

I worked for a white family that was Catholic. I would go to their house after school and help get the children settled in with their snacks and then I'd stay and help until I got them ready for bed. I heard them talk about the Sisters (nuns) in their church. So at one point, I thought that maybe I would be a nun. I knew I wanted to do something.

I had to do something that would allow me to do ministry and to serve. At fourteen, it was clear to me that there was a call upon my life. At sixteen, I shared with my pastor that I felt the call to preach. All he said was, "Just continue to stay in the Word. Read the Scriptures." By that time, I was already speaking in the church. I would take a passage and speak on it at the young people's service. When I was sixteen, the pastor stood up one day and called me out: "Sister, you have a message for us this morning." So I picked up my Bible and went to the pulpit and preached on the prodigal son. At sixteen years old! I was so bold about my faith.

A clear sense of call gripped Violet while she was in her teens, and she has never lost the conviction of the call or forgotten what it would require of her.

I knew, without a doubt, that God had laid God's hands upon me. After I started preaching, doors all over the shore and in many cities and towns on the Western Shore of Maryland were open to me. My parents encouraged me and supported me by taking me to these worship services. I was often invited to preach in Methodist camp meetings. Many pastors and leaders would call me to do one-night revivals—for youth days, rally days, homecoming. I didn't even know what I was saying, but I was serious. The people who were older would say, "She's different."

Bishop Susan Morrison likes me to tell about playing church when I was real young. I was always the preacher. We would turn tomato baskets upside down and sit on the tomato baskets in the backyard. We would sing, and somebody would get up and get the spirit and jump—my brother Billy would get the spirit—like those older people at church. I was the one who would preach. I would say, "See the birds fly. God made the birds. And the chickens running across the yard." I would preach on whatever was there.

Preaching here and there took a lot of time, but it did not deter the pursuit of education.

I didn't have a social life in high school. Our parents were very strict. There was just the church and family. I never even set foot in a dance or at the movies. I was different. I couldn't. The other kids could, but I couldn't. I was told by the older saints, "You are chosen. You cannot be like other young people. You must walk the walk and talk the talk. You must be an example."

While I was in high school, I started asking my mother if I could go to Bible college. I got my literature from Moody. I knew that I wanted to go to Bible college so I could preach better. My mother kept saying, "You can't make a living preaching. You've got to be able to make a living, Violet."

I had not thought of being a teacher, so I didn't take college preparatory classes. At graduation, I was the class chaplain and gave the prayer. Right after graduation, my mother and father said, "You've got to do something. Either you're going to work or you're going to college with Clementine." Clem had already finished two years at Bowie State Teachers College. So I went to college. My sister had a car, and she and my parents loaded me up and took me to college. My sister got me registered. I wasn't even into it.

In college, I did not have a social life on campus, because everyone knew I was a preacher. The black church always encouraged and affirmed me, and many doors were opened. I would preach weekends. My classmates would have their parents invite me to their churches for special days. Then I organized a gospel group. They would sing for me when I preached. I used to preach on Saturday nights all over the place, and also on many Sunday afternoons and Sunday mornings. In the black church, love offerings are taken for speakers and preachers. Being able to buy necessities for myself eased the burden for my parents who had the younger children to care for.

The sense of call never waned. Though she was prepared to teach—and was teaching—Violet's life was being an evangelist.

During my twenty-two years of teaching, I also served the King's Apostle Holiness Church as an evangelist and was later ordained as an elder. My call to serve in foreign missions began in 1969 when I was twenty-nine years old.

At a woman's conference, I met a woman from New Jersey who had recently returned from East Africa. Her talk and slide show whetted my appetite. I wrote letters to pastors in East Africa, asking if I could spend the summer working with children. I shared with them that I was an evangelist and would like to do some preaching. Responses came back from the leaders of these churches. I decided to go with the same church that sponsored the sister from New Jersey—The Voice of Salvation and Healing Church. It was the Church that was willing, basically, to get me started. It was one of the largest Pentecostal churches in East Africa. I spent the summer there and enjoyed it.

After I returned home and completed the work for my master's degree at George Washington University in Washington D.C., I was restless. I kept thinking that I needed to return to East Africa. In 1972, I took a sabbatical from teaching and returned for a year. I taught English as a second language and worked through church schools. We had crusades in the countries of Kenya, Uganda, and Tanzania. Three and four thousand people would gather in one area. What a powerful experience, being in the native land of my people and serving the church of Jesus Christ in so many wonderful ways.

Shortly after returning from the year in East Africa, I met a sister from Atlanta who had started a children's mission in Haiti. Because I had such an interest in children, I connected with her and made my first trip to Haiti in 1975. I continue to work at that mission. When I took my sabbatical as District Superintendent, I spent six weeks living in the orphanage with the children. Ministry to children became another passion for me. I like being with the children, holding them and loving them.

My passion to serve in other foreign lands was indeed birthed. Thus, I found myself in the Jamaican West Indies in 1974. I was on vacation with my godparents in Montego Bay. We got in a taxi and noticed that the driver had a sign across his dashboard that said, "I love Jesus, do you?" My godmother started a conversation around that and then told him that I was a preacher. He brought his pastor and the pastor's wife from The Church of the Open Door to meet me the next day. They asked me to preach at their church on Sunday. They also booked me to preach on Sunday night. Those invitations opened the door for me to return. I've made several trips back to Jamaica to preach. I have even taken crusade groups with me. I formed the Fisher Specials and took the group for a whole week's crusade.

After years of preaching and teaching under the ordination of the King's Apostle Holiness Movement, a hunger to "go home" arose in Violet.

Although I was ordained in the King's Apostles Holiness Church, I wanted to return to the church of my birth. I believed there was something there for me. I remember the nurturing I received in class meetings. I remember my grandfather, as a class leader, standing there after Sunday morning worship and saying, "So brothers and sisters, how is it with your soul this week?" There was something about those testimonies, their sincerity that tugged at my heart.

I had not done any work in preparation for ministry in The United Methodist Church, so I retired from my job as a teacher, sold my home in Maryland, and enrolled at Eastern Baptist Seminary in Philadelphia. I was in seminary while under appointment in the Eastern Pennsylvania Conference to St. Daniel's in

Chester, Pennsylvania. I went through the required three-year process in The United Methodist Church and was ordained Deacon in 1988 and Elder in 1990. The St. Daniel's congregation affirmed my journey into ministry as an ordained elder. After three years in Chester, I was appointed to Sayers Memorial in Philadelphia.

Her first experience of itinerancy caused some pain and offered a great ministry time.

I cried when I was sent to Philadelphia. The superintendent called and said he wanted to talk with me about an appointment. When we met the next day, he told me about Philly. I was scared to death of the city. I thought, I can't go to Philadelphia. Now I know that the Philadelphia appointment gave me the best opportunity for ministry that I had ever had. What a joy it was to serve that congregation and community.

When Bishop Susan Morrison called to set up an appointment with me, I couldn't understand why was she calling me. When we met, the bishop told me she had the gift of discernment and believed I should be a district superintendent (DS), serving on her cabinet. I wondered how I could say no to my superior who felt my work in Philadelphia was not yet finished. We agreed to pray about it. She gave me a time to call her back. I prayed and I prayed. Finally, I decided that if my gifts in ministry would serve the larger church, I was available. I served in this ministry role for six years, under Bishops Morrison and Weaver.

Violet honors an early heritage and opportunities given to her as a teenager as the source of her confidence.

I think the knowledge that I had something to say and the ability to say it came from my Scout leader first. Even though I was the only black person in Girl Scout competition, I won. My self-confidence and recognizing my own gifts came from that experience. That was success for me!

Then there were the opportunities that the church gave me to speak. It was important that the pastors and church leaders understood that I had something to say and allowed me to come into their pulpits, to preach at their camp meetings, particularly when there weren't a lot of young women preaching. I felt the call coming from these people, pulling me out and sanctioning what

I was doing. My youth president said to me, "God is going to use you and take you into places that some of us will never go."

My parents' affirmations and willingness to walk with me were crucial. My father sat in the audience and prayed for me while I preached. When I served in Jamaica and Bermuda, my mom, who also became an ordained elder in her church, was sitting there praying me through. The church really, really affirmed me.

The sibling relationship is dear and carries particular placement for Violet.

My brothers and sisters always treated me as if I was different. It was good that they acknowledged it. They've always given me a sort of reverence. I baptized all of their babies. What blesses me is, when my nieces and nephews are in difficult situations, they call me.

After Daddy's death, my sister wrote, "Violet, I just wanted to remind you how special you are to me and to our family. We all appreciate everything that you do to hold our family together. You know without a doubt that you had a special place in Dad's heart and he was truly grateful to you for going the extra mile to make life better for him and Mother. We all appreciate memories of our life with our father."

A sense of community expectation has always been with Violet.

The community felt that if you did well, you brought good to everyone in the community. Other people would benefit. I don't remember it feeling like a burden. I felt it was an expectation and that I could do it. I don't remember feeling as though I had to do something that I didn't want to do. I had high expectations for myself. But I never imagined I would end up being a bishop!

The journey was mapped out, all laid out.

When I turned off the tape recorder, I felt an overwhelming sense of wonder. Violet's unquestioning confidence that every step of her life is part of a divine plan that she has embraced with vigor is so strong and left me speechless for a while. When I think of the places she has proclaimed the gospel with force and delight, I am convinced with her that only God could open the doors that led to her travels and give her a message worthy of the invitations. When I hear her preach, I know she still moves in that river of assurance and knowledge of God in her life that has marked her story. It is consistent from beginning knowing of salvation to actively living out of the confidence of her salvation in her episcopacy.

Susan Wolfe Hassinger

The New Englandesque house sits in a quiet neighborhood. There Susan offers hospitality in simple surroundings. There are a number of family heirloom pieces scattered about. She points them out quietly. At home with herself, Susan invites visitors to be at home with her. Susan starts the saga of her grandparents and parents through the lens of their church involvement.

My mother grew up in the town of Hanover, which is about seven miles over the Mason-Dixon line in Pennsylvania. My maternal grandfather, Stremel, grew up in a Plain Brethren community in which musical instruments were not allowed in worship. But my grandfather had a lovely singing voice. My grandmother, Werner, had United Brethren roots in her family. So my grandparents began going to a United Brethren church.

My grandfather was German, and my grandmother was German and Scotch-Irish. I'm told that she spoke only German, and my mother and her siblings taught my grandmother to read English. They went to a little church in the heart of Hanover, which later became the fruit and vegetable store after the church outgrew that space. The church built another large brick building. My grandparents and my mother and her sister were very active in the church. When my mother was in late adolescence, the church split. My family was heavily involved with the split, though I'm not sure how so. My mother and my father ended up in that split-off church after their marriage. My grandfather on my mother's side was a Sunday school teacher. Both my grandmother and grandfather were very involved, but I think my grandfather more overtly than my grandmother.

My father grew up in Adams County, Pennsylvania, on various farms, with a good bit of time spent on one farm near Hampton, Pennsylvania. One of his parents had come from the Lutheran tradition, and the other from the Reformed tradition. He grew up in the Reformed tradition. That was not uncommon. In Pennsylvania, there were union churches in which Lutheran and Reformed worshiped together, and often families included both. The family was very much involved, primarily I think because of my father's mother.

Education was the norm of the household from the beginning.

My mother was school principal in an elementary school, and my father was a teacher. Today this might be called harassment. He was about three years younger than she was. They dated and then decided to get married. Mother was in her early thirties at that point, and Dad was twenty-nine, I guess.

My father's last name was Wolfe with the "e" added by his mother. Less of an animal, maybe. But she also had that German background, though my father was really more American and did not speak German. I think there may have already been some concern and movement away from Germanic roots with World War I, and definitely with World War II.

Talk of education is comfortable, and most of the story of life centers on the educational work of parents.

My mother was a school administrator very early, and she started out with two years of normal school, the equivalent to today's teachers' colleges. She then went to Columbia University in New York during the summers to earn a bachelor's degree, and then continued beyond that. It was the late 1920s, so it was unusual for a woman to keep going like that. She started teaching in a one-room school but didn't stay there long before going into the town to teach. Mother was at Millersville, and Dad was at Schippersburg. Both of them continued their education. I know they went to Penn State during the summers, even after they were married.

The same willingness to persevere I experience in Susan, I feel in her talk about her father. A career in largely modest situations did not hinder the expansion of mind and ability.

My dad kept pursuing education after we were born. My mother did not. At the time, the school system said that once a woman was pregnant, she could no longer teach. At one time, you could not be married and teach, but that rule was changed. When they were married, they moved my father out of my mother's school. Or, they may have gone to different schools. But my dad continued learning throughout his life until he could no longer concentrate on reading, in his older years. He eventually became administrator of a small school district made up of a couple of one-room schools and a larger school. As administrator, he consolidated them into one building with eight grades and then, eventually, helped them con-solidate with an even larger school district.

There were some years during which he didn't teach, but he always had something else going. He worked in a retail store sell-ing men's clothing and worked on a farm. During many of my older elementary and youth years, he sold insurance. He was not entrepreneurial in terms of starting his own business, but was always looking for more opportunities wherever he was.

Although Susan was a child of wartime and her father was away dur-ing her birth, her story is poignant beyond that. Only later did she learn of the wider trauma surrounding her birth.

I came in to the family in 1942, the first child. My father was old enough to escape battle, but he was conscripted into the medical corps. He was in Seattle in the Navy Medical Corps around the time I was born, and was not present at my birth. I'm sure it affected my mother. I was a twin, but the other twin died before birth. I'm not sure how far along in the pregnancy my mother was when she lost the other twin. And at first, she did not realize I was hanging on. I never knew that until I was in my late-thirties. She never talked about it. Finally, when I had children of my own, and they were early elementary school-age, she told me. I've never quite figured out what happened. I don't know that she ever worked through what happened.

I'm not sure she ever bonded with me. Her bond with my brother, who came fifteen months after me, was much, much deeper. I've had to come to terms with that. I don't know whether she ever fully grieved the loss of the other twin or if she, as a married professional, did not want to talk about it. Although she always cared for me, I couldn't have named the sense of distance I felt.

The sense of distance between mother and daughter was filled with love of father and grandparents.

I grew to be closer to my dad than to my mom. I was close to my grandparents, too. My grandfather died when I was five, and within a couple of months, Grandma closed up the house in town and came to live with us. Then my mother went back to teaching. Grandmother did a lot of the household chores such as cooking during the week. My mother did them on the weekends. Grandmother is the one who would sit down with me and read a book. She was a major influence in my life. She lived with us until I went away to college. She was a nurturer for me. I also knew she was a great woman of faith. I would frequently see her in her room, reading her Bible and praying, and I knew that that was important. She was a strong person, both spiritually and physically, well into her eighties. She died in her nineties. When she was in her seventies, she fell and broke her arm at the shoulder cap, and they thought she would never use it again. So she created her own therapy by carrying around a bucket and moving her hands with a ball. She regained use of it, almost completely. She was a very powerful presence for me.

Susan continues to admire her mother and her abilities.

From the time my father came home from the service, we lived in a house on Broadway in Hanover. My parents were there until 1988. I went to Penn Street Elementary School, where my mother was a teacher. I never knew school without parental involvement until I was in the sixth grade. She taught fourth grade. Since there were several fourth-grade classes, I did not have her for a teacher. She didn't teach my brother either. She avoided that. I think she was wise in recognizing that it's too easy for either people to see favoritism, or for the parent to go overboard not to show favoritism. She really knew the boundaries.

She was an excellent pianist and decent organist until her fingers were twisted by arthritis and she could no longer move them the way she used to. She and my aunt, her sister, were both musically inclined and often did duets. Sometimes they played for church.

Being in school was great for Susan. She was, and is, a strong student and an avid learner.

I enjoyed school—except for art in first grade. The art teacher was a close friend of my parents, particularly of my mother. She was a single woman who rarely took a shower or a bath, so she had this awful body odor! She was short, stout, and herself an excellent artist, but she taught art like an artist. If you did not do what she thought you should, she'd come around and hit your fingers with a ruler. I grew to have distaste for art and distrust in my artistic talent. I have never overcome that. Although I love to go to art museums, don't ask me to draw!

Friendships were more neighborhood- than school-oriented.

I was not a groupie at school. There was a group of kids in the neighborhood. That's where the group formed. Not so much with friends in the elementary school. These kids were often at our house and played ball in the yard. My mother was always glad that we were there.

When the seven-year locusts came, we collected the shells left on the trees. I can remember sitting down and making an orchestra— a pretend orchestra—out of them. And we would put on shows for the kids in the neighborhood and for one another. Like puppet shows. Mother had a portable puppet stage, and so we put on shows.

Quiet and reserved during her teen years, Susan found school intriguing scholastically, but social life less consuming than for other teens.

In junior high, the class work was not difficult. When I started school, I knew the names of a lot of teachers because my parents had known them across the years. And I had heard stories about them, some good and some bad. So I knew a lot of them as personalities before I ever had any contact with them.

In high school, the band and orchestra were formative communities for me. Although I had a choice, as everybody did, with what language I studied, I was one of the few students who chose to study Latin. I had Latin for three years. And then I audited a French class for two years because I wanted to learn a modern language. It was relatively easy for me. I feared chemistry and physics—and would have liked to stay away from them. But I loved languages. The Latin teacher was really a fine person and made a deep impression on me. Curiously, she came out of a Church of the Brethren background. I don't know how she ever learned to be so free. She didn't wear the head covering in class. But there was something about her presence that really impressed me.

When it came to gym class, I tried to find ways to get out of it. I did a little drama in junior high but was too shy to get involved. Music was my big thing. I was first chair flute from the time I was in eighth grade, I guess, and went on to do district and state events. So I did perform solo. In my senior year, I did a solo for the band concert. I also did choral music when I could, although the schedule made it difficult to do both band and choir. I did as much as I could at high school.

What couldn't be fit in at school seemed to find expression in church.

I sang in the church choir from the time I was in the ninth grade. Both of my parents were in the church choir. I loved to sing, and I learned early how to sing parts because I read music from playing piano and flute. I contributed mostly to the alto section. I could sing tenor, too. Oh, I love to sing! The only thing about singing next to me is that my usual pattern is to sing alto, tenor, bass an octave higher, and then the melody—at least you get some variety!

The young woman who became Susan's youth leader had a profound effect on her.

When I was in high school, our youth group leader was a young woman who was a public school teacher and eventually went into mission work. She began to feed me a kind of theology, and I started reading theology of all sorts when I was in high school. I can't remember the titles now. They would have been from a conservative bent because this young woman had come out of Intervarsity at Penn State. But these were books that she had, and she would hand them on to me. I didn't completely buy what I was reading.

She came to town right out of college. She taught in an elementary school and was immediately recruited to be adult leader for the church youth group. She was there only for a short time—maybe three or four years—before she went into missionary work in Mexico with Wycliffe Bible translators. On two occasions, she took me with her to visit her family in the Washington, D.C. area. It was my first real experience away from my family although I'd been away from home at camp and stayed with other family members. She was really influential for me.

Actually, it is not surprising that Susan would be able to comprehend some of the reading. Both the varied religious experiences of her parents and her exposure to the youth leader became strong formational influences.

I mentioned that my mother's side of the family was part of a group that split from their church to become an independent church. I think the split was more about personal stuff than about anything else. The church that split off called itself Otterbein. For a long time they were not in the conference and had an independent pastor. It would not have been called fundamentalist in the way that we use fundamentalist now, but it was obviously conservative. The pastor was an unlearned farmer and had to be called out from the field if someone needed a minister. He preached the same thing over and over and got people hyped up emotionally. There was shouting and jumping in the aisles.

It was hard for my parents to attend that church because they grew in faith as time went on. They were probably the only two college-educated people in the congregation. My father was a Sunday school teacher and Sunday School Superintendent, and my mother was a pianist. When my brother and I were in junior high, we stopped going to Otterbein. I don't know what happened, but I think my parents were accused of something. I think their education and their tendency to raise questions made some waves at Otterbein. At that point, the pastor of the church that had been my mother's church during her childhood and her youth invited our family to go there. And we did. It had been United Brethren but, by then, had become Evangelical United Brethren. My parents became very active in the church.

So reading that conservative theology and my feelings about it were relative. I was in that independent, almost fundamentalist, judgmental church. But it was in that same church that I had my first religious experience. It was somewhat expected that by the age of twelve one would have a revival response and go down the aisle to the altar to be saved from sin. Since I was accustomed to altar calls and had participated in them, my own revival response was meaningful to me at that point. This was the mind-set of the church I came out of, although The Evangelical United Brethren Church was a lot more open than that. Instead of revivals, the EUB Church would bring in great preachers and scholars and people of that sort for preaching. I was exposed to a whole different theological world. Even though I couldn't really comprehend it at that point, I had a real eagerness to learn, to increase my biblical knowledge. I remember in particular one book that was influential for me at the time was basically a commentary on Romans. Where did that hungering come from? Why would anybody have been reading that stuff in high school?

As pious as that background may seem, there was not an overly active religious life at home.

We did not do Bible study at home. We prayed before meals. My grandmother read the Bible. When I was a child, we had Bible storybooks that either my brother and I could read ourselves or were read to us. I knew that my mother kept the Bible and the Upper Room on a windowsill in the bathroom, which was the only place she could escape for a couple of minutes. Although she never talked any about it, I was very much aware it was there. You know, it was just part of the scenery. But we did not have family worship.

Susan is an introvert, and that introversion defined a good deal of her social life as a teenager.

I was not what I would call popular or a groupie. The primary group I was in was the youth group at church. We had a great bunch there. I also hung out with some band folks. I was not the "in" crowd, but I would unintentionally "collect" people. I would find myself listening to people, mostly to girls who had sob stories. I was the listener. I formed some friendships with people in the band, but not close friendships. I had one very close friend, but she was of the "in" crowd. Her father was head of a manufacturing firm in the town. But I couldn't run with that crowd.

I dated very little but did go to the big events—the proms and homecoming. I was a misfit. When I look back, it is somewhat painful. I always felt that I was different. Not that I wanted to be or tried to put myself in a different place, I just felt like I was different. Different because of the kinds of things that I thought about and read and so forth. So I wasn't dying because I didn't date, but it was clear that that's what the "in" crowd did. I was decidedly not the most popular girl in school.

What I loved was languages, literature, and music. I knew many musicals by heart. I loved the reading of theology. Those are some of the things that kind of intrigued me. I plowed through *Anna Karenina* as a teenager. The book *Peyton Place* passed through chemistry class. It went under the lab table. There wasn't much sex education. My mother, I assume, had some books on the shelves in their bedroom. That's where *Anna Karenina* came from. I surreptitiously borrowed the books. I'm sure she would have recognized they were not there.

So my teen years were a mixture. There was a lot of happiness, but also feelings of not quite belonging. I think my deep involvement with the church made me feel different. I sensed something there I couldn't fully describe and knew that it didn't fit with everybody else. But there were also a lot of really good times. I went to different children's Sunday school classes and played the piano. I got out of a lot of Sunday school. And I played for various groups and was the pianist for the youth fellowship. I had a place in the church.

At last it was time for college. There was never any doubt that Susan would go to college. Her love of learning would have propelled her even without the high value placed on education in her home.

There were high expectations in my family. After all, both of my parents were teachers. By that time I was in junior high, each of them had enough continuing education to have the equivalent of a master's degree. So education was just assumed. And school wasn't hard for me.

When I went to college, I assumed I would become an elementary teacher. That's all I knew. What else was there? I went to Lebanon Valley College in Annville, Pennsylvania. The youth group and the pastor there influenced me because it was an Evangelical United Brethren school. It was two hours away from home, so it was close. But it felt great to leave home and go off to college. I can't remember being sorry when I was taken there. I was ready.

Eventually I came to like dorm life. In my freshman year, I was in an old house with three students squeezed into a room. Two of us were fairly compatible. The third girl didn't know how to take showers and was overly tied with her home. She left at the end of the year. That house was a great place. I really got to know a number of folks in ways I don't think could have happened if I'd been a freshman in the larger dorm. One of those people invited me to Student Christian Association and Delta Tau Chi, which was the religious vocation group. At that point, I hadn't seriously thought about being a missionary. I had signed up at summer camp, but so what? I became part of both groups and, through that, connected with some other upperclassmen and upperclasswomen.

The next year, I roomed with the girl whom I had been compatible with during freshman year. After Thanksgiving, she tried to commit suicide and had to leave school.

Enter the college chaplain.

One of my primary influences at college was the chaplain, Jim Bemesderfer, and his wife. They would frequently invite students to their home. Mrs. Bemesderfer helped me improve the knitting skills that my mother had taught me. I eventually became secretary to the chaplain and his assistant in the Religion Department. He was very influential in my life.

After my first semester, I switched my major to English. In the house, there were quite a number of elementary education majors, and I began to watch how they would have to prepare projects for their classes—cutting and pasting and doing all of that stuff. It just seemed ridiculous. I couldn't imagine my education being based around that.

I was foolish enough, even as an elementary education major, to sign up for Greek. And I loved it. I took Greek all four years. I was beginning to get a taste of the intellectual life and just knew—this is the only way to say it—that if I was to become a teacher in an elementary classroom, I would not be satisfied. But I didn't know what else I was going to be. English seemed like a safe place to go, and I already loved literature. So that's where I went. Gradually I began to assume that I would be a college teacher in English. That's where I thought I was headed. It took only one semester to change direction.

Changes come in all colors and forms. They also come at varying stages of life. For Susan, college was a great turning point. Summers were a time of simmer and sizzle as Susan's dreams for the future were shaped.

The summer after my freshman year, I went to Washington, D.C. and participated in a program sponsored by the National YMCA and YWCA. Students from all over the country came together. We lived in an old hotel that soon after was knocked down. It had no air-conditioning and was near Union Station. All of us worked somewhere in Washington. Some of the women were in senators' offices. I worked in the government printing office. Some worked in House of Representatives' offices. All kinds of things. In the evenings and on the weekends, we would gather for conversation, lectures, and retreats. One time we visited Bobby Kennedy's office when he was Attorney General. It was my first acquaintance with a speakerphone: He called his brother, the President, and put him on the speakerphone!

One retreat—with somebody whose name I've long forgotten— tied faith to the political and ethical scene. Beginning to think about the relationship of faith, ethics, and politics was so mind-expanding for me. I *loved* being in Washington. My daily job at the government printing office was boring, but the rest of the experience was great.

The college chaplain provided the entrée to international experience.

The summer after my sophomore year, the chaplain of whom I spoke had put out information about an ecumenical work camp in Ecuador. I indicated my desire to go. He helped me get some funding. So I spent about two months in Ecuador with a group coordinated by a sociology professor with a Church of the Brethren background and from Texas. We were from all different denominations. We had Puerto Ricans in the group who, at that point, were considered international. Plus, young Ecuadorians would join us there. This trip was a revolutionary experience for me. That's where I started to raise questions about the Church, believe it or not. I saw some missionaries really connecting with the people. But one missionary couple acted in very paternalistic ways. They were actually in charge of the work camp. So, while the cross-cultural experience was mind-expanding, I also began to see that the mission of the Church wasn't what I had thought it was. As my understanding of the gospel grew, I began to see that kind of paternalism and racism as antithetical to the gospel. I came back with an internal struggle, both loving the Church and also despising what I saw the Church doing.

Engagement in the Civil Rights Movement of the 1960s marks this young woman's life. To this day, nonviolence and racial justice are hallmarks of Susan's way of being.

When I came back for my junior year—that would have been the fall of 1963—it was the very beginning of the Civil Rights Movement. I don't know how, but I was one of two people who went from Annville to Philadelphia for training in nonviolent civil rights action. It was really the beginning of my consciousness-raising about race as an issue of faith. I brought that back and began to do some talking and work on the civil rights issue at Lebanon Valley campus.

I went to the March on Washington, and I did local things, both in Pennsylvania and in Dayton. My folks—primarily my mother—were very traditional, and Hanover, being just across the Mason-Dixon line, was an anti-black community. Even a few years ago, it had rules on its books that blacks could not stay overnight. That rule goes back to the pre–Civil War era. There were no blacks in Hanover. Nearby York had a significant black community, but not Hanover. Until college, I had no interaction with black people other than going to York to do shopping and seeing them there. But college really opened my eyes.

She began to push the boundaries, partly in fun, partly because she was becoming one who would see no racial boundaries.

At the Ecuador work camp, there was a black Puerto Rican male who was a seminary student and brilliant. I thought I was in love with him. When we flew back into Miami, my parents and my grandmother had come down to meet me because we were going to travel in Florida and then drive home. I came off of the plane holding hands with this young man and got a very negative reaction, primarily from my mother. My father was quieter than my mother, but still not too thrilled with it. That would have been 1962. We corresponded for a while, but the relationship was clearly not going anywhere. In my parents' eyes, I flirted with danger in that connection. They knew I was heavily involved with the Civil

Rights Movement in college and seminary. They could not understand it, though they later came to accept it.

The summer after that, I was asked to go to three EUB summer camps to interpret the work camp experience and to invite others to participate. I was in Florida for several weeks, St. Mary's in Ohio, and New York, near Buffalo. During the course of that summer, as I was sharing my experience with others, I began to have a love/hate relationship with the Church, which I probably still have. In a couple of these places, they used me as a counselor, but it was more of an interpretive role. I began to sort through what I had begun feeling, but had not totally dealt with, the year before that.

At Camp St. Mary's, there was a laywoman counselor at the same time I was there. She was probably in her midfifties. And by this time, I had had enough religion courses that I thought that I knew a lot and challenged some biblical interpretations. I guess I acted pretty cocky. Well, she called me to account, both by her own personal expression of faith and by challenging me. I don't know how she did it, but she invited me to go back and think about a faith not just of the head, but also of the heart. Out of that experience, I renewed my commitment to Christ, as I confessed that I didn't know it all and that a head trip wasn't going to save me or anybody else. I wasn't ready to throw out the head knowledge, but I knew that that wasn't the core. That was a tremendous experience. It's one of those moments that you really think back on. I went from there to the New York camp. I have no idea now why, but in that New York camp, having just left that other experience, I had this sense of being called to pastoral ministry. And I knew—it was so clear—that my calling was not to be a Christian educator, not to be a missionary, but to be a pastor.

The decision put her at odds with her parents, who were always clear that education was the highest calling.

I did tell my family because I knew I had to. They assumed that I would teach some place, or at least go to graduate school. So I had to tell them. Their first reaction was disbelief: "You can't do that." But I remained firm. It wasn't just me saying this. There was something very deep within me, and I knew I needed to do that. Mother had been distressed that I went to Ecuador. She also hadn't been happy that I went to Washington. In essence, once I left high school, I spent very little time at home. In each of those cases, I did what I felt I needed to do. She wasn't happy, but by then I'd learned she would survive. Dad didn't say much at all. Only after I was elected Bishop did I learn that my father had thought of going to seminary but didn't. He had never shared that. So he didn't say very much.

According to the United Brethren rules, ordination of women was okay. But the people I was with were not UB. Bishop Kaebnick was from the Evangelical tradition. So Jim Bemesderfer said to me, "You'd better get ready. Somebody's coming." He's the one who gave me information on United Theological Seminary in Dayton, Ohio. Jim really gave me encouragement. Without that, I don't know what I would have done.

Intellectual curiosity lived side by side with spiritual searching.

I still periodically went to the EUB church on the edge of campus. When I went to Washington, I attended a Friends' meeting and Episcopal churches. I began to experience other liturgical traditions, other faith traditions. And I found things that I liked in all of them. Throughout my college years, I kept exploring the various worship traditions. During my junior year, I saw a notice about a Salvation Healing Holy Ghost Revival. I still remember. It was an Assembly of God church. I can remember recruiting a group of people—about five of us—who went in and sat in the back during this revival where there was lots of wailing going on. At first I had some hesitance about doing it. But it also drew me. I wanted to see what else was out there.

Susan reflects with gratitude on many people along her journey who opened doors to alternative ways of thinking, challenged her with new and stretching experiences, and affirmed her choices as they unfolded. Without naming names, she speaks of them.

Each influential person I remember encouraged me to try new things and to expand my horizons, even when I felt as if I couldn't. They always offered new opportunities, though I suspect I wasn't the only one to whom they offered the opportunities. That was just who they were. I think, for example, of the college chaplain. In 1963, when he heard about my calling to be a local church pastor, he could have said, "You're nuts. Forget it." Instead, he gave me all kinds of encouragement, talked with Bishop Kaebnick, and gave me the information about United.

The die was cast and United was on the horizon.

I was warmly received at United when I began in 1964. Harriet Miller gathered the women. Between the students in the Master of Religious Education and the Bachelor of Divinity programs, there were probably eight to ten of us. I received all kinds of encouragement from the faculty. Harriet was very important to me. Ed Burtner in preaching. George Frey. George Harner in New Testament. Probably one of the most influential people was the Greek teacher. I loved both Greek and Hebrew. Barr was the Old Testament professor. Biblical studies were probably my favorite courses. And I think because the professors sensed that, they were particularly encouraging.

Susan was married in 1966. Her husband graduated that year and was given his appointment, and Susan changed schools.

My husband graduated in 1966 and was appointed. I had to switch to Lancaster Theological Seminary, and my degree is from Lancaster. I very much wanted my degree to be from United, but United said, "In order to have your degree from here, you have to be here for your last year." And Lancaster said, "In order to have your degree from here, you have to have two years here." So, I essentially took one year's worth of classes in two years.

Then came ordination, but no appointment.

When I began the process of ordination and membership, the questions I remember them asking me were not about theology, but about my plans for a family: What happens if you get married? Or the bigger question: What happens if you get pregnant? if you have a baby? "I'll have a baby!" was my answer. And I wasn't trying to be disrespectful. But if you become pregnant, then you have a baby!

I was ordained Elder in June of 1968. All of my processing was done with EUB. The conference lines remained the same at that point, and the Board of Ordained Ministries that I went through was the former Board of Ordained Ministers. But, under the EUB rules, I didn't have to have an appointment. So, I was ordained but without an appointment for several years.

As a pioneer, Susan pushed boundaries in many directions.

I was the first woman to be ordained "in modern times." The United Brethren had that history. After my ordination, my husband was appointed to Manheim Salem EUB as an associate. A lady at that church remained as a kind of local preacher attached to that church. She really had more of a Christian education career, and I don't know if she ever served as a pastor. But she had some kind of ordination as a United Brethren. She was an older woman when we were there. I was the first Elder in what became the Eastern Pennsylvania Conference of The United Methodist Church.

Who knows what my conference relationship was. I hung out. I was ordained in 1968. In 1969, the District Superintendent came to me. It was fairly apparent that we should be moved. They offered us churches near his home area where I would have had a two-point charge. I would have driven past one of his churches to get to a second church. They were doing a stretch. I can't believe it, but we turned it down.

Instead, my husband went to Park Church in Reading, Pennsylvania, in 1969. We lived in Pennside, which is a suburb of Reading. In 1970, the superintendent came to me and said, "There's a church in Fleetwood where the pastor is retiring. He's been on what they call sustentation, and we've decided that we can't continue supporting him. So the church won't be able to afford a full-time pastor on its own." This was before part-time appointment was even allowed in the *Discipline*. In essence, he asked me if I would be willing to have a church, but only part time. And he said to the church, "You have a choice between this woman pastor less than full time, or you can close your doors." I don't think it was stated quite that harshly, but that was the essence of it. I had experienced real depression during those years without appointment, wondering why I had bothered. So I was willing to try anything. And the people were willing to try anything—at least some of them. Enough were willing, so I went. It was a former Evangelical church, which meant that when the Evangelicals had split, it had gone with the split. And it was the only church in Berks County that was a major Evangelical headquarters. In that whole area, it was the only one to come back into the Evangelical Association. So it had the Evangelical roots. But, of course, it felt more Evangelical United Brethren than it did United Methodist at that stage.

Thankfully, the superintendent and the church were willing to take a risk. I also took a maternity leave from that church before it was in the *Discipline*. I figured out how to do it and told the superintendent. The church was willing to do it, so I didn't think of myself as pushing the envelope. I just saw something and did it.

Although that little church had fallen on such hard times, they were marvelous. Within one year's time, they moved from having a pastor part time to having one full time. They were just marvelous people, had an excellent spirit. I was there for seven years, through the birth of two children, which also was a new experience. When a male pastor has a child born in the family, it's great but not such a big deal. But when the chair of the staff parish would say, "My pastor's pregnant," you get an incredulous and mystified reaction. Yet, by that time, he was proud to say it. And the church members were willing eventually—at least some of them—to go talk to other churches that were having difficulty with the idea of women pastors. Just imagine!

When I was pregnant the second time, I began to realize that it was going to be much harder to handle two children than to handle one. So, I asked to work less than full time after my three-month maternity leave. That worked out. Janet, a woman in her midforties, began to sense a call to ministry. She had worked at Western Electric in what they called the "Clean Room," putting things together. She was struggling with this sense of call in her life. So we worked it out that she would handle most of the program areas of the church and some visitation, and I would handle the majority of the preaching and some pastoral care. For a year, we did that.

When I moved on, my husband and I both became part of the staff of a large church, each of us working three-fourths of the time. And Janet became a local pastor in another community. How we got away with doing some of that, I don't know! Quietly devious. I'm still doing that.

Susan had been deeply involved in the Civil Rights Movement in college and seminary. Now her early ministry years overlapped the Vietnam conflict.

I was more involved with civil rights than I was with the Vietnam War. I was opposed to Vietnam and spoke out against it at seminary. I also spoke out about it from the pulpit as a pastor, although the way I dealt with it was devious. I wrote a musical, putting the Christmas story in the context of people fleeing on boats and a birth occurring on the boat. This put the nativity scene in a contemporary setting. For the music, I used familiar tunes but rewrote the words. Gosh, I forgot I did that. My word! But that was a devious way of helping people see the humanity and the desperation of the Vietnamese boat people. I also tried unsuccessfully to get the Ecumenical group in the town to host refugees. I was a young whippersnapper among old, longtime Lutheran and Reformed, but I couldn't make a breakthrough there. I would also include the issue, to some extent, in my preaching and my prayers. But I don't think I went out and protested against Vietnam, like I did during the Civil Rights Movement.

Some of Susan's heroes reflect her passion for justice.

Martin Luther King Jr. was clearly one of my heroes. Another one just came to mind, though I probably wouldn't have known about him before I was thirty-five: Desmond Tutu. Also John F. Kennedy. I can still remember, as many of that era can, where I was on the college campus when the word came about him being shot in Dallas. I had been in Washington early in his term, and it was an exciting time. New things were happening in the country and government, and he seemed to represent that.

I just noticed that all three I named were men! There was also Margaret Chase Smith. I just found it fascinating that she could be not only a state senator, but also a very prominent and thoughtful person. Since coming to Boston, I've realized even more how she was able to take a stand for what she knew—what she felt—was right, even if it wasn't totally with the party line. Queen Elizabeth was also inaugurated during the 1950s, and it was sort of a storybook experience. I was fascinated not just with the pomp and circumstance of it, but with the woman and the position. She had some recognition, though not a whole lot of power.

But in the last analysis, she returns to family and church-related people as her most abiding influences.

Probably the three people who had the most influence on me were my grandmother, the youth fellowship leader, and Jim, the college chaplain. Once I started serving churches, there were others. First, my husband was a mentor for me. I had no women role models. There were also understanding superintendents: "Barney" Mentzer and George Bashore (now a bishop). And the one who awes me the most is Jim Ault (also now a bishop). He could take everyday situations and reflect theologically on them. It was just his nature. He was such a teddy bear of a person!

It's a long way from a conservative little town in Pennsylvania to Episcopacy. Did she ever imagine such a life?

Oh, heavens! My imagination didn't go very far: Go to college; be a teacher. I don't think I did, or could, see very far beyond that.

But it is a gift of God to the church that God's vision reached further than Susan's vision. Her quiet obedience to calls and claims on her life that took her out of anything she might have imagined is reflected in the way she carries on her work now. Though she is soft spoken, her wisdom and understanding of life's twists and turns and how people and institutions interact make her a powerful woman in the midst of trouble and conflict. Though she may not think of herself as a pioneer, her leadership helps people move into the new understandings and ways of being. Deeply rooted spirit, quiet leader, and wise counselor are all appropriate phrases to describe this woman of God.

Janice Riggle Huie

This interview took place in a small house located in the middle of a cow pasture on a ranch near Beeville, Texas. The house has been used as a guesthouse and a house for ranch hands. It is furnished sparsely, some of the furnishings being from the Huies' first household. Cattle graze in the huge flat pasture surrounding the house and stick their heads through the fence to enjoy the weeds in the unmowed yard surrounding the small building. Far on the horizon is a tree line, beyond which lies a "tank," a watering pond. It is not visible from the house, but a ten-minute walk takes one to a beautiful view of the next sweep of pasture where the tank is located. Janice had insisted that any understanding of her would arise from being on the land that nurtured her.

My mother grew up not too far from here. She grew up in Bee County, and her mother and father ran a dairy for a while. My mother's father was a tenant farmer. If we were to use more colloquial words, he was basically a sharecropper. By the time I was growing up, my mother's parents lived about three miles from here. My mother shared lots of things with them, including me. Sometimes Mother and her mother washed together on Monday, and on Friday night, my sisters and I got to spend the night with my grandmother and my grandfather. That was a big treat for us. When Mother and Daddy went to the high school football games, we got to spend the night with them. My first memory of their home was a house with a fireplace and a wood-burning stove. Later on, they moved to a little frame house in a pasture by a creek.

That's where I learned to walk these creeks. That's where I learned to pick grapes and make jelly. My grandfather always had time for the grandchildren, and we walked in these pastures. One time we discovered an old graveyard out in the middle of a pasture. Seeing the untended graves, many of which were the graves of children, made a big impression on me. I sensed a mystery that is still with me today.

Grandmother images are very strong in Janice's memory.

My two grandmothers were very strong women, each in her own way. My mother was also a strong woman in her own way, although more circumscribed by culture than, I think, probably her own mother was. My grandmothers were dominant figures in their families. In both cases, my grandmothers were stronger than the men they were married to. I think that was apparent to me growing up. The men had the formal roles, but the women shaped the household. My grandfather was a lot of fun. But my grandmother figured out how to get things done and knew how to do a lot with a little. She was a person of great strength.

My grandmother's mother died when she was fourteen years old. She had six younger siblings. My grandmother took care of her mother throughout her illness. Just a few hours before her death, my great-grandmother took off her wedding ring, gave it to her oldest daughter, and said, "Take care of the children." And so, my grandmother became the caretaker of this brood of children. Her father would eventually marry someone else, but at the tender age of fourteen, my grandmother became an independent woman at great sacrifice to herself. All of her hopes and dreams gave way to taking care of these younger ones. She became independent and strong. My own mother, the oldest daughter in her family, now has my great-grandmother's ring. She also has much of her own mother's strength.

I was in high school when I saw firsthand my grandmother's strength after the death of my grandfather. He was only sixty-two. With the breadwinner-farmer gone, my grandmother had to go back to work to provide an income for herself. She was also in her early sixties. She went to work as a cafeteria worker and worked until she was seventy-something. She cooked for hundreds of children in an elementary school cafeteria. She made her way—independently. A few months after my grandfather's death, I said to her, "Well, Mamaw, are you going to get married again?" And she said, and I quote, "I ain't gonna take care of no more old men."

I've got plenty of my grandmother in me—too much at times! When I have to, I can summon that kind of strength of my grandmother, whom I loved dearly and grew up around. That part of my grandmother is mine, that kind of self-sufficiency.

Grandma Riggle, on my dad's side, is the grandmother of faith. I watched her be very much involved in her church and her personal devotional life. When I was in high school, one of her sons-in-law gave her the J. B. Phillips translation of the Bible for Christmas. She told me privately that she'd take her King James Bible, thank you, and she didn't want that thing. Then she said to me, "Well, honey, if you want to take that and read it, you might enjoy it." Remember, I'm a reader. I sat down and in two days, I read the New Testament from Matthew to Revelation. I loved it. That was the first contemporary Bible I had ever seen.

I had these two really strong grandmothers in my life who were very much a part of a multigenerational family that's still all around here. At the time, I saw my grandmothers as strong women, stronger even than I saw my mother. Now, looking back, I think that wasn't true. My mother was strong in her own way. But I leaned into the strength of my grandmothers whom I saw as pioneers, as quite independent women.

Before my Grandma Riggle's funeral, our family told stories about her. My dad told me that when I went off to seminary, some family member said to grandmother, "Oh, Janice is going to seminary. She wants to get a MRS degree" (*meaning I wanted to get a husband*). And Daddy said, "And you should probably know that it was your grandmother who said to them, *"Hush, I don't want no more of that. Janice is doing what she is called to do."* When my grandmother told someone "hush," that was the end of it—at least around her! As far as I know, the talk ceased. I never knew about it until her death. Even today I think about what a gift it was for my dad to tell me that story. I believe that there was something in Grandma that allowed her to sense that there was more going on with this oldest granddaughter of hers than could be seen on the surface.

Out of her parents' life stories come life stories for her own children. Janice's dad farms and ranches. Janice and her husband's older son, Matt, has always wanted to follow in his grandfather's footsteps. When Matt entered his junior year in high school, he insisted that he wanted to spend the last two years of high school with his grandparents so that he could learn how to farm. The Huies reluctantly agreed, after exacting from him a promise that he would get a college education before he began farming and ranching. He did. Now Matt and his family live a mile from his grandparents' home, and he farms and ranches several thousand acres.

My mother graduated from high school in Beeville, and my parents met here in Beeville in 1944. At the time, my mother was working at the office of the Agricultural Stabilization and Conservation Committee. She and my father went down to Corpus Christi and got married. It was during the war, so it was a big deal. They got married in the living room of a Methodist preacher, spent one night in Corpus Christi, and then came back and went to work.

Dad wanted to farm like his father had done. Mother and Daddy lived for a few months in a little apartment before they got this land. As I recall, they got two hundred acres of land for a thousand dollars. They borrowed the money. By that time, mother was working in the bank. They have lived where they live now since maybe six months after they were married. The first house was a small house, a little white frame, shotgun house. I think it had five rooms originally: two bedrooms, kind of a living area, the kitchen, and some sort of little dining area. It was small! I was born in 1946. My roots are here out here on this land.

There were early lessons about frugality and living off the land that have left an imprint on Janice.

From the time I was a child, I heard stories about Roosevelt. Because of the Great Depression and how it affected the farmers, I grew up on stories about what it was like during the Depression. Of course, my parents are very much formed by that. Since I was born in 1946, I'm technically part of the baby boom generation. But in many ways, because of my own upbringing, I bridge backward a little better than I bridge forward. And so not owing money and being careful with spending was very much a part of my own growing up.

I started school when I was six years old, and by that time, I was so conscious of saving money. I have always been concerned about financial matters, which, I'm sure, comes from those experiences when I was young. We were conscious that we had to make it with what we had. There was talk about Mama going back to work when I couldn't have been more than six or seven years old. We didn't want Mama to go back to work, and by that time, my sister, Cherry, had been born. She's two years younger than I am. Mother did everything. She made every single dress we ever owned. I was thirteen years old before I ever bought a dress. I remember when we went to buy it. It was a huge thing. Mother made all of our dresses and we had a big garden. We had a cow at that point. We had chickens. During that time, we did everything to be self-sufficient.

The land and its importance, for past and future, is illustrated in a story Janice tells in many settings.

I was just beginning first grade when the drought of the 1950s scorched South and West Texas. It was terrible. Cracks in the earth were so wide, a little child could step in one and break a leg. For two years there was no crop at all. The grass died. Daddy sold nearly all of the cattle. He burned pear wood for the remainder. It was a tough time.

One evening, Daddy asked me if I wanted to drive to the pasture. I liked to do that. We drove out. He stopped the truck. He turned off the ignition. Even the evening breeze was hot. "Janice," he said, "what do you see?" I didn't know what to say. Old scrub brush with more thorns than leaves. Desolate, dry earth. Finally, I said, "I see brush—black brush and bee brush and juisache." I knew the names of brush like my boys know the names of video games. There was a long pause. I knew that I must not have given the right answer. I looked again. Nothing had changed. I tried again. "I see a jack rabbit and a rattlesnake." I didn't really see a rattlesnake, but I knew he wanted to hear me say something else. I knew rattlesnakes were out there, so I said I saw a rattlesnake. There was another long pause. I sneaked a look over at Daddy's face. There were two little furrows between his eyes. I knew I'd said something wrong, and it wasn't just because I made up that story about rattlesnakes.

"Daddy, what do you see?" I asked. We both looked out at that barren land. "One day, Janice, this land will all be knee-high grass. We'll graze three cows to the acre." He pointed to a little depression in the ground. "We'll put in a tank over there and stock it with catfish. We'll leave brush in the fencerows as ground cover for the quail. One day, Janice. You'll see." I didn't know the words then, but what I witnessed that late afternoon was the power of hope.

It took years for that vision to come true. The grass has all come back. And the cattle graze. Daddy bulldozed the brush, plowed the ground. Then he sprigged it in coastal grass and dug that tank. It's a couple hundred acres of some of the prettiest land you'll ever see, the kind that rolls a little bit. He left the oak trees and a few mesquite trees for shade for the cattle. Today he could lease those tanks out for more than he gets, but he isn't about to do that. Or he could lease the field for deer because there are deer on there now, but he doesn't. It is beautiful land.

Questions about Janice's mother provoke yet more stories.

My mother is this wonderful, sort of stereotypical woman. She was a homemaker. She is very nurturing and would die in a ditch for her children. Her idea of fulfillment is that you do whatever it takes to raise your family successfully. So mother was the on-site caretaker of the daughters.

Reading became an important outlet for Janice and a means of expanding her consciousness of the world.

Reading became a tremendous outlet for me. When I wanted to go to some other place, I did it through books. It is fair to say that I read every book in my elementary school library. Of course, now that I look back, it wasn't a very big library. I read every book in my junior high library. That was my way of going to a different place. That's how I discovered that not every girl was a housewife and that there might be something in addition to being a housewife and mother.

Winston Churchill said, "We shape our buildings and afterwards our buildings shape us." I think that the environment shapes us more than we give it credit for. We were only five miles from town. I had to ride to school on the bus. I caught the bus at seven in the morning and then rode forty miles all around this area to get to school at 8:30. Then in the afternoon, I got on the bus at 3:00 and was the last child off. Think of all those hours I was on the bus. What do you do with that? Most of the kids who rode the bus out here were Hispanic and spoke to one another in Spanish. I couldn't understand them. I had some Hispanic friends, and we talked a little, but mostly I coped with those long bus rides by reading. I read almost a book every day. That went on until I was fourteen years old and got a driver's license.

Out of that kind of arrangement came another lesson for Janice, which carried into many other parts of her life.

When Daddy was elected to the school board, one of the issues attended to was the fairness of the school bus route. If you're the first one on in the morning, then you ought to be the first off in the afternoon. Then Daddy said, "Well, we can't do special favors for my daughters." So, that long bus ride went on forever because no special favors. Here's another lesson from growing up. Just because you have whatever privilege, there are no special favors. If you're a girl and you want to work alongside men, you don't ask for special favors. I would think it fair to say that the lesson of not asking for special favors because of who you are was imprinted on my mind. When I drove a truck, which I did later, Daddy said, "Now, the men will probably offer to let you go in the front of the line because you are a woman. You tell them no thank you. You take your turn like everyone else." I've done that my whole life. The good news is that I don't function with a big sense of entitlement. The bad news is that I function far too much out of a sense of works righteousness.

In spite of the isolation of the ranch and the clearly defined role expectations, Janice did not feel fenced in. Yet, in retrospect, she sees some family patterns that she did eventually come to see as limitations.

I don't think I was aware of my life being limited at the time. I started to figure it out by the time I got to high school. This is a wonderful, safe, secure place. There weren't a lot of reasons to push against it. My sister was here. My sister Cherry is two years younger than I am, so we really grew up together. My other sister, Patty, is ten years younger than I am. So that stretch meant that she grew up an only child, in effect.

I graduated from high school in 1965. Everybody wanted me to be a teacher. That's what you do for good insurance, my parents said. Get a college degree and teach school. So the world they expected was really this world. Big country world. The same world that their parents and their parents' parents had lived in. The expectation was this world would also be my world. As much as I love this place—it's so much a part of me—it was just too small. I think that was probably true from the time I was as young as five or six years old. When I started to read, I learned there was another world out there and wanted to experience it.

Janice's father had a strong sense of service to the community. He served on the school board in 1956 and 1957, during the time schools were being integrated. From his example, Janice picked up this commitment to service, political activity, and a strong sense of justice. It began to show in high school.

By the time I was in high school, I was a far-out liberal. We were pursuing the war in Vietnam. Between the church and my family and hearing all the stories about FDR, I was a raging liberal.

When I was a senior in high school, I was nominated for a Rotary award. Teachers nominated students, and those who were nominated were interviewed by a group of men from the Rotary Club. In the interview, I was asked about the Vietnam War. I told them how wrong I thought it was. Little did I know that every guy on the committee was a Republican. I unloaded on them all of my liberal Democratic leanings. I laid out all the issues involved because by this time, I could talk politics with the best of them. I was used to doing it at home with Daddy and had been reading the paper. When I told Daddy what had happened, he said, "Oh, Janice, they're all in favor of that. Well, you didn't win that one."

A couple of days later, they held this big assembly and announced that I won. My Dad was there. The men from the Rotary club were his friends, though he was never a member himself. He told me that I was the only one who knew what had happened and could talk articulately about it. So, whether his friends agreed or not, they had to give it to me—even if I was a little overzealous. Being able to talk politics was a pretty important part of my family culture.

When Janice talks about church, she doesn't start with a congregation.

My first experiences of the transcendent and holy occurred not in church, but rather in nature. That's another thing that connects me with this land so much. The house wasn't air-conditioned, so I'd lie out in the yard under the chinaberry tree and watch the clouds. You could feel the wind in your face. You'd feel the earth, and the earth was sometimes hot, sometimes warm. I remember how the grass felt underneath me. I remember how the sky was with the clouds, changing shapes. The gulf breezes would start, maybe at six o'clock at night. Then it started to cool off. I didn't know what to name it, but I knew there was something more, something larger than me from the time I was a little girl. There was something that I was a part of and it was a part of me.

Before I knew there was church, I knew there was something else. Then church came along. But what I now understand as The Holy or Mystery was experienced before I really understood what church was all about.

In 1994, Janice's thirteen-year-old son, David, was killed in an accident. The land became her solace once again.

After David's death, I was a total basket case. It was horrible. I was called to the scene of the accident right after it happened. I saw David out there, my beautiful child, dead on the asphalt. I went to Beeville to grieve. My husband was here part of the time. You just have to grieve and do the best you can in your own way. I came home.

I had terrible flashbacks. I'd wake up, sometimes at midnight, sometimes at one or two in the morning, with a flashback. I'd be trembling and crying. So I'd get the quilt and go outside on the porch swing. It might be eighty degrees out there in late June, but I'd wrap up in the quilt. I would lie down on the swing and put my head so I could see out. I'd lie there and let the wind blow over me, looking at the stars and the moon. I would hear the coyotes. And I'd sometimes hear the cows. Finally, I would stop shaking and go back to sleep. Nearly every night Daddy would get up and check on me outside on the porch. Sometimes one of the first psalms I ever memorized, probably in high school, would come to my mind: "Where shall I go from your Spirit, where shall I flee from your presence? If I ascend to the Heavens, you are there, if I make my bed in Sheol, you are there. If I take the wings of the morning to the uttermost parts of the sea, even there Thy hand shall lead me" (Psalm 139:7–10). That would kind of flow in and out, and I'd go back to sleep. I was probably there a month. When I started sleeping through the night again, I took the stars with me back to my bed. Then I knew I could probably go back home to San Angelo.

This terrible story comes tumbling out in the midst of beginning to talk about church. The story always goes back to the land and that early sense of Holy. So when in grief, Janice returned to the mystery of holy that preceded any cognitive understanding. When there was no way to understand the loss of David, she turned back toward the mystery of her first knowing.

So, before I knew church, I knew the Holy. I knew the Sacred. I knew Mystery. I had to learn ecclesiology. Ecclesiology is not my first language. My first language is much more contemplative. Ecclesiology is my second language, not my first.

I've been going to church since I was six weeks old. I was in church every single Sunday. The Methodist line is on my dad's side. On my mother's side, there wasn't much—maybe some Catholic way back. My dad's mother read her devotionals and her Bible. We had prayers with her and this was very much a part of my growing up. My dad grew up in that, and when my mother married my dad, they went to a Methodist church. So, when the door opened on Sunday morning, we were there. Daddy was a leader in the church as a young man. He actually did some lay speaking.

In junior high, I was the president of the Methodist Youth Fellowship, though I don't know how I got into that. Later, in high school, I was a leader in the district, and this experience was formative for me.

By that time, I was also starting to get involved in conference work. I went to the first Tri-Ethnic camp that the Southwest Texas Annual Conference ever sponsored. This was a great breakthrough in race relations. I was probably a junior or senior in high school. We had a camp at Mount Wesley that brought together African American high school kids who were Methodists, Hispanics from the Rio Grande Conference, and Anglos. Of course, the Anglos dominated because there were so many more of us. I was very much involved as part of the leadership team. I was involved at the district level. I don't ever remember when I was not in charge of something.

Vocational decision making was difficult because of the role expectations. But there were early intimations that never went away.

I was quite young, in elementary school, when I did my first funeral. Religious children that we were, we held a funeral for nearly every bird and frog whose carcass we found. Almost always, I was the one who conducted those funerals. We dug graves for those little creatures and made a little cross out of two sticks. Sometimes, if things were really bad, we'd have to bury puppies or something like that. That would be harder. We buried the creature out in the plowed ground. I think that I've always understood "earth to earth."

When I was in high school, I started to wonder what I was going to do. My parents were very clear that I should be a schoolteacher. They wanted me to go to Southwest Texas State Teachers College, which was a good school only ninety miles from here. That way, I could get a good degree, and if, God forbid, something should happen to my husband after I was married, then I would have a way to support my family. My parents assumed I would move in that direction, although my mother once remarked, "Janice should never teach the slow learners, because she has no patience. She wants to move and move quickly, and she has a low frustration level with people who don't keep up with her." Mother was right. Working quickly is a blessing and a curse. I tend to get impatient with people when decisions and processes don't move quickly. I make my biggest mistakes then. I get frustrated with myself. Slowing down is an important spiritual discipline for me. Life is much more than just producing.

Teaching was what my parents wanted, but I wanted a bigger world. I knew there was a bigger world out there because I read about it. And I dreamed about it. But I didn't know how to get to the bigger world. I had a real sense of God calling me by the time I was a sophomore in high school.

I never signed a vocational commitment card, but I did walk down to the altar one time in high school. I had thought of full-time Christian vocation by then, but not pastoral ministry. One night, the pastor preached a sermon on serving God in a full-time

Christian vocation. He asked for anyone interested to come down to the altar, and I walked down the aisle that night. Looking back on that, it's so ironic. When our pastor and others gave those invitations, I know now that they were intended for the boys in our group. Those sermons were preached to the boys. I'm confident it never crossed their minds that a girl would walk to the altar unless maybe she was going to be a Christian education director or a missionary. Those were your two choices. Being in Christian education sounded far too much like teaching school to me, although I served as a pastor for education in my first appointment. I also saw Christian education as second-class status. Christian educators were never the "in charge" persons. So I tended to pull back from that. I also had a hard time imagining myself going to Africa. I just knew being a missionary meant leaving here, and that was too big of a stretch to think about. I wanted a bigger world, but not that big!

My folks weren't thrilled. But at that point, they thought it was a phase and that I'd get over it. After all, I was only in high school then. I think that some of my friends just thought, "Janice wants to be in the spotlight." Somebody actually said that to me. It hurt my feelings because I was filled with this sense of God's calling. I was thinking I was living the words of the song, "I'll go where you want me to go, Dear Lord. I'll do what you want me to do." By the time I was ready to go to college, there was a lot of conflict in me. This is where you look back and see providence at work. Not in the beginning, but later.

But the decision was made, and Janice left the ranch for college.

In the beginning, I made the decision that my parents and high school teachers wanted me to make. I went to Southwest Texas State College in San Marcos. I had wanted to go to the University of Texas instead and had been accepted in their honors program. At that time the University of Texas was considered a hotbed of radicalism. It was 1965 when the war in Vietnam was heating up. So I didn't go there. I chose what my parents wanted me to do—the safer way.

My teachers and my parents' friends had also lobbied hard for me to go to Southwest Texas. One of their refrains to me was, "Yes, Janice, you're bright, but you're not that bright. You're capable in a little setting, but you're not capable in a bigger setting." That assessment wasn't true, but it took me years to make that discovery. What I know now is that while there are many people who are far more capable than I am, I am smart enough. I also know how to work with people. I have a lot of desire. I work my heart out. And these are characteristics that can overcome some intellectual inhibitions, or lack of ability.

I was so unhappy at Southwest Texas. One of the things that disappointed me was that everybody looked like me. The courses I had taken in high school that would now be called advanced placement weren't recognized. So I had to take classes similar to high school. I talked to Mother and Daddy about getting out of there. I said I really wanted to go to the University of Texas. They couldn't understand why I wasn't happy there. I told them it was just not academically challenging.

I made it through the first year, and that summer I got a job. Here enters divine providence. I looked around, talked to my pastor, and decided I wanted to be a youth director. I was struggling for ways to try a bigger world and to learn what God might want me to do. I also think I was trying to listen to God by getting in the shallow end of the pool. I went to work as the youth director at First United Methodist Church, Port Lavaca, Texas. The agreement was that I would live one month each with three different families because the church didn't have enough money to provide housing. That was fine with my parents because they thought I'd be safer that way. The church hadn't ever had a youth program, but since I'd been involved in youth stuff since I went to church, I thought I could figure out how to start one.

Never give up on a dream. God's grace and guidance meets us in unexpected ways.

Here's where the prevenient grace starts to show up. One day, I was talking to the pastor, and he asked me what I wanted to do. I said I wanted to go to the University of Texas at Austin. And he said, "Well, why don't you?" I said, "My parents have told me I have to live in a dorm. All the dorms are full at UT, so I'm stuck." And he said, "Not unless you want to be." He picked up the phone and called this old Methodist deaconess who ran an off-campus dorm. And he said, "There's room for you there if you want to go."

The dorm was just awful, but I didn't care. I'd already been accepted at the University of Texas, and now I had a place to live. So in January, I went to the University of Texas at Austin.

That pastor was God's voice for me. I didn't know who to talk to. I really wasn't getting much help. The school counselor, my English teacher, all those people who would have been people you would ordinarily expect to help were telling me, "You know, Janice, you can't do this. You're not smart enough, you're not this, and you're not that." A lot of barriers were there—the same boundaries that had once brought a sense of safety and security now brought a sense of being hemmed in.

Janice immersed herself in the larger world of knowledge and experience available to her at the University of Texas.

At the University of Texas, I was in a bigger world. I loved every moment of it. I took advantage of all the opportunities I could. I learned speed-reading. I took an art course and other subjects that I would be too scared to take academically, but I wanted to explore. It was an incredible time of exploration for me.

I got really involved in the Wesley Foundation because it was a safe place. I knew church. At that time, we were doing our own worship, which was a version of contemporary worship. I suppose one of the reasons I don't get too stressed out about contemporary worship or about people trying new things is because I was writing liturgy for worship services by the time I was twenty. Even with guidance from the campus minister, I realize that those liturgies were pretty weak. It was a wonderful learning experience for me—another opportunity for exploration and creativity. It was a wonderful way for me to spread my wings.

But the real action wasn't in the church; the real action was in the world. So I signed on to be a VISTA volunteer.[1] When I told my parents I was going to be in VISTA, they were truly horrified and sure that something terrible would happen to me. My dad arranged for a friend of his to offer me a job that summer at the company where his friend was an executive. Then my Dad put major pressure on me. "Look, your sister's starting school. We're going to have two of you in college. If you stayed home and worked, you could save all the money that you earn. You could work, and by staying home and eating at home you would almost be able to pay for UT

because it costs more than going to Southwest Texas State College."
Although I was accepted in the VISTA program, in the end, I stayed
home and worked. That experience was an incredible turning point
too. It was one of those strange ways that God works through
awful things.

*Strength of character is built in difficult circumstances. It is a blessing
when in retrospect one can claim such circumstances as a gift.*

I worked that summer as the executive's secretary. He engaged
in sexual misconduct of the first order. That is the best thing you
can say about it. I was nineteen years old, truly a babe in the
woods, and not very sophisticated in the ways of the world. I was
naive about what people who go to church and sit in front of you—
your parents' friends—could do to you when the doors closed and
other people left. It was awful. It was a disaster. It's so ironic looking back on that. My parents tried to protect me by not letting me
go to VISTA.

I was really at major risk. I didn't know how to tell my parents.
It got really bad. I got sick, and I got real thin. At the same time I
was also volunteering at the church as the Junior High Youth
Director. It was my salvation that summer. I finally told my mother
and dad what was going on at work. First I told my mother what
the executive had done and was doing. Mother said, "I knew he's
been doing that from the time I worked there." Of course, I was
angry with my mother for a time. Why didn't she tell me? When I
finally asked her, she said, "I never thought he would try to do that
to you." Of course, at that time, we didn't know about sexual
predators.

But the lesson was yet to come.

Then Daddy and I talked. I think I was expecting Daddy to be
my knight in shining armor or something like that. I think I
expected him to go in and tell the executive that he was a jerk. I
think I expected that Daddy would say that I could quit my job and
stay home. Looking back, I know that was unrealistic, but I think
that is what I expected. At any rate, my dad said to me, "Janice, you
have to tell him he can't touch you any more." And I said, "I can't
do that." And he said, "Yes, you can." We role-played what I would
say and do. I sat in the rocking chair and rocked and cried. He sat
on my mother's dressing stool. He would say, "I'm going to be him

and you're going to tell me that I can't touch you any more." And I said, "I can't do it." "Yes, you can. You can do this. You are going to do this. You are going in the morning." We went through this drama again and again. And I said, "Well, what am I going to do when he doesn't believe me?" Daddy said to me, "You're going to tell him that if he touches you again, you will tell his wife." I can't tell you what a feeling of power this was. For the first time since I went to work there, I thought, "I have the power." The next morning when I arrived, I'd been crying all night. I was a wreck. I'm sure he figured that out. I walked in his office, sat down, and said in one big sentence, "I don't want you ever to touch me again, and if you do, I'll tell your wife." I worked the rest of the summer there. He never touched me again. It was an incredible kind of experience. On the one hand, it was a horrible experience. On the other hand, it was probably one of the most empowering experiences of my life. I had enough strength and power and courage to face down an executive and I came out victorious. My grandmothers would have been proud. I know my dad was proud.

I've often wondered what would have happened if Daddy had rescued me. My life probably would have been different in some ways. We used to laugh about this later on, though it was no laughing matter for them. I said, "Well, that event made a feminist out of me. You made a feminist out of me." I was so bad! I didn't let them forget it for a long time. "You wanted to take care of me and look what you got me into."

But, see, it helped me draw a line. It helped me draw a line to know that my parents don't always know best. I grew up thinking that parents always know what's best. So, I went to the school my parents wanted me to go to. I tried to take the paths they wanted. But that summer, I discovered that, as much as they love you, parents don't necessarily know what is best. That was a failure of major proportions. Not that they ever intended it. But it was a failure of major proportions.

When Janice returned to school, there was a growing awareness not only of her own questions and desires, but also of God's call.

The next semester, I went back to the University of Texas. I kept feeling this call of God for my life, but I didn't want to make my parents unhappy. So I just rocked along. I was still involved in the

Wesley Foundation. I got to my senior year, second semester. I was really torn then because I felt like God really wanted me to do something. I had so many faith questions about who God is and what God is like and how God might be calling me.

I talked to the Wesley Foundation director. By this time, I began thinking about going to seminary. I wrote on my application to seminary that I was going to attend for just one year because I had all these faith questions that I had to answer. My Wesley Foundation director was thoughtful and open and encouraged me. I applied to Perkins and Union and some place out in California. Perkins offered me a full scholarship. This was good, because I knew if I went to seminary, I'd pay for 100 percent of it.

I decided right away to go to Perkins. When I came home at Easter, during my senior year, I drove in from Austin in my little Volkswagen and knew it was going to be grim. I waited until Easter. I know my parents were wondering, "What in the world is Janice ever going to do?" We all sat around the table, and I said that I had been accepted at Perkins and would be going in September. My mother cried and cried. The tears were running down her cheeks. And she just kept saying, "The church is no place for a woman. The church is no place for a woman." Oh, she was so stressed. "They won't like you. People talk ugly about the Methodist preacher. You're a girl." Oh, she cried and cried. My daddy tried to persuade me logically. He said, "You know you're not going to make any money working in the church. You won't be able to make a living doing this." And then he said, "Just because they're offering you a scholarship, you've got all these other expenses. Financially this isn't going to work." And I said, "Daddy, I already have a job this summer, and I'm planning to save a thousand dollars. If I save a thousand dollars this summer, then that's enough." He said, "Well, you can't save a thousand dollars." And I said, "I will save a thousand dollars this summer." He said, "You know, I'll bet you a hundred dollars you can't save a thousand dollars." That was not a good thing to say, because he had to pay up.

Finally he said, "Well, I'll send you to law school. You're really too smart to be a Methodist preacher. If you go to law school, I'll pay for it." Now I understand that they were so scared that I'd be hurt. They were trying to keep me in the safety and security of their circle, their world. It was a good and loving world, but I was being called to a different place. There was no doubt in my mind that I would go to Perkins that fall.

Janice was seminary bound, still not sure what she was going to do there or where it would lead.

I was determined. I was a typical clergywoman of my generation in that it never crossed my mind that I would stand in the pulpit. I couldn't visualize myself in that. But I had this incredible tug that God wanted me to do something special. There had to be something more than being a missionary or a Christian educator. I just didn't know what it was. Somehow if I went forward in faith, I would know. So I got to Perkins that fall. Oh, what an incredibly wonderful fall that was. I never dreamed life could be so good. Doing biblical studies after all that English background—I couldn't get enough of it. It was like Thanksgiving, and you just eat and eat and eat. It was like I was eating with both hands. JEP and D² became my best friends. I loved every minute of it. I did struggle. I had a hard time with philosophy courses and I was scared. We had some pretty tough faculty at Perkins. But it was a wonderful time, and I knew I was in the right place. I got there and I didn't know what I was going to be, but within two weeks, I knew I was in the right place. My parents thought I'd be in school forever.

One of the great stories of my first year at Perkins concerns the class picture. The dean sent out a note that said that the class picture was going to be made and that everybody should wear a coat and tie. Several of us organized the women, and virtually all of us showed up for the class picture on the steps of Perkins Chapel wearing a coat and tie. Of course, the skirts were so short in those days. I think I looked like the only thing I was wearing was a coat and tie. The dean was none too happy, and pretty embarrassed!

Life wasn't on hold for Janice. She had met her future husband at UT. He preceded her at Perkins and when she arrived, the relationship flourished.

I had met him at the University of Texas. He was involved in the Wesley Foundation. We had a coordinating council. There were many young men on that council, and they all asked me out. He was one of them. I hadn't dated much until then, because I was focused on going to school. But I really liked him. So we dated a couple of times before he went off to seminary at Perkins a year ahead of me. Since we had dated only a couple of times, my decision to go to Perkins had nothing to do with him being there. But once we were both there, things heated up between us during the spring semester. His mother died in January, and we decided to get married around Easter.

So begins a detour that is not without its lessons and not without its signs of confirmation that God's call was still waiting to be actualized.

My husband was interested in campus ministry. It was where the action was. He got a campus ministry internship at Buffalo State College and Erie County Junior College in Buffalo, New York through the old Board of Education in Nashville. We got married in June. We both worked that summer and then went to Buffalo in September. My parents thought I'd gone to another part of the universe.

I knew when I went up there that I had to get a job because I was going back to seminary after he finished the internship. So I applied at churches, and they wanted me though they didn't want to pay me. I applied at the Buffalo County school system. I had taken all of these education courses, and I needed the money. I interviewed one morning and when I got back home around 2 o'clock, the phone was ringing. They were short on teachers, and even though I didn't have a teaching certificate, I had a pretty decent-looking transcript. The woman said, "We need you to report this afternoon."

I taught sophomore and junior English that year in an inner city high school in Buffalo. It was 1970, and this high school was in a changing neighborhood, a working-class neighborhood with African American kids getting bused in. The thing was just on the edge of explosion. They locked the doors from the inside because there was such a problem with gangs coming in. There was a lot of school violence at that point, violence against teachers, and just a lot of acting out. The next year, the school was closed for a couple of weeks because it did explode.

It was a wonderful and hard year and a great learning opportunity for me. I learned a lot more than I taught. I knew how to work with kids. My teaching practice was in the church, but I had skills. I was probably as good of a teacher as they had. I was supposed to be teaching Shakespeare but had kids who couldn't read at a third-grade level. What do you do with that anyway? By the end of the year, I lost my voice a bunch of times, and it was real clear to me that God was not calling me to be a public school teacher. I finally put all of that stuff from my parents to rest. Absolutely and completely.

It was a good year. We traveled all over New England every time we had a school holiday. We saw the leaves turn. We went to every anti-war protest. We were at the march on Washington. We were part of a big anti-war group out of Buffalo. We were involved in some heavy duty protests with arrests and all that. I never told my folks. My husband was really involved.

At the end of the school year, his internship did not end the saga of exploration.

That summer, my husband got a job as an intern with General Board of Global Ministries called Board of Missions. He told them that his wife had to have a job, and so I worked at the United Methodist office at the United Nations. Now if that doesn't radicalize you, nothing will. They wanted me to write this paper on South Africa. Of course, how do I know anything about South Africa except what I read? I wrote a paper that wasn't very good, because it wasn't radical enough. But I kept saying "How are people in Texas going to read this?" It was a great time to be in New York. We were there for ten weeks, or maybe twelve.

By the end of the summer, a Texas-hungry Janice and husband returned to Perkins where things took a significant turn.

We went back to Perkins to finish school. By that time I really was interested in being a missionary. We were accepted by the Board of Missions to go to Uruguay. There were two things that put the brakes on that. One was that my parents were just dying at the thought of me going to South America. Another thing was that there was the coup d'état and Uruguay exploded.

And again the vision shifts. First, there is activism and leadership on the campus, and then ...

I was involved with student government at Perkins. I was a student member of the Senate. The Senate was made up of the entire faculty and two students. I was one of the student representatives. When a position in Old Testament department came open, they hired a woman, Dr. Bird. She was the first woman on the faculty at

Perkins School of Theology. The dean announced to the Senate that we were hiring a woman. Then he proceeded to describe her physically. I was livid! I just stood up in front of all those faculty members and said, "I hope that the next time you introduce Dr. Bird, you will pay as much attention to her academic credentials as you do to her appearance." And I sat down. The faculty was mortified. All of those things my dad had taught me about being diplomatic just went out the window. I was so mad when he made that statement about Dr. Bird. So a faculty member took me aside later and said, "Janice, it isn't good to embarrass the dean in front of other faculty members." Here the dean had hired the first woman faculty member, and I criticized him for doing it. I wasn't sophisticated enough to say, "Dean, thank you for your courageous leadership in bringing a woman on the faculty."

Upon recollection, Janice realizes there were skids greased for her early in her seminary career.

When I decided to go to seminary, which would have been 1969, I told my pastor here. He talked to my dad. I didn't ask him to. He just did. He saw to it that I got a license to preach. The Board of Ministry of those days was good about making trips to Perkins, and they also helped me get going in the process. I still didn't have an image of myself as a pastor. I didn't know what to do. My husband didn't know what to do.

One night, we went over to talk to John Deschner, one of our professors at Perkins. I sat on his couch and cried the whole time. Then he prayed. We sat there on his couch, and John prayed. As we were walking back, somehow I knew we were going to come back to the Conference and serve churches here. We got back into our little apartment and it wasn't three hours before the phone rang. The senior pastor of University United Methodist Church was on the phone, and he said "Janice, we've had a position open at University United Methodist Church. The Associate Pastor of Christian Education is leaving, and I'd like for you be associate pastor here." I was blown away with the events of the day. I said, "Well, what about my husband?" He said, "If you say yes to this, then there's a church and the District Superintendent will be calling him. It's thirty miles away, and you'd live in the parsonage in Leander. He would be the pastor in Leander, and you would be the associate pastor at University United Methodist Church." So my husband and I talked about this, and I called the pastor back. When we'd said yes, the pastor was so funny. He said to me, "Now, young lady, I want you to tell me every good thing you've ever done, every award you've ever won, and I don't want you to be modest. I want you to tell me right now."

They went for the introduction. The pastor at University United Methodist Church, in his inimitable way, introduced Janice, and it was all over. Janice would meet several people at University United Methodist and at other places who would become lifelong friends and mentors.

Margaret Berry was the first woman to chair an administrative board at University Church. She was the Associate Dean of Students at the University of Texas at the time. She thought it was a good idea to have me and was a great supporter. University United Methodist was about the only place you really had professional women who weren't teachers. And they were so happy to have me in that position. There were also hard parts because I got ugly notes in the offering plate. That was my first encounter with anonymous letters. Oh, I was so stressed out.

That's also where I met a woman named Lerlene, who took me on as a project. She was one of the first professional women in the public school system in Austin. She started in the classroom teaching, but then moved to administration. Like many women of her day, she never married. After I left University United Methodist, she decided to take me on. She wanted to keep in touch with me, and fortunately for me, I didn't really pay attention to the rules that said you weren't supposed to have friends with your previous congregation. She was the only one with whom I had a long-term friendship that lasted until she died. And I took care of her as she died. She died in my arms. She would tell me stories about being a professional woman and how hard that was for her. She would tell me I had special gifts and that she wanted to help me fulfill those gifts. She did. When I got into Mason later and wanted a Doctor of Ministry degree, Lerlene said, "Well, of course, let's talk about how you're going to do this."

Two women appear often in our stories. Nan Self was a member of the first General Secretariat of the General Commission on the Status and Role of Women, an organization whose advocacy was beneficial to all of us. Jeanne Audrey Powers was among those first women elders in The United Methodist Church. She was eloquent and outspoken on behalf of women, both in her years as a campus minister at the University of Minnesota and later as Associate General Secretary of the General Commission on Christian Unity and Interreligious Concerns.

Jeanne Audrey Powers was another person who was truly wonderful and responsible for sustaining me in those years. I knew her from being in New York. Also Nan Self. By that time, we had the Commission on the Status and Role of Women. Nan was always the one I related to. In her mothering way, Jeanne Audrey looked after me during those years. She would occasionally call and just check on me, and that kept me connected to a larger world. I was now back in a more constricted environment where the roles were much more circumscribed. Jeanne Audrey was a real link to a larger world. I'll always be grateful to Jeanne Audrey for that. And for Nan, too.

And finally the affirmation she most wanted.

Then we wanted to have babies. I think my parents had hopes that I'd come to my senses, or that once I had a baby I'd settle down. It was after Matt was born that my parents came and I preached and Daddy said, "You know, Janice, when I see you up there, it's almost like you're a different person. This must be what God wants you to do." Oh, it was wonderful.

A last walk across the field toward the "tank" (pond) topped off a time of listening that had truly put together in my mind this child of the earth and daughter of faith wedded from the beginning. She grew up in a story-telling story and is a master of that art, herself. Most of all, she is grounded both in the stories of her familial heritage and in The Story, which has come to be the map for her journey of faith. No matter how difficult the circumstances, Janice has always found the way to find God's grace and guidance, evidence of which spills out in her ready laughter and her intense sense of self-assurance. Child of Texas soil, daughter of God's baptismal waters, she lives The Story.

NOTES

1. Since 1965, over 120,000 Americans have performed national service as VISTA Volunteers. VISTA (Volunteers in Service to

America) places individuals with community-based agencies to help find long-term solutions to the problems caused by urban and rural poverty.

2. Biblical scholar, Julius Wellhausen and others, developed the JEPD Theory, or Documentary Hypothesis, in the nineteenth century. According to this theory, the Bible's first five books (as well as Joshua) were oral tradition written down many centuries after Moses, by at least four or five different authors: Jehovist source (c. 850 B.C.) for passages where the divine name is used; Elohist source (c. 750 B.C.) where the word *Elohim* is used for God; Priestly source (c. 450 B.C.) for verses pertaining to the temple; and the Deuteronomist source (c. 622 B.C.).

Charlene Payne Kammerer

Western North Carolina's episcopal residence is set in a lovely neighborhood and is tastefully furnished, as is the custom in that area. Around the furnishings, Charlene and Leigh have placed their own mementos and signs of their heritage.

Charlene's story begins with a poignant reality that sets her in a place of grace unlike the rest of us. Note, however, the total lack of disappointment or feeling slighted because of the circumstances of her childhood.

I was raised by my grandparents in Winter Garden, Florida. My mother lived with our family off and on, but I was always in the home of my grandparents. I have an older sister, Sue, who is fourteen months older, and a younger brother, Al, who is four years younger. My father was in the Army, but I never really knew him, because my parents were divorced before I was school-age. I met him when I was older but never had a relationship with him, although we tried to encourage that. It just never happened.

My grandparents, Sudie and Allen Brown Kannon, were founding settlers of Winter Garden. They came from Tennessee. We had a lot of extended family in Winter Garden and close by. My grandmother came from a family of nine children, and my grandfather came from a family of six children. We were always surrounded with great-aunts and great-uncles and cousins. My mother was an only child, so we did not have any aunts or uncles, but we had a lot of family.

My grandmother was a schoolteacher. She taught for fifty-two years, well beyond retirement age. She taught English in the Orange County school system. My grandfather was a citrus grower and a truck farmer and did well with fruits and vegetables. He helped central Florida become an orange and citrus production center.

I was born in 1948 on January fifth and went to my grandmother's immediately from the hospital. My sister was born in San Diego, and my brother in Miami. Those were places where my father was posted. There were times when the whole family was together, but my siblings and I were always in our grandmother's home. It was clear that my grandparents and my mother agreed that it would be better.

Winter Garden had a population of less than ten thousand people. The Methodist Church was three blocks from where Charlene lived. Everyone in the community knew one another. The elementary school was just one block away. There were lots of children in the neighborhood to provide playmates.

I grew up in a nurturing, extended family setting and in the family of faith. I related to church from the time my name was put on the cradle roll at First Methodist Church until I left there to go to college. My grandmother was a founding member and first president of the Women's Society of Christian Service at that church. It was really through her that I inherited my faith.

Being raised by her grandparents rather than by her parents seems not to be a big issue for her. But Charlene does recall an incident that was sad at the time.

I remember a painful experience in my early elementary days. It actually happened at church. It was approaching Father's Day, and we were asked in a church school class to make a card for our fathers. I made one, but I didn't have a father to give it to. I remember that being very painful for me. Later, as an adult, or really as a teenager, I was able to claim that the teacher was insensitive and didn't pick up on the fact that I didn't have a father at home. I probably wasn't the only one in that situation.

When Charlene speaks of her mother, it is with a gentle tone and a respect that excludes any judgment or feeling of rejection.

My mother has been emotionally ill for most of her adult life. I think at some level my siblings and I always knew that she just couldn't be depended on. She could not trust herself caring for us. I accepted that. But I have always been able to connect to my mother and have a relationship with her. I think that of all of the children, I'm probably the closest to her. It's almost as if she were an adult friend because my grandmother was both grandmother and mother to me. My grandmother was such a strong presence and formative spirit that I never felt unloved or uncared for or undirected. I really feel as if I reflect much of her spirit and vitality and her mannerisms.

I am proud to be my grandmother's granddaughter. It wasn't until I was a teenager and then a young adult that I began to contemplate what kind of sacrifice my grandparents must have made to take on raising three children in their midsixties. They were both retirement age and could have had a peaceful life. My grandparents made enormous sacrifices to see us grown. My grandfather lived until I was a junior in college. My grandmother lived until I entered seminary, right after I was married. I always felt like my grandmother had made her own pact with God in regard to all of the children: "Just let me live long enough to do what I want to do for them." And she was able to do that. It was an extraordinary gift, one that I understand a lot better now than when I was younger.

Grandmother was a force to be reckoned with, always pushing the limits of the children's thought.

She was a teacher who revered the English language. There was never a mealtime when we would not have to leave the table and go to the dictionary and look up the meaning of a word and report back. She drilled my sister and me. We were both spelling bee champions. My brother never had enough persistence to make it, but we were both spelling bee champions beyond our local school level. There were a lot of word games in our family. And she exposed us to reading very early on. We spent lots of time selecting books at the library and entering coloring or reading contests in the summers. I know my grandmother instilled in me a love for learning and reading. We did not travel much, so I traveled through books.

I read all of the Nancy Drew books. In particular, I read historical novels or books about people, about their lives. This inspired me and perhaps opened my horizons to thinking about what my life might look like some day or what I could do. I think my grandmother always strongly encouraged my sister and me to teach and even assumed we would become teachers. She was so splendid at it herself.

The ethos of her grandparents' home was still forming Charlene, whether she was aware of it or not. The expectations were high, and Charlene still lives with those high expectations of herself and others.

I'm not sure I was aware of those expectations until some point in high school. I had always experienced my grandmother's presence and her direction and her advocacy and the way she lived her life as fierce love for me. I really didn't experience her expectations as a burden to achieve or perform for her. I think she had expectations because she saw things in me.

A lot of my grandmother's expectations of me had to do with school and learning and her sense that I would need whatever that education brought me. She expected me to do my very best in school. I excelled because I usually worked very hard at it. Not in the early years, though. I didn't need to do that so much. But when I started getting advanced courses in high school and classes I didn't particularly like, I worked really hard. I played a lot, too! I was also involved in other kinds of activities. Because my sister had dropped out of college after a year to get married, I felt the burden of being the first in my family to finish college. And I really wanted to do that and certainly had that goal for myself. The day I left for college, I found a note from Grandmother on my dorm study pillow. It said, "We're expecting great things from you."

While Grandmother Sudie was warm and hands-on, Grandfather was not so.

The relationship with my grandfather was not very good. He was not a hands-on father substitute. He had an alcohol problem. But of the three children, I was closest to my granddaddy. I talked to him and spent time with him. He was a big Yankee baseball fan. I have a lot of memories during the baseball season of watching ballgames with him. The other kids didn't seem interested, but I would do that even though I didn't really like baseball. It was a way to hang out with him. Though he was somewhat distant, I always knew that my grandfather was aware of things that were going on with us kids. People from town such as the barber or the bank president or the drugstore owner would always tell me something that either my grandfather or my grandmother had said about us. My grandfather and I were connected in strange ways. I was very close to his sister and other relatives from his large extended family. And they were always very affirming of me. When we were together in those settings, I knew that he was very much involved in the care of us.

My grandfather was in his late-sixties when he was raising us, and I don't really know what impact it had on him. It's very hard to sort that out. He died from a melanoma when I was a junior in college. He died rather suddenly to my way of thinking.

Other adults filled in the holes of family for Charlene. Although her grandparents provided the security and comfort the children needed, Charlene is still grateful for these "extensions" of family.

There was a woman, Diane Shepherd, who was a formative influence for me. She and two of her friends were in their mid-twenties when they arrived in Winter Garden to teach, fresh with their college degrees in hand. They were all from Alabama.

One of my high school classes was to be an office assistant, and Diane worked in the office with me. I became her friend, and she allowed that. She was a very special person in my life during high school. Although I liked the other two women, it was Diane I looked up to and knew more about. I would go over to their house sometimes, always invited. She was a really friendly and warm and fun adult presence. She was probably ten years older than me. She was just a great person.

There were other couples who acted as surrogate parents. I guess, in my own way, I was getting needs met that couldn't get met at home. All of these people were active in the First Methodist Church, so they knew a lot about our family. I was always fortunate to have some significant adults around me, in addition to my grandparents. I think they helped shape me quite a bit. I wanted not only my grandparents, but also these other adults in my life to be proud of and pleased with me. In many ways, I wanted to be like them, even though I couldn't have articulated what that meant at the time.

Another example of the role some significant adults in my community played in keeping our family unit together was when my grandmother was diagnosed with colon cancer. I was in middle school at the time, and this was a frightening family event. My grandmother was well into her seventies by then, and at that time, there wasn't much success with surgery and treatment. There was a lot of talk among people at church and among my extended family about what would happen to us if she didn't live. We were not part of the discussion in terms of real involvement in the decisions. I don't remember anyone ever asking, "What would you prefer if this happens?" But it was decided that we would go to the Methodist Children's Home. There were adult people ready to help do all of whatever was necessary. The thought of losing her and of having to go to the children's home was very frightening.

She went through surgery and had much of her colon removed. I think that's when she really did bargain with God about letting her live to finish her commitment to us. It took her months to recover. Her bed was moved into the Florida room of our home. People trooped in and out of our house visiting. Her sister, my great-aunt, cared wonderfully for her. We all helped care for her, but we also continued to go to school and carried on our routine. She was absolutely determined that she was going to recover, and she did. She had a very strong will and a very strong understanding of herself. I always felt her forcefulness as love.

There was a stirring in the community—a racial stirring. These early events became the foundation for later expansion of consciousness.

When I was in high school, the schools in my community were becoming integrated. There was a black community on the edge of my town that was very, very separated from the white community, the majority community. It would have been the early 1960s. I can remember the called meetings about integration in the school auditorium. My grandmother went to the meetings, so we would also go. I can't remember all of the content of the discussions, but I do remember there was extraordinary anxiety about black children coming to our schools and the security precautions and what that would mean.

At the same time, I was in Methodist Youth Fellowship at my church. I was an officer and can remember to this day sitting in an official board meeting as the youth representative. I listened to adults whom I had admired make plans to bar the church doors to keep black people out of our worship. There was fear of integration developing in our community. I really remember being stunned at why all of this was happening. It was my first real awareness of racism and what that does to people. To my knowledge, we never had black persons try to worship in my church. We were truly separate in every way you can imagine.

Still, her grandmother was more liberal than Charlene realized at the time.

As a child, a preschooler, my grandmother took me with her in the evenings to the black community. It was called the "colored quarters." I didn't know until later in life that she was teaching both adults and children how to read. While she taught, the people in the house would play with me and take care of me. She spent many an evening teaching black people how to read.

During her college years, Charlene became friends with African American students, and this strengthened her desire to work toward removing the barriers of race.

I went to college at Wesleyan, in Macon, Georgia, which is a United Methodist and all-women's school. During my second year there, African American students were admitted. We had some international students from the mission field context, but no African American women. I volunteered to be one of the resident advisors who would shepherd the new students. I felt very committed toward that and, I think, was one of the few who did. But that was important to me.

During college, I was a student leader in several organizations, one of which was the YWCA. I have vivid memories of going to Atlanta for weekend training and having lots of interaction with African American students. I began to realize it would be very difficult to bring some of my new friends home with me, either home to Wesleyan or home to Winter Garden, Florida. I think the awareness of that has certainly stayed with me and made me want to do everything I could to help change that reality.

Charlene's friends, and Charlene herself, often describe her as "focused." As she talks about her teenage years, that sense of focus, of drive, becomes apparent.

I was always told that I was mature for my age, whatever that means. By the time I was in seventh grade, I was already thinking about college. No one in my family had been to college. My grandmother had gotten a certificate for teaching from a good school, but it wasn't a university. My mother had not gone to college, and at that time in my life, my sister didn't know if she wanted to go. But it was a burning desire for me.

There wasn't a particular college I wanted to go to. And I didn't know if my family could afford to send me to college. I was afraid to ask. I thought that was too much to ask for. I didn't know scholarships were available for good students. But from seventh grade on, I was focused, wanting college to be possible.

Extracurricular activities were not entirely eliminated in favor of academics.

We had a piano. My grandmother purchased one so that we could learn to play. My mother played by ear. She had a gift and could play without looking at music. I guess my grandmother wondered if one of us had that gift, too. Both Sue and I took lessons. But I didn't like it, because I had a rigid teacher who rapped my knuckles with a ruler if I made a mistake. I did learn to play enough that I could play most of the hymns. I think that if I'd had a different teacher, I might have liked it. But I always enjoyed singing. I was in the choir from about third grade through youth choir. I did some duet and trio work, but it was all church music.

Focused, always focused.

I continued to love school, even with six regular classes instead of just basic subject matter. I was active in student government. I was a cheerleader in seventh through twelfth grades. I loved sporting events. I tried to play, but cheerleading was one of the few sports possible for girls. Women didn't run track or play soccer. There were no organized sports for women in my high school. Since there were no other options open to me, I did cheerleading, which was fairly athletic.

High school began to sort out the academic disciplines that were comfortable and challenging.

I got into math and science, and I would say I peaked at about ninth grade in terms of really liking math. The rest of solid geometry and trigonometry I did because I had to for my degree program, but I didn't like it. I liked the biological sciences, I think, more than the others. I was always, always clearly interested in liberal arts, particularly English, history, and foreign languages. I even thought about becoming an interpreter at United Nations and took Spanish, Latin, and German. I worked really hard to get good grades so that I could go to college.

Her brain did not completely outrun adolescent interest in friends and that other gender.

I dated a good bit. I wasn't allowed to date until I was in the ninth grade. We didn't do a lot of group dating then. You paired off and "went steady." I did that with many boys. Leigh was one of those boys. I met Leigh in the seventh grade. He grew up in a neighboring town, but it was seven miles away, and we went to the same high school. We were in all of the same classes. He was into sports, and I was a cheerleader, so all of those things kept us close. I was a good student, but Leigh was an excellent student. He excelled in all things. So we dated all through high school. I think we felt very committed to each other early on, but that scared both of our families, so his parents told him he couldn't date me until he dated so many girls in between. He would date my friends so he could come back and date me some more. We would have been considered a couple in high school. Then we went to separate colleges, but we would date during the summers. We dated for about seven years before we decided to commit to marriage. So we were long-term friends, which was good. We have been through a lot of stuff together for a very long time now, after thirty-three years of marriage (as of August 2003).

Early church experiences were fairly conservative, but blessed with another element, too—grace.

In my home church, I would say the theology was conservative, United Methodist, and evangelical in expression. But in no way was it fundamental. That was the Baptist church down the street. I knew enough to know that there were differences between me and my friends who were either Baptist or Lutheran. We did have one small Catholic parish in town and independent churches around. But I think that I got solid Wesleyan theology and a lot of pride in my home church about what it meant to be Methodist. That was before we became United Methodist. And I think it's always been true in my life that the concept of grace was something I knew before I could articulate it. Grace intervened in my life—through my grandparents, through other adults, through the faith that was given to me by my grandmother. I always experienced grace in my life.

That emphasis on grace softened what could have been hard and fundamental. Rather than inhibiting further learning, it provided a foundation.

Most would think I had to do a lot of unlearning when I took religion courses in college. I was so eager to learn higher criticism and study the Old and New Testament that I absolutely absorbed it like a sponge. There were some laypeople in my church who earnestly prayed over my soul when they learned I was going to be a religion and philosophy major so I wouldn't go astray. I didn't understand their concern at the time. But in seminary, I understood it better.

What would a woman from central Florida who attended a southern college think of becoming?

I thought about being a missionary. Missionaries came to our church, and I was intrigued and inspired by them. The only church work I could envision was being a missionary. I did have the stirrings to do something. I never talked to anybody about that. I had never seen another woman pastor until I actually landed in seminary and hadn't considered being a woman pastor. I never had a pastor or youth minister who said to me, "Have you ever thought about being in ministry in some way?" If I had someone I trusted and respected ask me that question, the clarity would have come sooner than it did. My grandmother expected me to be a teacher.

When I got to college, I loved school so much. I think I changed my major five or six times by the end of my sophomore year. In addition to German, I loved social studies, I loved religion and philosophy, and I loved P.E. I was all over the map. I was ready to major in any one of those areas, and when I finally told my grandmother and other friends and family that I had declared religion and philosophy as a major, they were horrified. "What can you do with that? You need to get a teaching certificate." I couldn't tell them what I was going to do with it. I just wanted to keep studying it.

Once again, Charlene was gifted with extended "family" who helped her find her way.

I got to Wesleyan through a friend of mine. Her parents were surrogate parents for me. I've had several of those wonderful people in my hometown who, I think, looked out for my sister and brother and me. They filled the gap in my generational family history. My friend's older sister had gone to Agnes Scott, which is a woman's college in Atlanta. And she also wanted to go to a woman's college, but she didn't want to be with her sister. When she decided to interview at Wesleyan, her parents asked my grandmother about taking me with them. So I went with her family to visit Wesleyan College. I interviewed with the Admissions Office and fell in love with the place. It was the only place I applied.

College opened a wider window on the world and offered involvement in the Civil Rights Movement.

I began to see a wider world in college. I went to a Washington United Nations seminar in college. And I was always involved in social issues on campus. The Poor People's Campaign, a march organized by Martin Luther King Jr. in 1968 to bring attention to the plight of the poor, went through Macon, Georgia.[1] It happened during final exam week of either my junior or senior year. There was a route mapped out, and there were police escorts and so forth. I heard about it and felt a need to participate. So I walked across the campus, joined in the line, and learned as I went by, listening to the conversation. At one point, we all stopped and there were speeches. A picture of me and other students participating in the march appeared in *Time* magazine. It really scared some people in my hometown.

College was the foundation for that later activity. But first, she had to settle on some future goals, which took a while to figure out.

I had never settled on the notion of a career but also never felt that homemaking was my destiny. Then Dr. Gilmer, my wonderful religion professor, began to talk to me about seminary. Almost as soon as he had said it, I knew. In 1970, I applied for a Christian education program because I didn't know about anything else.

At long last, the steady relationship of many years issued in marriage, and the newlyweds headed north.

Leigh and I got married on August twenty-ninth of 1970. We spent our honeymoon driving to Evanston, Illinois, to enroll in the fall term at Garrett as students. Leigh had been an anthropology major at Vanderbilt and was active in their campus religion program. He became interested in the Rockefeller trial year in seminary,[2] as an alternative to graduate school for anthropology. The Chaplain at Vanderbilt talked to him about going to seminary. Since I was going to Garrett and there were places in Chicago he could go for graduate school, Lee decided to apply for the fellowship.

Given Charlene's strong feelings about her southern culture, Evanston must have seemed a very long way to go.

We went to Egypt. We didn't go to Asbury, Emory, Duke, or some other southern school. It was a big leap to go to Garrett and live in another geographical area. There was definitely culture shock. But being away from home was also part of my education, part of my formation. There were lots of theological and cultural differences. The midwestern environment was very different from the southern climate that was my heritage and that so shaped me. Exposure to students from around the globe was important, too. John Kurewa, who was the first president of Africa University, was a doctoral student at Garrett. He and his wife and their three children were active in our local church. One son of Bishop Muzorewa—Bishop of Zimbabwe—was there. Two sons of the first Director of World Evangelism of the World Methodist Council were there from Australia.

In seminary, she found the world at her doorstep, in more ways than one.

During our first fall at seminary, the United States invaded Cambodia. Nonviolent anti-war movements were very strong across the country and in some seminary settings. Our whole campus shut down, and those students who wanted to marched in the streets in protest. I was a part of that. A peace institute was born out of those protests. And the Institute of Black Church Studies was in place at Garrett. There were seven black faculty members, which was unheard of in United Methodist seminaries. The Institute was very strong, and the impact was great on all of us. Bishop Edsel

Ammons was a significant mentor for me. After that, I participated in many marches for equal rights, both in seminary and beyond. I was still active in the movement when Chris, my son, was born and can remember taking him in the stroller to march with me. And I was always aware that my grandmother would have been right there if she had been living.

By the early 1970s, women were entering seminary to study theology. But Charlene studied Christian education.

It never occurred to me that I could have entered as a Master of Divinity student. There were over eighty of us in my entering class, which included a large number of women, almost all of whom were in the Master of Divinity program. I was stunned. I began experiencing women preaching, teaching, and being pastors. Many of them were married, and some were mothers. There were all different kinds of women from all different parts of the country. I immediately knew deep inside that that was who I was. I was like them. But I didn't know what I could do with that knowledge. I still didn't know anything about the ordination process or the Boards of Ministry, and I'd never known a district superintendent. So I stayed in the Master of Christian Education program. It was a wonderful program. Dorothy Jean Furnish was my advisor.

I grew up there on the North Shore of Chicago. People pushed me to think about what I really wanted to do. One fall morning, I remember sitting down and thinking that I could finally say I felt called to preach. But without those people and those experiences, I never would have had the courage to do that.

Despite her confidence in her decision and her relief, she still had to deal with the reactions of her family.

When we called my family and Leigh's family to tell them of my decision, I reverted back to a little girl, voice and all. It was a strange thing. They didn't seem surprised at the news but also didn't want me to be hurt. They knew more than I could have imagined what hurt would come. They were concerned because they didn't know any women pastors.

But she also had much support and encouragement from other quarters.

At that time, Leigh and I were very active in Wheaton United Methodist Church, and we grew spiritually strong there. We had good friends from seminary who were very encouraging. And I was surrounded by faculty support and encouragement. When I found out how to apply and prepare for the Board of Ordained Ministry and went to interview, it was my middler year.

Those interviews with the board proved to be rough and sent her scurrying for some starch in her spine.

During the interviews, I came up against real sexism and questions about whether I should be a preacher. The board turned me down. Now I realized I was back in a culture that treated women quite differently than what I experienced in the North. So I signed up for assertiveness training at Northwestern as an elective. I aced the class. None of that was required, but I really got better in touch with myself.

I finished my year of classes and wrote my Board of Ordained Ministry paper, not knowing I shouldn't have done that, and asked for another interview. Apparently, there were big discussions about that, and they sent the registrar of the board to Evanston to check me out and see if they should even consider interviewing me again. He learned a lot about me. By the time he got back to Florida, he had become my advocate.

So I was interviewed again, and there was just enough openness this time. I didn't know that one of the main issues my first time around had been what they would do with me. There weren't any women appointed in Florida, and they didn't know what to do. They were not prepared as a Cabinet for that. But I didn't know that. And so in the second interview, a DS from the Jacksonville District, whom I did not know, offered to take me in his district. And he did. And I think that's why I got in. The senior pastor of my first appointment, Caxton Doggett, mentored me well, and we remain dear friends to this day.

Then it all happened so quickly. In two months time, I was accepted as probationary member and candidate for Deacon's Orders, graduated from seminary, and went to my first appointment. Two years later, when I was on track for applying for Elder's Orders, I was the first woman to do so in my home conference. Of course, it was an all-male board, so I just squared my shoulders. I felt like I was walking through the gauntlet. During the interview, Bishop McDavid came in, sat down, and remained throughout my whole interview. He did not say a word, and when they finished the interview, he left. He had heard what had happened during my first interviews, and he was trying to signal that the Church would treat me fairly and would ordain women.

The members of the Commission on the Status and Role of Women in my home conference were great supporters. They wore yellow ribbons in celebration of my ordination. I had been appointed to Belmont after Annual Conference. The average age in the congregation was seventy-five years old. My first Sunday there, I walked out for worship, and they all had on the yellow ribbons. They didn't know what it meant, but they had seen it done at conference, so they did it, too. I was almost speechless, but then, honestly, it was just God's way of conveying to me approval and the presence of the Holy Spirit.

It was this same small-membership church that welcomed our son Christopher. With only four day's notice, we brought our adopted baby home to the parsonage. The congregation provided the basics of care for an infant and granted a maternity leave before such provision was in the *Discipline*. The miracle of Christopher's arrival made motherhood and ministry intertwine.

Charlene is another southern woman who became a feminist. How does that happen?

I think some of it has to do with understanding that some doors were not open to me, which I wasn't really aware of before. One of the lessons my grandmother did teach me was that I could become anything. I think I first became aware of the barriers in high school, though we didn't talk about how boys and girls were treated differently in school. Some subjects were considered more suited for boys than for girls. Boys were encouraged more in math and science and analytical studies, and girls in English and reading. But in college, particularly in a women's college setting, there were a lot of women faculty. I read a lot of feminist themes. Betty Friedan came to our college after *The Feminine Mystique* came out. And I became immersed in the feminist movement before the Christian feminist movement. But it was an easy transition in seminary to embrace the core of my faith and heritage as being feminist. And that's how I would talk about it. My faith compels me to be a feminist.

Jesus was a feminist. How can anyone question that? One of the women first irregularly ordained in the Episcopal Church was across the street at the Seabury Western Seminary. During the time we were at Garrett, there was much interchange among the women seminarians. We'd pray for them and support them. Then on our campus, some of us founded the Garrett Women's Caucus. Out of that came the Georgia Harkness Chair, and Rosemary Radford Reuther was hired in that position. So, interwoven throughout my whole seminary time were varied opportunities for an activist expression of my faith, which always felt so right to me.

So I was formed and transformed by my faith. But in the context of everything, I was never that radical. I was aware of going through enormous changes of faith and having my horizons extended in every way during seminary. I graduated in 1975, so I was there five years, which was good. It took a long time. But given what I would have to face, I think the experience really shored me up and enabled me to deal with the barriers. I'm not sure I would have survived the early years in the Florida Conference had I not been immersed in Garrett and what happened there.

Just as there had been extended family at one time of life, now there were strong women who accompanied her on her new journey.

While I was at Garrett, D. J. Furnish was really the only woman tenured faculty member. We had some women instructors who would come in and teach pastoral care, but they were not on the tenure track. We also had the members from the early Commission on the Status and Role of Women come because that was all happening in Evanston at the same time. Nan Self, an executive at the General Commission on the Status and Role of Women, did some teaching and was supportive of women's groups.

I really think Sharon Rader (now Bishop Rader) has been one of the influential women in my life, though she would be surprised to hear that. The gift of who she was and her centeredness and authenticity in her many roles, one of which was minister, was so profoundly reassuring to me. When I was struggling with how to be a minister, a mother, and a wife, she was already doing it all. How she lived her life was a profound message to me. I've always looked up to her even though we were in different jurisdictions, not regularly in touch, but always readily connected if the Church brought us together. She was an ideal I always held up.

There was also a laywoman, Rose Thomason, who was present at many intersections in Charlene's life.

She and her husband, Robert, were waiting for us in my first appointment. Rose helped with the birth of Florida's Commission on the Status and Role of Women and was part of the Women's Caucus. She was from south Georgia and married a lawyer who later became a preacher. She was brilliant and had a Ph.D. in English. She taught at the college level and also did some writing. When we were still in Evanston waiting to move, she wrote me a welcoming letter—a welcome to her new pastor—although I was the Associate. She said that she had been waiting to meet me all of her life and had been praying for a woman pastor. And I just couldn't take that in.

Rose continued to push the envelope, to push the edges of the local church where I served. She was a strong feminist but also a very articulate and caring person, which allowed her to get away with what some people considered very radical thoughts. But she was always a consistent and persistent presence. Our friendship with her and her family has continued layer upon layer over the years. She followed my appointments in Florida. They often came for a Sunday here and there. We did a lot of visiting. But I always found that Rose was out ahead of me on many issues. She always told me that she had more freedom to do that as a layperson. I remember asking her if she might have a call to ministry, but she was very clear that if she remained laity, she would have more freedom. She taught me a lot.

She had breast cancer and, sadly, died in 2002. Her retirement life revolved around the illness and the treatments and brief moments of intermission. She talked with me very directly, as I expected her to, about her illness, what it felt like, how she had come to understand it. She published a book about it. She needed more people to be totally honest with her and just needed to be with them. It was an extraordinary privilege to officiate at her memorial service. So, here's a woman who pushed me, who celebrated me, and who hung in there with me. She gave me good advice—whether I asked for it or not—all along the way, both because she cared about issues and people, and also because she cared about me.

As we closed the conversation, Charlene expressed gratitude over and over for the abundant grace given to her by Christ and The United Methodist Church. She clearly sees direct lines of influence that, together, weave the tapestry of a life over which she muses with some amazement and great thanksgiving. The thread of the influence of the Church runs seamlessly through her life, beginning with her early introduction to religion at her grandmother's knee and continuing into the present. Her gracious demeanor and intense desire to do what is right frame my experience of Charlene.

NOTES

1. This march took place in 1968 and was organized to bring attention to the plight of the poor. This large gathering of people from across the South culminated with the rally on the Capitol Mall and the famous "I have a dream" speech by Martin Luther King Jr. on the steps of the Lincoln Memorial.

2. The Rockefeller Brothers Theological Fellowship Program was set up for the purpose of recruiting students of superior quality to the Christian ministry by offering fellowships that would enable those who were willing to consider the ministry as a vocation, but who had not decided on it, to spend a trial year at an accredited theological school. This program ran from 1954 through 1976.

Leontine Turpeau
Current Kelly

The senior living woman bishop, Leontine, grew up in the home of a Methodist pastor, educator, legislator. Her story is a uniquely placed one, with the particularities of life in African American parsonages in the 1930s and 1940s. Much of her family's remarkable heritage is told about in the book Breaking Barriers *(Nashville: Abingdon Press, 2001) written by her daughter Angella Current. Bishop Kelly's story is full of insight into a Depression–era African America pastor's family. Being our "senior sister," she has lived in times that none of us know directly. The stark realities of poverty and racism are throughout the stories she chose to tell during the taping session. Her story starts in Washington, D.C.*

I was born in Washington, D.C., in the Georgetown section, in 1920. My father was pastor of Mt. Zion Methodist Episcopal Church. I was the seventh child living. My mother had lost twins somewhere along the line. I had a brother who was three years younger. My sister, who was five years older, had not been well. Mama and Papa never took her bed out of their room; so when I came along, my bed was in the bedroom of a woman Papa hired to stay with us and help Mama.

Then when my younger brother, Mickey, came along, he became my mother's heart. He was the only one of us who looked so much like Papa. He was a little brown baby with sparkling eyes. Years later, when my sister tried to help me walk through some parts of my life, she said, "Mama really never nurtured you, but she loved you."

Two moves ended with an extended life in Cincinnati. And there, Leontine's childhood became unusual and, although apparently pampered, quite isolating.

We moved to Pittsburgh, and when I was seven, we moved to Cincinnati. There were two women in the church who didn't have children, and both of them fell in love with me. I was teeny, a very small child. Mama would let them take me home with them. One of them I loved. She was the most wonderful person and was as a mother to me—in fact, to a whole group of children. Later, she did have a child, a little girl. She formed us children into a sewing club, all of these little girls. She could sew anything. I grew up going to her house. Her daughter was an only child and had a mother and father who doted on her and gave her all kinds of toys. That's the only place I ever saw in a house what was on display in store windows, so it was always a joy to go to their house.

The other lady who really fell in love with me was domineering. My mother and father didn't know her well, although she and her husband were members of my father's church. They had a beautiful home, and she won gardening awards almost every year. But she couldn't relate to many people. She would go to church only on Sunday nights.

She didn't have any children and asked my mother to give me to her. My mama said, "No, I'm not going to give any of my children away." This lady said, "But you have so many." Mama said, "I don't care. I'm not giving any of them away."

I visited her house from the time I was about eight years old until I was in high school. When my mother and father would go to her house, she would show them "my room." It was a gorgeous room—the wallpaper had blue roses—but I never slept in that room. Instead, I slept on a trunk in her bedroom. At a time when most bathrooms were white, this bathroom was painted to match the room. But I wasn't permitted to use that bathroom. I couldn't tell my parents.

Her sisters saw what Leontine couldn't tell for a long time. But the charade continued until she was in her teens.

It did something to me. She would have my clothes made. I just loved the clothes she gave me, but she wouldn't let me take them home. My sister Florida always called me "poor little rich girl." I had this beautiful brown coat with a beaver collar and a beaver muff and a beaver hat. I'd go for the weekend, and she would take me to church on Sunday evening all dressed up, with patent leather Mary Jane shoes. She would take my other clothes to the church, and after the service, she would collect everything I had on and take it back to her house. My sister Florida wasn't much older, but she said, "You know, you're living with a crazy woman." And she used to tell Mama, "Teenie's not happy." Mama said, "Well, Teenie loves going there." It wasn't until I was twelve that I was able to tell my parents that I didn't want to go. I was waiting for the elementary teacher who lived near the woman to pick me up and take me, and I went in the bathroom and cried. Mama knocked on the door and said, "What's the matter?" And I said, "I don't want to go."

I had been going all of those years. The time that really got me was when Papa took the whole family to the World's Fair in Chicago and they stopped by to tell me good-bye. She had told my mother in front of me, "Teenie said she didn't want to go." And Mama said, "Are you sure you don't want to get in this car?" And I said, "No ma'am," because I was afraid of her. They never knew that she whipped me. That's why, after I became a mother years later, I was very careful where I let my children go.

They were good people, but she just had this quirk. She had worked in white peoples' homes for years and had this taste for the best of everything—the best china, the best linens. She and her husband had all of these apartment houses, and she used to go collect rent on these apartments. She had somebody to drive her in a big car. She had delusions of being a wealthy woman. It wasn't until after her husband died that we found out that those apartments were owned by the bank. All they did was take care of them. She just picked up the money, dressed in her furs, and I was right there with her dressed in my furs, too.

All of the things she got for me appealed to my ego and vanity. There were all of these things that I had at her house, the dolls and everything. But my sister Florida knew that I still wasn't happy.

My hair was just ringlets of curls. She brought me home one Sunday with straightened hair slicked down to my head. And Florida, who always said whatever she wanted to say, said, "You've straightened my sister's hair." The woman said, "I do what I want to do. She's my little girl." Florida said, "She is not your little girl." She fussed like she was my mother—and she was just five years old! She said, "She's not your little girl. And I wouldn't be in her shoes for anything. I wouldn't stay at your house. I don't care how pretty it is." But I had that sense of not being able to rebel, and not being able to share that experience until later in my life.

Finally, in her teens, Leontine found the courage to push back. The last straw came after the woman's husband, who had always been kind to her, died.

When I was sixteen, I really looked at what that had done in my life. My older sister also told me, "I don't think it was fair for Mama to let you go over there." I said, "Well, they didn't know. I wouldn't tell them anything."' When I got older, my sisters all talked to me about not going because I became ill when I went.

I rebelled when her husband died. The first time I ever saw him in their gorgeous living room was when he was in his casket. They kept the living room covered up when they didn't have company. He didn't go in there when he was alive. He couldn't smoke in the living room. He wasn't allowed to do anything more in the house than I was allowed to do. She wouldn't let me use the gorgeous bathrooms. I didn't know that he couldn't use the bathrooms either. They had a downstairs toilet that he used. He was a big man, and I don't know how he got in and out of those tubs. He put up with so much.

I remember a time after her husband was gone that she and I were sitting on the porch, talking. I felt sorry for her. I was just about to finish high school. She said, "If you come live with me, I will pay all of your college expenses. With you and your sisters, your father will have three of you in college at the same time. Why don't you come live with me and let me?" But I said, "No, I'm not going to do that." That's the first time I ever said no to her. I didn't have any animosity about it. I just knew that that part of my life was over. I was not going to get back into that.

Leontine believes her mother favored her sons. She also describes a mother who was strong and the head of the family, regardless of the public image that the father was head.

My brother Mickey was brilliant. When he was four years old, he would stand up in a chair and recite the Twenty-third Psalm. He was the little preacher. My mother adored him! She plugged into all of her boys. She loved her girls, too, but she didn't give us any attention. My mother was such a strong woman. I didn't realize until my mother came to live with me after David's, my second husband's, death, what Papa had really been up against.

I remember seeing my father getting himself ready to stand up to my mother, but he never did it. When I look at the picture in Angella's book of me sitting on my father's lap, I remember it as the only time I ever sat on his lap. But he was a great provider. He was a great preacher and a great church administrator. He and Mama worked together as a team at the church.

The phenomenon of being a white Negro was central to Leontine's mother's life. It was not until the children were older that they began to grasp the decisions their mother had made and what those decisions cost her. Leontine's comprehension of some of this came out of what is, in many ways, a funny story, but also indicative of the demeaning treatment she and her family experienced as she was growing up.

When we were older, we figured out that when she was a girl, she couldn't go to the white school and the kids at the black school wouldn't accept her as black. She was blonde and blue-eyed. She was "octaroon," or whatever they called it in New Orleans. One time my father was driving with all of us children in the car. My three older brothers and sisters tried to convince the three younger ones that if they used Sunday school chairs, they could make a limousine out of Papa's car. We'd been down in Kentucky for a District Conference. Coming home, I had to sit on this hard chair—nothing comfortable about it—with my head on the door. Florida sat by the other door, and we put Mickey in the middle. He was the baby, and he had to lean his body up against the seat. I had fallen asleep and was awakened by a police siren. Papa never drove fast enough for my teenage brothers, so I couldn't imagine what a policeman was stopping Papa for. It was about ten o'clock at night, I guess. Papa pulled over, and the policeman put his flashlight in my father's face and said, "What are you doing with a white woman in the car?" And my mother flipped on the switch and pointed to us in the back and said, "I think you're a little late asking."

This must have happened sometime between 1928 and 1930. Well, he started turning red all the way down to his collar and then told us to go on. When I first heard the term "redneck," I remembered how that policeman looked and thought that's what a redneck must be!

Papa drove off, and everybody was silent for a moment and then started laughing. I laughed and I laughed and I laughed. Papa said to Mama, "How'd you happen to think of that?" And she said, "When you're born my color, you know all of the answers." I couldn't go back to sleep, because I couldn't figure out where the white woman was. I remember very vividly going through the whole incident in my mind. Was he talking about my mother? Is my mother really white? Is she one of *them*?

I thought about not being able to go anywhere. We couldn't go to any of the theaters downtown. We could walk downtown from my house, but we couldn't do anything. Those were the days. I just couldn't believe my mother was one of them. Even if she were, I still couldn't understand what a policeman would have to do with whom my father married. I didn't know I was hitting the root of it all.

I knew that the subject was very sensitive, and I couldn't ask my mother. It took me two years. Finally, one day when she was combing my hair, I asked her if she was white. And she said no. She told me that her great-grandmother had been a seamstress on a plantation, and she had a child of the master. Mama told me about slavery.

Her mother's hair was blonde. One time when her mother was six years old and had just washed her hair, she ran out in the hall. When the mistress saw her, she picked her up by her hair and threw her down the steps. My mother's grandmother picked her up and took her out in the yard and said, "Don't ever let her see you again." Her mother had to take her to work with her but kept her daughter hidden in her big skirt. My mother looked like her mother, with blonde hair and blue eyes. So that carried down through successive women for two more generations.

My mother had never talked to me so freely as she did that morning. When she had finished combing my hair and putting ribbons in it, she said, "Oh, we're going to be pretty today." See, my mother could go anywhere she wanted, unless she took one of us with her. She could pass. I was in my teens before I realized my mother chose to be a Negro woman.

Leontine's mother was a strong woman not only in her own right, but also in her community. She had the courage to be true to her heritage when she could have "passed," and she married a man she did not know. Then she became a tour de force for the community in which she lived.

She made a choice, a strong choice. She was at Gilbert Academy and was in school with three of my father's sisters. His sisters wrote him all of the time and introduced my mother and father by mail. They did not see each other until she went to Washington to marry him. They were both supposed to wear roses so they would recognize each other. He had gotten a picture of her, but it was one of those old tintypes. When she arrived at the train station, she recognized him because he looked just like his sisters. He wore his red rose and she wore hers, but he told me later, "I wasn't about to get lynched over this woman I hadn't even touched or seen before." So he walked behind her and picked up her bag, and they waited until they got outside of the train station to meet. He had a horse and buggy waiting, and they went to be married at the Methodist church. She always told us, "Don't ever marry a man you don't know anything about!" But they were an amazing team, and they loved each other.

She was one of the founders of NAACP in Cincinnati and also a founding member of the Urban League. She and my father both worked in the NAACP and in the community. She was quite a politician. When there was an opening in the Legislature, the Republican Party asked her if they could run her. But she said, "No, but if you run my husband, I will support him." Even after Papa died, they came to her and asked if she would run, but she said, "No, but there's a young lawyer here in the community who really needs to be in that spot, and I'll support him." She would never do it herself. She was active and we were reared with a whole sense of church and the community and school. She was president of the PTA for years and took part in YWCA management.

Her father's story is one of grace and generosity, also.

My father's mother had eight children—four girls and four boys, just like my mother's family. His mom went to New Orleans because she was born in New Iberia near Lake Charles. Papa was very close to his mother. One year, a group of folk, much like our Volunteers in Mission, came down and built a building at Gilbert Academy. Papa was an excellent cook, and he cooked for the builders. When they got ready to go back to New York, one of them who had taught carpentry there asked Papa's mother if he could go with them. He was a young teenager. The folks said, "If you let us take him, we will see that he gets an education." They were Methodists.

This Methodist family from New York sent my father to Bennett College in Greensboro, North Carolina, before it was a woman's college. Then when he graduated, they put him with the only black couple in the town. He joined Mt. Kisco church. And Papa always called those people Pap Mosley and Ma'm Mosley. They were the only grandparents I knew. The family house still stands. Papa said he ate with the brothers and everyone at the table. They were strong Methodists. His room was up in the attic, but he loved that room because he'd never had a room of his own in his life.

And then he had a terrible accident. That summer, he worked as a janitor at the family's factory. One day, the factory was behind in production, and one of the brothers who ran a machine wasn't at work. They were trying to fill an order. Papa said, "Well, I can do it." They showed him how to do it, and he was doing whatever it was. One of the brothers came through the factory and said, "Oh, David! You are doing fine," and slapped him on the back. Papa's hand slipped, and he cut part of his hand off. He had only two fingers on his right hand.

Somebody told him that he could have sued the company, but he said, "That was my family." Whenever he was in a picture, he always hooked his fingers in his pocket. He had to train his left hand to do everything.

In the home, Leontine and her siblings came to understand their own heritage. The strength of her parents and stories of their past built into them self-esteem and dignity.

Papa and Mama knew how to help us understand our history long before black history became important during the Civil Rights Movement. We had been reared with that. And we had a wide sense of the Church, because when any of the leadership of the Church came to Cincinnati, they stayed at our house because black people couldn't stay in the hotels. When I was in elementary school, many people who would become famous came through the church. I met great leaders. My mother was active in the community at that time. There were always friends at our house. We never sat down at the table to eat when there wasn't somebody else with us.

You see, Papa and Mama came out of that Mississippi/Louisiana ethos, and it shapes you in some way. One day Mama was on a bus, and this white woman got on. She told my mother, "I'm going to sit here by you, because if you wait, you won't be able to get a seat. All the niggers get on at this corner up here, and I don't want to sit next to one." Mama didn't say a word. When she was ready to get off, she said to the lady, "Before I leave, I want you to know you've been sitting next to a Negro all along because that's what I am."

As a preacher's kid, Leontine was nurtured in the church. She proudly relates how the church in Cincinnati flourished under her father's leadership.

The people of the church loved us. I grew up in Calvary Church in Cincinnati. It was one of the large churches in the Lexington Conference where they held Annual Conferences. Papa had been at a church in Pittsburgh for four years and had paid the mortgage off on that church. After Annual Conference was over, the bishop called Papa and asked him to go to Cincinnati. With the help of the Board of Missions, Gloster Bryant[1] had purchased a whole block for a new church building. The Bishop said, "I need your expertise for this little church that is going in there to be able to handle all this. You can do it." Papa was a very strong administrator. That took us to Cincinnati.

Faith, endurance, integrity, grit, and wise management made it possible for this household to survive in times of great scarcity.

Ours was a home based on faith. We never had much materially. But my parents were committed to making sure that all of us would be educated. This was during the Depression, and my father never made more than $4,600 a year. My mother never had a second Sunday dress. After my father died, I took her downtown to get a new dress. She found two dresses she liked but couldn't make a decision between them. I told her to buy them both, but she couldn't imagine having two good dresses. And I said, "Well, you go out more than once." Oh, how they sacrificed for us!

Elementary school years became a formative time for Leontine. She was fortunate to be near a black elementary school where education was excellent and self-esteem was nurtured in its students.

I went to a black school in Cincinnati. The Harriet Beecher Stowe School was founded by Jennie D. Porter, the first black woman to get a Ph.D. from the University of Cincinnati. She started her own school because black children were not having good experiences in the integrated public schools. She believed that black children needed a program geared toward lifting them. I went to kindergarten through second grade at an integrated elementary school in Pittsburgh. I remember when I was able to read, my teacher had a book, *Little Black Sambo,* and she always wanted me to read it. I was the only black child in her class.

Dr. Porter, who was our principal, never had any children, but all of the children in that school were hers. From the time we hit Cincinnati, she told my mother that she wanted to get the younger ones who were still at home in her school. Harriet Beecher Stowe shaped us because that was the first place we had gone where we as black children could participate. My older brothers and sisters who were in school in Washington, D.C. went to black high schools, so they could be in the dramatic club and other things.

Public poise was an early lesson, and leadership opportunities were seized and used to good advantage.

I was introduced to the YWCA when my mother was on the Board of Managers. In high school, all of us had leadership ability. I never knew I had any. My mother said when I started preaching, "I can't believe this is the same little girl." That's because we always gave family concerts or family programs, especially when Papa was on the district. Mama used to write these big pageants, and we were all in it. She recited Paul Lawrence Dunbar's poems. She was excellent with it. Everybody did something. Some of them sang. My piece was, "I have a little shadow that goes in and out with me," but I could never remember. Every time we'd go out to a church to perform, I would forget it. I said, "But, Mama, I don't like that piece. I don't like a shadow following me." And she said, "Well, you're not going to use another poem until you learn that one." She was a strict disciplinarian. So when she later sat in my congregation and heard me preach, she couldn't believe it!

Talented, bright people with obvious leadership potential, the children of Leontine's family experienced racism in so many ways as they moved through school.

As teenagers, we couldn't do anything at the high school. The schools in Cincinnati were integrated, but the black students were not permitted to participate in extracurricular activities such as choir or swimming. Our activities were all through the YWCA and YMCA. My sister Florida got in trouble one time because a music teacher told her she had a beautiful voice. So she tried out for the choir, but the choir teacher told her that she was too "light," meaning "slight." She was browner than I am, but she was very thin. And Florida said, "You don't mean I'm too light, you mean I'm not light enough. You just don't want any colored kids in your choir. Why don't you just come out and say that?"

That was my experience when I found the map of the Underground Railroad. The principal had called a special assembly to tell the school that a young Negro boy was going to be the valedictorian, and we all knew it. Then he said, "No Negro will ever stand on this platform as long as I am principal." When I was thirteen, I found a map showing that there had been a station for the Underground Railroad under our house. I went to the principal, and I said, "You can't treat us the way you treat us in this school. Look at this map! There was a station of the Underground Railroad underneath this school, under the public library, at the Jewish Synagogue, at our house, and at church." And I said, "I really object." He sent for my mother. But when she came, he got in trouble! Mama was always there for us. She and Papa always stood with us and told us we were children of God no matter what anyone said.

141

When I was a junior in high school, we were talking in class about what we had done during the Christmas holidays. The teacher had gone to Boston for Christmas, and she said, "Would you believe that in the middle of the city of Boston is a big statue of a nigger?" See, teachers could say things like that if they were inclined to because that's the kind of principal we had. I stood up and said, "You cannot use that term in this class. I don't want to hear you ever use it again. That's the statue of Crispus Attucks, who was the first person to die in the American Revolution, and that's what it's doing there, and you cannot use that word." She sent me to the office. That's another time Mama came to school. The principal didn't want to see my mother. She wanted to get him out of the school system.

I had both white and black friends at school. By the time I was a senior, I was President of the Girls' Reserves in Greater Cincinnati. The YWCA had a conference at our high school, and I told the Y secretary, "Well, our principal said no Negro is ever going to stand on this platform." She said, "Well, you're standing on there because you're the president. And you're going to preside from that platform." And I did. So there was always reinforcement.

One of the reasons we couldn't develop friendships with white people outside of school was because they could do many things we couldn't. The high school prom was held at a country club, but we weren't allowed there. So we made up our own little prom and held it at the colored women's club. They did a lot of things that we couldn't, such as going to amusement parks. My daddy, as a legislator, helped write legislation that undid those things.

You see, that's the kind of parents who raised us. They had no fear. They understood who they were, and they were very deep persons. That was also the tenor of their marriage, and all of us were affected by it. They determined early that we would all go to college. Papa always said, "As many children as I have, I will educate them."

Even as Leontine began higher education, she encountered the crude racial stereotyping and talk of the times.

I started out going to the University of Cincinnati and stayed at home, but I didn't adjust to it at all. It was like still going to the same high school. I couldn't belong to any clubs or organizations just like in high school. There was a lounge where the black kids would meet and socialize, but we weren't a part of anything. So I transferred to West Virginia State. West Virginia State was a black college then. I was ready to major in extracurricular activities and was a cheerleader and was involved in several organizations. I was president of the pledge group for Alpha Kappa Alpha, the sorority of which I'm now a member. I had a great deal of leadership opportunity. I majored in French. It was one of the first colleges to integrate schools. When they integrated, all of those white kids living up in the mountains came down to West Virginia State.

Her relationship with her father had been one of admiration yet distance. It took a crisis with her mother for them to speak honestly with each other.

I hadn't had a real conversation with my father until my mother had a stroke when I was a freshman in college. He was sitting on the trunk waiting for the doctor and was just beside himself. He said, "What can I do?" I said "Go make a pot of coffee." I found out I had to take over because he couldn't do anything. Here was this strong man I'd been scared of all my life, and he doesn't know what to do. That night he said to me, "Teenie, I'm very proud of you. But when you speak, you keep still because you're trying to preach." "Not me," I said. "None of your daughters are even going to marry preachers." We made that covenant. But I broke it all the way through!

The conversation moved back and forth through the years, this time returning to memories of heroines and significant organizations.

When I was a teenager the YWCA executive secretary was my hero. Oh, I just loved her. I wanted to be a YWCA secretary. My sister Angella became a YWCA secretary. Papa never said, but he and Mama had agreed that if we wanted to join an organization, it had to be an organization with a purpose. We couldn't belong to social clubs. So the YWCA was okay, and my father was active in the YMCA just like my mother was in the YWCA.

Then there was Mrs. Bethune. I remember her, oh so clearly. I could see her figure through the window of our front door. I opened the door. I'd just come down the steps at the Calvary parsonage, and she stood there and said, "Young lady, what do you plan to be?" I didn't answer her. And she said, "You must plan to be somebody." And then she said, "I'm Dr. Mary McCleod Bethune of the Bethune Cookman College. I have come to see your mother and your father." I showed her into the living room and I went in the kitchen. I said, "Mama, there is somebody in that living room." She had on all black—black dress, black shoes, black coat, and real black cotton stockings. I just knew she was somebody. She became my hero because she was an amazing woman. When I later preached at Bethune Cookman College, it was just like being on sacred ground.

Conversations in the household were significant and inclusive.

My family always had discussions. And there was always somebody there to tell us what was going on in the church. We talked about everything. And we never had a deliberate family council, because we didn't have to. If you wanted to do something, you talked to Mama yourself. But around our table, it was connected with what's going on everywhere, with Negroes everywhere. And oh, the jokes around the table. We always liked Bishop Lorenzo King from New York because he gave me a dime and gave Mickey a dime. He was always so good and would play games with us even if he just had two minutes. So we came to know all those leaders. I never understood how much that would affect our lives.

There was a sense that the whole community expected something of you. You didn't just live. We had great speakers. We had Mary McCleod Bethune and Lorenzo King and others preach or lecture at the church. Papa always opened his church to the whole community.

When I read Breaking Barriers, *I was left in awe at the depth and contribution of the Turpeau family and the family Teenie raised out of that heritage. The aggregate influence on the Church, the community of Cincinnati, and the political life of Ohio staggers the imagination. Here were strong people pushing against cruel and wrong systems that tried to deny their worth and block them from society. But this family never grew bitter and never caved in. They did what they could with courage and serene dignity and left foundations upon which many parts of the Civil Rights Movement was built.*

But when I heard these highly personal memories, I was almost in tears. That so gracious and lovely a woman could have experienced so much wrong at the hands of a world she did not so much create as adapt to, left me freshly grateful to share a bit of life with her.

The stories of the other African American sisters all carry the tinges of this same kind of living—pushing against the walls of racism in different times and places, but still the same walls. These women are extraordinary in that they have emerged in the life of the Church in spite of racism and those social realities that sought—and seek—to ignore such talent and devotion. Thank God that they were given the strength and encouragement to endure by their families and their churches (in its faithful moments) and the God they so clearly understand as their rock and redeemer. We are blessed to have them among us as leaders of the Church in a new century.

But one wonders: Will there come a generation of women—and men— who will tell different stories, these stories being only their distant heritage rather than a continuation of what we have learned from these sisters?

NOTE

1. Gloster Bryant was the grandfather of Gloster Current, who would become Leontine's first husband.

Linda Lee

Linda met me at the door dressed in jeans and a long shirt. I took delight in seeing her so relaxed. We entered the large Episcopal manse and settled ourselves in a room with three walls of windows looking out into a walled garden. Large African American depictions were hung on the wall, and drums and other artifacts were on the hearth and mantel.

I was born in Cleveland, Ohio, in 1949. I was the first child born to my parents. My mother had been barren for seven years before I was born. She tells the story about how she prayed to have a child for seven years. One night in the seventh year, she went to a revival. The preacher told the people in the congregation that if they would come to the altar and pray that night, God would give them whatever they asked for. My mother went to the altar that night and prayed for a child—I don't know whether she specifically prayed for a daughter. But within a month or so, she was pregnant with me. My mom said that after I was born, she did like Hannah and gave me back to God. Later, when I was elected Bishop, she wondered if it was because she had given me back to God, as Hannah did with Samuel. It is an awesome thing to think that this could be the case. And actually, I believe it is.

My mother is a seamstress, and my father is a plasterer. They were part of the migration of African Americans from the south to the north in the early to mid-1940s. It would have been the early 1940s because they came to Cleveland some years before I was born. My father and his brothers moved to Cleveland from Alabama. My mother was from Mississippi.

My father's family had been landowners and farmers. His father was a teacher. The family also owned a store. My father's mother was the businesswoman. She took care of the business records, supervised the work on the farm, and all of that. My mother's mother was a teacher and her father was a farmer. Both families left agricultural and educational legacies as well as some business management experience.

I knew both of my mother's parents. Every other summer, for most of my growing-up years, we traveled from Philadelphia, where I grew up, to Mississippi to visit them. We would stay with them in their farmhouse, so I got to know them pretty well. I used to love visiting them. Their farm was a place of freedom and peace for me. And it was very different from our two-bedroom apartment in Philadelphia.

My father's mother died before I was born so I never knew her. But my father's father always told me that I was his favorite grandchild because, according to him, I looked exactly like my grandmother. I always felt special because he said that.

Linda is not sure about the physical resemblance. But as she has grown older, some of her interests tie her back to that grandmother whom she never met.

Based on the stories I've heard about her, I feel that my resemblance to my grandmother is more in spirit than anything. For example, she knew how to make herbal remedies for her family when they were sick or wounded. When I became a mother, I discovered that I had allergies to several commercial remedies and several foods. I discovered herbal teas and dietary remedies for myself and my family. My grandmother, who was from Native American parentage, used to go out in the woods and pick the herbs. I found my herbs in health food stores. I wish I had had a chance to meet her and talk with her about these things and many others. I still feel a spiritual bond with her.

Linda and her younger brother are very close, in spite of their differing views about church.

My mother had difficulty having children, but my parents had one more child, my brother. So my mother has a girl and a boy and that's what she said she always wanted. She was satisfied. My father never said.

My brother is three years younger than me. He lives in the Chicago area. He's an advertising writer. He's been self-employed, the CEO of his own company, his whole adult career. Since he started, he has kept his business and stayed in business for about twenty years. We are close, not in terms of talking a lot, but in terms of keeping up with each other. We get along well. We always have. He is not a churchgoer, although he has attended on special occasions, such as my installation as Bishop. The rest of the time he lives the high life of an advertising executive. He used to talk more about it to me before I went into the ministry. Probably because of age and circumstance, we talk more now about religion and politics.

Life in Philadelphia is remembered as happy and good. Linda especially liked school.

It was in elementary school that I knew I wanted to play the violin. I was in the third grade or so when I started. Playing became an important part of who I was and what I did. I studied at the Philadelphia Institute of Music. I didn't start there, but that's where I ended up studying. There was a man at the Institute who wanted to take me to New York to play. My mother didn't want me to go because she couldn't afford to quit her job and she didn't want me to go alone with him. So I didn't go. I stayed in town and played around different little places and at church and things like that. I really love the instrument. I was in the orchestra at school. I really enjoyed school. I'm a good student. Mainly As and Bs.

Leadership came to her naturally. She said she just emerged as the one who was taking responsibility.

I really like people and counseled them. I remember in elementary school thinking about writing a "Dear Abby" kind of column, though I never wrote one. But somehow I ended up counseling other people all of the time. I think for that reason people liked me. Some of the teachers were affirming, too.

I was gregarious and outgoing. I remember talking a lot. I used to get in trouble for talking. Even though I need privacy and solitude to renew myself, in elementary school, I used to get in trouble for talking. I would be talking with my friends.

I had a best friend. And then we had a whole group of girl friends. In elementary school, I didn't have boyfriends. In fact, I didn't have an interest. The one guy who did like me, I didn't like. The ones I liked didn't like me. Girlfriends were really important.

Home life brings mixed reviews and signs of having overcome a great deal.

My father had a drinking problem during my growing-up years. Home life had its challenges. Most had to do with things going on between my parents rather than things that were happening to me directly. They would argue, and he would binge. He would leave for days, and we wouldn't know when he was coming back. I always worried because I was not sure he was okay. And he would break promises. He would say he was going to take us somewhere and then wouldn't take us. Those are the things I lived with—their arguments, his broken promises and absences, and my uncertainty about where he was.

My brother and I got along very well. We were compatible. He was also caring. One time there was this girl who wanted to fight me at school. I didn't want to fight. He was going to fight her for me. She was bigger than me, and I was big. She was about twice as big as my brother. So I had a little respect for him. I thought, "Well, he's got heart."

I was left to watch us when my mother was at work. After school, I was responsible for making sure we got home and did homework. There was a lady who lived next door. Her name was Helen. She was white. The neighborhood was mixed. There weren't a lot of white people, but there were some. We were in an apartment. She was the person I was to call. I knew she was there when I came home from school. One time I had an accident and had to get stitches. She came and took me to the hospital. I knew she was there if I needed someone. But mainly I was responsible.

My mom did something with us that I don't think I did with my children because I was overcompensating. When I was about nine or ten, my mother wanted a baby-sitter to be there with us during the summer while she was working. This girl came from the church to baby-sit, and she sat around the house. I said, "Well, Mom, you don't need to pay her to do what she's doing. I could do that." So, she quit having her come. She really wasn't doing anything, and we weren't either. We'd watch TV or play cards or whatever. When I think back on it, I realize that I'd never let a nine- or ten-year-old baby-sit my child while I was at work. But we were fine. Every now and then I would get claustrophobic and leave my little brother, who was three years younger than me, alone in the house. I would go up to Fifty-second Street and Market—which was a shopping area. I'd go to watch the people and to be outside. Didn't have any money. So I'd go watch the people, and then I'd come back home. Whenever I needed to get away, that's what I'd do.

Church was part of the family experience. Though Linda's father was seldom there, her mother was always part of a community of faith and immersed her children in it.

I was active in church. That's really where a whole set of friends came from. We went to a black Presbyterian church in Philadelphia. We had some progressive pastors. The first guy was older, so he retired while we were still there. But he had gone to Africa and brought back slides of the things and the people that he had seen in Africa. He showed us slides of palaces with guards and gold. Some of the other things were really beautiful. It was then that I knew I wanted to go to Africa and see what he saw.

The pastor who came after him was a younger pastor. I was in the choir. Every now and then I'd do a solo. The younger pastor invited me to teach vacation Bible school for the littlest children— around the ages of four and five. I didn't do it by myself, but I was allowed to teach the class. I guess there was something going on.

My mother taught Sunday school. As we got a little older, there were some guys there. We had a youth group. It was good. There were some good relationships. I had a good experience at church.

Life in Philadelphia was stable, and though there was the difficulty of a father who could not be trusted, there were other helpful adults around and influences and opportunities that made life happy. But mid- and late adolescence brought a change.

I grew up in Philadelphia and attended school there from kindergarten through eighth grade. Then we moved to Cleveland. Going into the ninth grade was a big change, but it was an okay year. It was the year I met one of the women I am still friends with now. The school did have a music program so I was able to continue that, and that was a kind of stabilizer for me.

I came to this new place with people I didn't know and told them I was the leader of a girl's gang in Philadelphia so they wouldn't mess with me. I was so far from a girl's gang, but I did go out with gang members. The people who were my neighbors were part of the Forty-ninth Street Gang, which was one of the toughest gangs in Philly when I was growing up there. In the summer, gang members were the guys I would sit with and talk to. They would tell me about their life and what it was like to be in a gang. They were preteens and some were close to my age. So I got an understanding of what it meant to be in a gang. At the same time, I would hear about some of the things that they were going through—fights and people getting hurt. So when I went to Cleveland, I did have some knowledge of gang life. I don't know why I had this impression that they were going to test me. People filtered through all of that, especially when I got to the music class. That's where I met some people I could relate to. I found a home there.

I went to John Hay High School in Cleveland. It had just changed from being a girl's vocational school to a regular coed high school. It was a smaller black high school. They didn't have a lot of strong college prep at the time. So I really didn't study. I did struggle with math and biology, so I guess I should say all of the humanities were a breeze. But I really don't remember studying or taking a lot of time doing schoolwork. I also worked on the school newspaper and in the school bookstore to take up some of my time and energy. School was not challenging, but the newspaper was and that was fun.

Linda always liked to read.

We went to the library in the summer when we were still in Philadelphia. Mother would let us walk the eight blocks to the library alone. We'd go a couple of times a week. I didn't know about black history and black studies at that time. The only black person I remember reading about was Louis Armstrong. When I was in elementary school, I did a book report on him. I was fascinated with him. I also read all of Louisa May Alcott, and especially liked *Little Women*. I read the encyclopedia, too.

I read Gandhi's autobiography when I was sixteen or seventeen and went back to it later when I was an adult. I remember wondering what I was doing reading that title when I was in high school. I had read the whole thing and had underlined parts. I think I read Gandhi because I watched TV during the Civil Rights Movement. I must have picked up on what he had done in India. I knew enough about what he had done in liberating his people that I wanted to read about him. Then when Martin Luther King Jr. referred to him, I decided to read about him. I don't remember reading about MLK Jr., because he was living.

Linda was on the front lines of the Civil Rights Movement, for Cleveland had some severe shudders during the 1960s.

It was pretty hot while we were there. During the riots in Cleveland, there were tanks up and down the streets. We would pass them as we were going back and forth to school. A shootout happened around the corner from my house. We could hear it while it was going on. It was strange. We didn't know enough to understand it at the time. I was in the eleventh or twelfth grade. I graduated in 1967. This had occurred before that.

I think there was some teaching in school about desegregation. I don't remember much. I felt engaged and knew it was about me and my people. I think that's why I got caught up in Gandhi and Martin Luther King Jr. I remember watching TV and police in the south sic dogs on the rioters and use fire hoses on them. I remember thinking that it didn't make any sense. I was affected by it. There wasn't a good reason for it.

She lived in a black community for most of her life and had minimal contact with whites. But even within her community, she found some discrimination.

High school was mainly black. I went to a large black Presbyterian church that was in its heyday. At the time, the pastor there was what we called "High Yellow," meaning he had light skin and wavy hair. The church had a color hierarchy. I didn't understand it when I got there, because I had come from a church in which we were all part of the group, no matter what we looked like. We had children there, some were light, some were dark. But in this church, I discovered first of all that I was coming into an existing group, and they did not know how to assimilate a new person into the group. I also found that the people who were invited to do things were all light-skinned people. I don't think anybody would have said anything to me directly, but I do think there was a hierarchy in that church at that time. So I didn't get the leadership opportunities I had in Philadelphia. And that's when I quit going to church; there just wasn't much to do.

I had gone to Sunday school one day, and the teacher said, "Yeah, you never know who you sit next to in church. Nothing but a bunch of hypocrites up there. They do one thing on Saturday night, and then they come here on Sunday and act as if they are holy." That day, I kept looking at the man sitting next to me in church and wondering what he had done Saturday night. It wasn't really the contradiction that bothered me. I was just suddenly suspicious of everyone. So I didn't go back because of what that Sunday school teacher said and because of my experience. I never found a place.

High school social life revolved mostly around music.

I related mainly to people in the band or the orchestra. It was actually the people in the band who ended up being my friends. I played the bass drum. I couldn't play anything except the oboe, and that wasn't a band instrument. I wasn't interested in learning to play a whole other instrument. I figured I could keep rhythm, and they needed a bass drum player. So I played the big bass drum, which I liked. I would rock and march. We never won a game. But I beat the drum and loved it!

As to happiness in her teen years:

I don't know if I was happy, but I think I was. I do remember a period of time when I stopped speaking to my family. I don't know how long it was. I was fed up with them. So whatever they were doing, I just thought, "I've had enough of this." I couldn't move so I just stopped communicating with them. Whenever it was over, I started talking again. I don't know if that constitutes unhappiness or not.

I had a boyfriend, and I was in love. We were going to be married. My mother had a fit because she had heard about this guy at the beauty parlor. He had been a member of a gang when I first moved to Cleveland. About that time, all of the adult gang members were arrested and put in jail. My boyfriend was the same age as me—fourteen or fifteen. He hadn't been involved in some of the gang stuff for a while. I guess they nipped it before he got into the rest. He was in high school, played football, and did regular stuff as far as I know. Maybe my mother knew something she wasn't telling me. One summer he was gone, and my friend and I met two guys somewhere. We decided we would go to a movie with them. When my boyfriend came back and found out I had seen this other guy while he was gone, he slapped me—hard. He never did it again. But I fell out with him, though we did come back together again. I finally broke up with him my last year in high school. It broke my heart. I knew it was for good. I just cried and mourned. I remembered him slapping my face and never forgot that. I knew I couldn't stay with him.

The first try at college was not a happy experience.

I went to Adrian College for one semester in 1967. I met James Cone there. He invited black students to his home to talk about what it meant to be black, what it was like to be in that institution. That was a nurturing developmental experience for me. But at the end of the semester, I was ready to go because of some of the other things that I experienced there. Even though I am an introvert and need some time alone, I am still a social person. But at the time, there were only twelve black students on the Adrian campus. There were so few of us that people still looked at us when we walked across campus. I would go to social events such as dances thinking I would have fun, but that never happened. My roommate had never been around black people and would say something that would just set me off. It was, "Where have you been all of your life?" I just couldn't deal with it. It was absolute culture shock.

After that first semester, I left and went to Ohio State University. It was a little more like what I was used to—it was larger, it was a city. I was there in the fall of 1967 while all of the unrest was going on. These were civil rights acts. I participated. I don't remember sitting in the administration building, but I did sit in on things in cafeterias and went to the meetings. You were intimidated if you were black and not there. There were bomb threats in the dorm. I ended up flunking out of OSU. I couldn't get it together. I blamed myself for years until I figured out: How much studying are you really going to get done when you have bomb threats in your dorm, people harassing you about meetings, and other stuff going on?

That was a great shame. I never told anybody, but I think my parents knew. I was paying most of my own way anyway. My mother had saved up and was paying some of it. So I vowed that she would never have to pay any more money for me to go to school. I left there the following year and went to Temple. I went home to Philadelphia. That was a good decision.

Though she had continued to play the violin at Adrian, she underwent a major shift at Ohio State and Temple. She put the violin down, as it were, and turned to black studies. Church and campus religious functions were not on her calendar.

I did pray. I never quit praying. Even when I was studying world religions and searching for meaning, I never stopped praying. I remember that. I didn't get involved with the church, but that's when I started reading the Bible for myself. Though I had been taught about it and learned some things, I had never actually read it. I started reading the New Testament. That was the beginning of my spiritual journey.

The return to Philadelphia also put her in the path of the man she would marry.

I got married while I was in Philadelphia. I ended up going to the University of Pittsburgh where I entered the music program. I studied at the school of music for two years but graduated with a liberal studies degree because I didn't finish the piano requirement. Otherwise, I would have had a degree in violin. I still can't play the piano.

Career goals were fuzzy.

I thought about becoming a musician. But it is so competitive. I just didn't feel I wanted to do that as a vocation. Then I began thinking about becoming a nutritionist or going into arts management. My husband and I graduated the same year—he received his Ph.D. and I got my B.A. He got a position at the University of Dayton, and we moved.

The move to Dayton did not quickly bring Linda employment outside of the home. She worked for a year with children with disabilities—just four students—and seemed to enjoy that. Yet, being a teacher did not beckon her.

I decided to get some kind of degree. I wanted to get into administration in the school system or something. I did not want to end up in teaching. I had tried that at Temple. I was a student teacher long enough to figure out I didn't want to be in the classroom every day.

She interviewed with the Dayton Public Schools but did not get the job.

They gave the job to somebody else. They told me I was too assertive in the interview. I don't remember being particularly assertive or aggressive. I still don't know. What I figured was that they really wanted whoever else it was. I guess I said something somebody didn't like.

Linda continued searching for direction, still looking for the right road to take for her life. As doors closed, she searched for one to open.

Somebody had told me about the book *What Color Is Your Parachute?* (by Richard Nelson Bolles [Berkeley, Calif.: Ten Speed Press, 1971]). I read the Martin Luther King Jr. biography and reread Gandhi's autobiography. Then I ended up being curious about the place I kept driving past called United Theological Seminary. I had no idea what "theological seminary" meant. I had no concept. But one day I went in and found out that it was a school where you could take classes. I was led to go and take some classes there. People kept asking, "Are you going into ministry?" And I kept saying, "I don't know. I don't know enough about it yet." After the first semester, along with a few mystical confirmations, I knew that was what I was supposed to do.

Those confirmations had to do with lights.

I had stopped going to church on a regular basis in high school. But by the time we moved to Youngstown where my husband had employment, we had two children, and I had decided it was important for us to go to church. So I decided to find a church. At the time, we were living in an old house that we were renting for forty dollars a month. We redid the house—we put in a new kitchen floor, painted, and bought new appliances. There was a light on the front porch that never worked, even after we replaced the bulb. But the day I went out to find a church, the light was on when I came back. It was just on. There was nothing we could do to get the light to work. But it came on that day. When I decided to go to United, we had another porch light that wasn't working, and my turn signal wasn't working. When I went to the seminary to find out what I needed to do to become a student, the turn signal worked on the way home. And when I got home that light was on. I think they were really just signs. What can I say?

Once that confirmation came, ministry became part of Linda's life.

I thought about turning back. I wanted to. But I haven't.

When asked about other formative experiences, Linda turned to a kind of determinative understanding of herself.

I think some of it was just the way God made me. My father likes to tell stories about the kind of questions I used to ask when I was little. He remembers one time when he was talking about the stars and the moon and I asked him whether they stayed up there. I wanted to know what makes them stay. It was that level of questioning he thought was different. I don't know what other children ask at young ages. I was three or four years old. There was something about the way I asked the question that really stuck with him. I still ask those questions. Sometimes my husband says, "Why do you want to know why?" I just want to understand. I think my father was the same way—inquisitive and interested in people. He never meets a stranger. My mother takes time finding out who people are and then makes a decision. But my father is the kind of person who just meets people. So am I.

A number of teachers, especially music teachers, left a lasting influence on Linda.

The choir director at the church I attended as a child got pregnant out of wedlock and was fired. I remember feeling really bad because she did such a good job with us. All of the children really liked her. She was a caring person. She asked me to do solos from time to time. But I wasn't the only one. She developed us.

I remember a teacher at the Philadelphia School of Music who really inspired me. He required a lot of work and pulled a lot out of me. I remember that I wanted to achieve it and worked hard to do that. I didn't have to be told to practice. My mother didn't really know how to help me excel—she had been a seamstress and had lived on a farm. Though she did encourage me from time to time, it really was mostly internal. She was very influential.

There was also a music teacher at my elementary school who was always affirming to me. I remember that she always acted like she was glad to see me and always had a good word to say to me. Even though I wasn't with her all of the time, she had a real influence. The fact that she was black was important. I suspect she did this with other black students to help build our self-esteem.

Then I had two other teachers, actually three. One of them is still around in Cleveland at Harry Davis Middle School. My first music teacher in Cleveland was the sweetest man. He was so wonderful. He's the one who got me into the Cleveland Institute of Music. He was a wonderful, kind, loving person. I felt cared about and affirmed and nurtured. Another influential teacher had this real rough exterior, and a lot of students didn't like her. But I was able to see behind the gruffness, and I could tell that she really cared. There was a man who was Jewish who was also very good.

Growing up during the Civil Rights Movement sensitized Linda in ways that caused her to turn to great leaders of liberation in addition to King and Gandhi.

Rosa Parks, Shirley Chisholm, Angela Davis, and Patty LaBelle were all leading women in the Civil Rights Movement and had a profound influence on me. Those were the people to whom I paid the most attention. When I went back to the church, there weren't many women leaders like them. One notable exception was Jeanette Cooper, an African American clergywoman in the West Ohio Conference. She was a leader in the conference and was one of my heroines. Judy, you were also one. You were the first woman bishop that I knew or that I had. I remember meeting you one time in the bathroom, and it was really a thrill. I hadn't experienced a woman bishop before, and that really meant something to me.

The journey has not been without difficulty.

I did encounter some challenges, and it took me a while to come through them. But I've been able to use those hard experiences as a tool for spiritual development and deepening my faith rather than allowing them to destroy me or tear me down. So I've discovered that I have a pretty good amount of resiliency. I am able to bounce back really well, especially if I use support, which I make sure that I have. If I turn to my supports, then I am usually able to get through the stuff that I think could have been debilitating otherwise.

Being a bishop has brought its own particular challenges and has taught her many lessons.

I think I have learned to be more organized, to prepare myself ahead of time more often. I have learned to take a minute and look through the minutes or sit down and think about what's on the agenda, just to think ahead about things I have to do or that are before me. I think I've also developed my ability to focus because that's the only way I can do this. I found that what I need to do in any setting is focus in on what we're doing in that setting. So I've learned to do that. But I've found that you have to be able to do two or three different things at the same time!

I have also learned some management and leadership skills. I don't think I've had any trouble with being a leader and making decisions. In fact, sometimes I need to stop and *not* make decisions. What I haven't quite grasped is the magnitude of the job and how to use that in leadership. How do I use this position to speak out and use my voice on certain issues? I haven't done that. I've done this in the area of spiritual formation. But I haven't when making contact with secular leaders or being involved more ecumenically with leaders of other churches. I just haven't entered into the arena the way I could and the way I still feel I need to in these times.

The extent of her office and its responsibility still overwhelms from time to time.

Today, when I was driving back from Grand Rapids, I saw the name of a little town where we have a church. I said, "I have responsibility in that place." Then I thought, "Oooh, I have a whole lot of places where I have responsibility for oversight."

Writing is another thing that I feel I need to do, though I don't have any idea when I'll have time. I need to tell my story. So I need to start writing down memories and connecting them with things that are going on. Even in my sermons, I haven't done much telling of my story. I intentionally did it this last week when I preached because it felt like it was time to do that. I'm beginning to remember and record my experiences.

I haven't so much changed as a person since becoming a bishop as I have developed as a person. The office grows us. In that way, I don't think *who* I am has changed, but rather *how* I am. The other day, I was at a social function and talking with some women in administration at Michigan State University. One of them asked me how I ended up being a bishop. I told her that's a question I still ask myself!

Linda's closing comments made me smile. Who of us knows how we came to be bishops? Being a bishop was no childhood dream (although we hope it will soon be that for little girls). Linda is clear that she has been under God's guiding hand, through both times of disappointment and times of great surprise. She lives out of her sense of prayer and self-care, tending to her soul without fail, no matter what else goes on around her. It shows in her thoughtful and deliberate way of leading and modeling living "in the Spirit."

Susan Murch Morrison

Susan's home is beautifully decorated with artifacts and those symbols of her travels—paintings tastefully hung, statuary and abjects artistically displayed. To walk through the rooms of her house is to walk through the journeys of her life.

When Susan Morrison talks of her family, she begins with her paternal grandmother.

My grandmother was the oldest of ten children and came to America from Wales. Her father was a gentleman farmer and decided that there wasn't a future for his children in Wales. The oldest would inherit the farm, but what opportunities would there be for the others? They had cousins in New York who kept telling them about this wonderful country, and so my great-grandfather decided that moving to America was what the family needed to do. Mary Matilda, my grandmother, was eighteen years old when her family decided that she would come to America. She would meet the cousins in New York City who would take her upstate where she'd find a farm and buy it. Then the rest of the family would come to America.

The story of my grandmother's journey to America is a legendary family story. My grandmother had a ticket to travel on this new boat that was going to America, a famous, unsinkable boat called the *Titanic*. The family, I think, was very uneasy about Mary Matilda going all by herself. About a week and a half before she

161

was to come over, they talked a cousin into going with her. The problem was that all of the tickets were sold. So she had to trade in her ticket. She and the cousin went on a ship that would come to the rescue of the *Titanic*. What interests me—and I didn't think of it until I saw the film *Titanic*—is that she would not have been traveling in first class. She would have been in a lower-class section down below where passengers were not allowed to come up to the deck.

When Mary Matilda bought the farm, the family came over. Then she was sent to normal school—the equivalent of a teachers' college—to be a teacher. I think it was somewhere in St. Louis. We believe something happened to her there because when she came back home, she didn't teach. She did some menial work, living in a family home taking care of the house. To make a long story short, we think my grandmother had an emotional breakdown. But in those days, no one knew what to call it, or what it meant. And there was also, I'd guess, the embarrassment that something had happened. She would have been twenty or twenty-one.

She met my grandfather, who worked at a bank, in a little western New York town. He was an interesting character in his own right because his father had run off with his cousin. They just disappeared. No one knows what happened to him. His mother couldn't take care of him and his sister, so he went to live on a farm south of Buffalo. He helped on the farm. One day, he went out hunting with the father, and the older man mistook him for a deer and shot him. He lost one eye. The family name was Morrison, and he eventually adopted that name.

My grandmother retreated into a religious world unconnected to her daily life. She wasn't quite right. She was an odd character, but her extended family loved her and cared for her. All of her brothers and sisters deeply appreciated her because she enabled them to get to where they were. I had never understood why there was such fondness for her. She talked religion and laughed and prayed all of the time. This was my first experience with the faith, with religion, and it was kind of negative because she was intimidating to a child. She always asked us prying questions such as whether we were going to church at home. She even paid us to go forward. And, of course, that did it.

When visiting my grandparents, we always had family devotions in the evening. My mother seemed to get out of them. She sneaked out before they got started, and that infuriated my brother and me. We had to go down on our knees to pray in Grandma's living room. This all influenced my early feelings about religion and the church.

My grandmother wanted a preacher in the family. She had twin boys, one of whom was my father, and a daughter who died at childbirth. Grandma was in a Free Methodist church that had broken off from the Methodist congregation in the town. That church in Rushford, New York, was her world, her life. Since neither one of her boys became a preacher, she worked on her only grandson, my brother. At those evening devotions she would get my brother to read the Bible because he was going to be the preacher. The irony of all ironies is that the preacher turned out to be her granddaughter.

To finish that story, there are a lot of threads to my grandmother's influence. When I went on the mission field, well, that was great. She had a granddaughter who was a missionary. That was important. But it wasn't the same as having a preacher in the family. When I went to seminary and told my grandmother I was going to be a minister, she just could not compute that. At that time, there were, of course, no women in those kind of roles, so she would tell everyone I was studying Christian education.

But I'll never forget what happened the day she first heard me preach. My folks brought her down to the church in Silver Spring, Maryland, where I was an associate in a large suburban church. To this day, I can remember her coming into the narthex. The wind was blowing, her wig was a little crooked on her head, and she was almost overwhelmed. She had lived her life in this little teeny town and had never been in a church facility that size. My parents helped her to a seat about four pews back from the pulpit. After the service, what a change there was in her! While I was greeting people, she was whipping around the narthex, greeting everyone, and saying she was the grandmother of the preacher. She was the grandmother of the preacher! I never, ever forget that day. She would have been in her seventies.

My early experience of faith was my grandmother's faith and the way she lived it. And it made me uneasy. When I realized later that she had had that breakdown, it changed my whole picture of my grandmother. Now it seems to me that my grandmother had risked and risked and risked. And I think her life had just one too many risks. That's how I understand it. She probably would have liked to become a preacher. I'll never forget a comment made by one of her nieces who took me to dinner when the Council of Bishops met in San Diego. She said, "You know, my mother always said that your grandmother was by far the smartest in the whole family." But that was never the image we had. I had such mixed feelings about my grandmother as I was growing up. Partly some embarrassment, partly some intimidation because of the way she lived her faith. But she really was the only grandmother I knew closely. We always went to her house on vacations and holidays.

So in a way, I think I've lived her life, finished living her dream. I lived out the potential of who she could have been. That understanding came to me in an odd way, and it could be why the memory of her is so important.

Great affection and admiration for her mother are at the center of Susan's being.

My mother was an incredibly wonderful woman and the parent with whom I was closer. She was a gracious and elegant woman, which is an interesting contrast to me. She never said a bad word about anybody. She was always very good at interacting with people. My brother has more of my mother's personality. My sister and I are more like Dad. Mother had some Native American Seneca heritage in her and began exploring those roots as she got older. She was always interested in studying, taking a class, or reading something such as the *New Yorker* or the *Smithsonian*. She had a lot of curiosity.

My dad was a sensitive, gentle man who was seen as the intellectual. I think, in some ways, my mother was a bit intimidated by that. Although she had a wide range of interests and knowledge, she never saw herself as an intellectual type.

My parents met at Houghton College, a very conservative school near Buffalo, New York. It was where my mother could afford to go and where my father had gotten a scholarship. They were married there, and my mother finished school after Dad was drafted.

Susan is the eldest of three children. Her brother is two and a half years younger, but her sister is ten years younger. Both Susan and her brother were born during World War II, when her father was away fighting in the service.

My father was drafted before he finished college and was away fighting in World War II when I was born. In fact, he was in the first American unit to go in to Auschwitz. And you should see the pictures. Some of his photos are now in the Holocaust Museum in Washington. My brother and I both were born when he was in the service.

Dad had not finished college, and when he came back from the war, he still wanted to be a professor of English. He finished up at the University of Buffalo and worked at night. My mother's invalid mother lived with us for those first years until she died. When Dad graduated, he went to Cornell to graduate school. He was working on his doctorate there and was working part time in the industrial relations area at Cornell when he was offered a job with the DuPont Company. So we moved to Wilmington, Delaware, where he worked in public relations.

Much of Susan's childhood was spent moving from place to place.

We kept moving when I was a kid. It happened to be the timing, nothing more than that. Dad had started college, had a family, was drafted into the war, came back, finished college, and went to graduate school. We didn't have very much money, so we rented houses. A couple of times the house we rented was sold, so then we had to move to another. And then he got this great deal. We lived out in the country on a little farm. It was a wonderful setup. They rented that for years. My parents finally bought their own home after all of us were out of college and away from home. They started out with nothing.

It was different for my sister. When my brother and I were growing up, my father was in transition. I don't think I went to the same school more than two years in a row until I got to high school. But my sister, being so much younger, went through the same school system.

When I was in the tenth grade, we moved outside of Wilmington. I managed three years in a row there at the same school—the longest time I had been with the same kids. I constantly had to make new friends, I was always a leader. I was very active and into sports. I was a tomboy in the traditional sense of a tomboy. I was rarely in the house, and there were always lots of kids around. We lived in small towns and, in those days, had the whole neighborhood in which to play. You could climb hills and discover pastures. There was never any sense of being confined to a house.

Though there were certainly some good things about moving and Susan was able to adapt pretty well, there were also times when the moving was heart-rending.

In seventh grade, I was in Ithaca. I was going to be president of the student body the next year. And then we moved. I was very involved in school, in sports. I was student of the month. And then we moved. Our last move, when I was in tenth grade, almost did me in. I not only changed schools, but also moved to a school with a different cultural environment. I went to a public school that participated in a private school league. A lot of my friends had debutante parties. There were levels of competition and sophistication that I was not prepared for. I did survive it and was accepted well, but psychologically and emotionally I think I lost some self-confidence that I only partially regained when I went to college.

Yet, family was a stable reality, and now Susan is the stable center.

I'm the one who keeps all of the family scrapbooks, everything. I am rooted by those symbols. I've clearly become the matriarch. My brother said to me, "You're the heart and soul of the family. Don't let anything happen to you. You're the heart and soul of the family now." It used to be my mother.

I've always thought that moving around freed me to be a risk taker. I realize the openness in which my family lived. In some ways, I had a mutually intertwined relationship with my mother. But the family structure gave me the security to go out and do things.

Susan links her lack of involvement with church to the constant moving around.

I was not strongly connected with a local church. My transformational faith experiences came in other ways. It's amazing that I've gotten this far with so little foundation. I've always felt as if I had to catch up.

Susan has a unique relationship—or lack of relationship—with church that sets her apart from the early experiences of the other women bishops.

Mother's family was Seventh-day Adventists. I think they went to church regularly, but it didn't dominate her life. The church did dominate my father's family's life. But to some degree, this turned off my father and uncle to church. When I'm interviewed, I often say that I did not grow up in the church. When I do, my mother always feels insulted by that statement because her friends will see it in the paper. But when I was little, I only went to my grandmother's church. My mother might have taught Sunday school someplace. I have a memory of her one time building a tabernacle for a class. But because of our almost nomadic life, we never really hooked up with a congregation. So I don't have any tradition of church other than when we had to go to my grandmother's church. I listen to my colleagues or cabinets talk about their camping experiences and their Sunday schools, and there's this huge fondness. They also talk about the pastors who touched their lives, but I don't have any of that tradition. In some ways, I don't have some of the baggage I would probably have had to let go of. But I do think that I missed the deep appreciation for growing up in a congregation.

Living in so many places coupled with being a natural introvert colored her early activities and relationships.

I am more of a sideline organizer. I like building community and am good at it. And I'm really good at choosing personnel. But the specific way I organize comes out of my introversion. I'm very much people oriented. I'm sometimes too self-conscious to claim my own authority. That's always been an issue for me. I listen well. I'm extremely intuitive. I can usually tell by a gesture when someone's upset or that something is wrong with him or her.

I have had several close friends in whatever situation I've found myself. From school days on, I have known a lot of people from different groups, not from just one group. I usually connect across groups.

When Susan speaks of her brother, she smiles, and you sense the warmth of their relationship.

Growing up, my brother and I were closer. In many ways, it was just my brother and me because we moved a lot and my sister came around so many years later. Mom and Dad said we never argued. Well, I don't believe that. I do think my brother struggled with being my brother because I was an achiever and more athletic.

He's the outgoing one. He's the storyteller. You sit down with him, he knows everybody. To this day, he goes to the small town of Rushford where my grandparents lived. He talks to my father's old friends and our cousins. He stops by at the diner, has coffee with the locals. There isn't a person whom he's met who isn't his friend. And he's a raconteur, a storyteller. I've never seen myself that way. I was the quiet one.

Sports were a big part of Susan's life.

My mother was always into tennis. She played until she was in her sixties. Back in college, she played on the basketball team at Houghton. They had to wear these thick net stockings. Of course, she used to paint them on instead of wearing them and was called in more than once by the Dean. My mother was the rebel of Houghton College. I think my parents enjoyed sports, and it was also inexpensive family entertainment. My parents always had season tickets to the University of Delaware football games. They'd go with friends and tailgate. We were sports oriented, though perhaps my sister less so, although she played sports growing up. And now most of the next generation is playing sports and are very good. It's in the genes. That's what I tell nieces and nephews, meaning, teasingly, that it came from me.

I wouldn't have minded being a Billie Jean King. That is to say, I wouldn't have minded being a pioneer in the sports world. With the ability I had in those days, I think I could have gotten far. My high school was one of a few places that had women's sports teams because it competed with the private school leagues around. That's really where women's athletic sport teams started; but there still wasn't much of an avenue for women in sports after that.

So, I just was not in the right place at the right time. That would have been fun. On the other hand, I was clearly in the right place in the right time for my journey. And I would take nothing for the journey!

Academic achievement grew during Susan's school years. She is probably a much better student than she exhibited or claims.

Academic achievement was important to me until high school. Prior to that time I had done well. But then I ran into a level of competition that intimidated me. I don't think that I was intellectually inferior. But I dealt with the style of that school by being friends with everyone, by being an outstanding athlete, by playing in the band. But I didn't compete academically There's another factor. I think I have ADD (attention deficit disorder). If you were to see a video of me, you would see that I'm never still. My body moves. My eyes are always wandering. I don't focus long. I was never diagnosed or treated for it, but I suspect it has played a part. When I hit college I did okay, but I was still doing everything except studying. I really began to connect when I went to seminary. I graduated second in my class. I think I had matured and had confidence and could then succeed in that area.

Most people have some kind of vocational aspiration in high school. Susan's had an interesting hidden side.

When I was twelve or thirteen—the classic age for this kind of experience—I was riding in the car to my grandparents' and something came into my head and said, "Be a missionary." I didn't know what a missionary was. It was a mantra that went through my head over and over. Now I think it must have been the Spirit. At the time I didn't know what it was. I never said a word to anyone about it, but it stayed with me.

When I was in eighth or ninth grade, we had to choose professions. I chose forest ranger, detective, and missionary. And I hid the paper. Afterward, the strangest things happened. I'd open up *Life* magazine—we didn't have religious magazines in the house—and there would be an article on a missionary. A friend mentioned that her aunt who was a missionary had visited. This idea of being a missionary was always there, a part of me, but was something I was embarrassed to admit. I never told anyone. I didn't really know much about it. But when I applied to colleges, I chose church-related colleges. It's as if I had to make some connection.

At last, off to college and a campus ministry that turned her life in a new direction.

So, I went to Drew University in Madison, New Jersey, a church-related college. In reality, it was a campus ministry that turned my life around. It was the 1960s. What a glorious time! I remember going to chapel on one occasion and a woman minister spoke. I turned to a friend and said, "I just don't see women in ministry. Maybe they could be counselors or something." Can you believe that? But that missionary thing stayed with me.

I led in the student group and was president of the Student Union, the official student government. I was an officer in my class, very involved. Friends and connections were really important to me.

College was the "great time of her life." Susan has a sense that she was at "the right place at the right time."

Really, this sounds corny as can be, but a significant decision changed my life between my junior and senior years. At Drew, the big office was to be the senior boy or girl elected to be in charge of Freshman ("Frosh") Camp. They were elected the same time as the next year's student body president was elected.

I was majoring in religion with a minor in political science. I had to take philosophy, which was known as the hardest course in the school at that time. I took it my junior year but wasn't doing very well. But I thought I could always take it my senior year. At the last moment I decided that I needed to finish what I had started. And so I did.

That year I had also decided to run for Frosh Adviser, and I ran unchallenged. Since there was no competition, I knew I would be elected to the position that I had wanted since coming to Drew. Then I went to a meeting of some kind and realized that I could go to the London Semester in my senior year because I was a political science minor. So I had to make what was, for me, an enormous decision. What to do? In a sense, it was a symbol of the past versus the future—the past being those roles or those things that kept you where you were and the future being something that was a step into the unknown or a step into the future. I chose to go on the London Semester, and my college roommate became Frosh Adviser. I was able to go to London in the fall because I decided to hang in there with philosophy and didn't have to take it the first semester of my senior year. That semester in London gave me the world perspective.

That decision was pivotal and was really my first act of "stepping out on the promises." Moving so often as a child had helped me learn to be a risk taker. And when I stuck with the philosophy course—hanging in there and finishing something that was tough—it was possible for me to step out into something new and let go of something I thought was terribly important. This was another transforming point in my life.

The Civil Rights Movement was a magnet for Susan. All sorts of liberal movements and influences began to converge.

When I came back from London, I became involved in the Civil Rights Movement. I went to Alabama. I protested in the barbershops in Madison. I went to New York. But none of my friends were interested, which was very hurtful to me. Some people who were very into faith were not interested, and I couldn't understand why everyone wouldn't get on the bus and go with me. Now, I wasn't obnoxious about it. But it marked a point when I began to distance myself from those to whom I had been close before because they either were scared and worried or were tied up in their own worlds. I went with other people, other kids, a whole busload from Drew. But none of my close friends who were important to me were on that trip.

She keeps returning to the campus ministry and the influential campus chaplain.

It was the campus ministry program that absolutely put a lens on a faith that I could live with and become grounded in. Something Jim Sessions, the chaplain, said changed my life. During a retreat, we talked about how we could invite people in our faith. We were using the word "in." After about an hour and twenty minutes, Jim Sessions got up and said "You arrogant folk! Who do you think you are that some people are in and some people are out? I need to tell you now, everybody's in; they just may not know it." It was like a light, and it transformed me. "Everybody is in." And that's who I am to this day. That's who I've always been in terms of my witness in the church.

Susan begins to explore the call to ministry that she had heard so many years before.

Then I decided to go to seminary because I still had this notion of being a missionary hanging over me. I decided to apply to the General Theological Episcopal Seminary in New York because I liked their liturgy. Drew's worship always had high Wesleyan liturgy. I got this letter saying, "Dear Miss Morrison, we are deeply honored that we received your interesting application, but we do not accept women." And I remember taking that letter and laughing at myself. "Wasn't that crazy of me?" I didn't realize what it all meant. It was just before the women's movement.

I was in my senior year, and I said, "I've got to deal with this conflict within me." I talked to Jim Sessions about my call. He was the first person to whom I ever said anything about it. He just listened to it like it wasn't some crazy idea and said, "You know, next week a woman's coming from the Board of Global Ministries about a short-term program that The United Methodist Church has. Why don't you meet with her?" I went to the meeting and, among other things, talked with her about my fears of going alone. She said, "Oh, but this year, we're putting together teams of young people. We're sending an urban team to Brazil and a rural team to Bolivia. And I think you should apply for one of those teams. And then you would not go alone." So I applied, and do you know who headed the missionary personnel committee? Jim Ault *(now Bishop James Ault whom Susan succeeded in the Philadelphia Area when she was elected to the Episcopacy).* I was interviewed by missionary personnel and accepted on the Brazil team.

When I arrived at Greencastle, Indiana, for missionary training, an interviewer talked with me about my local church support in the mission field. When he asked me what United Methodist church I went to, I told him that I wasn't Methodist. (I don't think they'd accepted anyone at that time who wasn't Methodist.) Then he asked me what my local church was. And I said, "I don't belong to a church." Then he asked where I had been baptized, and I told him I had never been baptized. And he got up and left me at the table. About a week later, I got a call suggesting that it might be helpful to get baptized. The application for short-term missionaries had asked if you smoked or drank, but it never asked about church membership. After that they changed the application.

Brazil becomes the glue in Susan's life. After all of those important turning points in college, this experience sets the tone of her life and her being.

The experience in Brazil put everything together for me. I was part of a team of six young people. We were sent to a very, very poor community outside Rio. We quickly invited Brazilians to join us on the team. I connected with the kids and learned the Portuguese slang. Most of us lived with Brazilian families. One of the women on the team lived with a wealthy doctor in town, and she used to tell about everything she had eaten. I had rice and beans and beans and rice with my family. We were not apart from the community; we were part of the community. I became very close to the family I lived with, and to this day, that family is still connected with our team members.

While we were there, we developed a community center. Missionaries were usually part of institutional life, so their training in language and their experiences were usually in schools or in hospitals or in organizations. But The United Methodist Church came up with an idea of placing a group of young people in a community and telling them, "Okay. You be the church, whatever that means to you." We always began with a morning ritual and worship based on the Ecumenical Institute. We worked out of a small elementary school that was given to the Methodist church of Brazil. That became our community base. Different people did different things. We did some literacy training for individuals, but we mainly trained Brazilians to teach literacy. We vaccinated children. I worked with the kids, with games. I'd walk the favelahs, the urban slums, and would have a group of fifty kids running after me.

We started out with six Americans, and then we had Brazilians that came in and out during that period of time. All of them, by the way, are now leaders in Brazil. One became a bishop. One runs the seminary. We led in a way that developed leadership. That team became famous in the Brazilian church history, and other projects were modeled after it in different ways through the years. We were there three and a half years. Prior to that we had seven months of language training, longer than usual because we were going to be put in situations in which we would have to speak the language. I became fluent enough that I can, to this day, talk to the bishops from Angola and Mozambique in Portuguese.

I was in my early twenties, right out of college. It was an idealistic time—living in a different culture, being part of a sense of community. It was an incredible experience. Really, it was the Church at its finest.

Though Susan's experiences in Brazil gave her a powerful sense of the kind of community the Church should be, she largely experienced this outside the institutional church.

I was not interested in being seriously involved in the church there. Some of the other team members got very involved in churches and in the youth groups, but I didn't. Nothing like being a missionary and not going to church! My Brazilian family was Roman Catholic, and in Brazil, you always went with the matriarch or the patriarch of the family, wherever they were on Sunday. To be polite, I went to church with my Brazilian family on Sunday morning.

At some point, the team did suggest that I get involved with a church, so I went out to this little rural church for about six months and played the organ. I only knew three songs by heart, but that was more than they knew, so they were grateful. But other than that, I always went with my Brazilian family on Sunday to the family events.

Still more protests for Susan to enjoy and enter. And she begins to think theologically.

After Brazil, I came back to the States, and it was another time of protests. It was the Vietnam era. I went to Boston University School of Theology in the early 1970s. It was an exciting time for me because I had experienced another culture and had seen things from a different perspective. When I came back to the States, I connected my theology and my story to the experience I had lived. I thrived. I did well.

So what was this all about?

I guess I thought I was going to be a minister. But I don't remember. It did seem like seminary was the next thing to do. I never even thought about another path. But I don't remember having a call to it as strongly as I had to, for instance, the mission field. It's as if once I went to the mission field, I had done what I had been called to do. Out of that, I took the next step, and the next step. But I was still in no rush to get involved in the institutional church. When I was in seminary, I did my field work in other settings. I spent a summer organizing welfare rights in Minnesota. Another semester I did clinical pastoral education at Massachusetts General.

I graduated from seminary *magna cum laude*. That's when I had really put it together academically. I was awarded many fellowships, and I decided to study overseas. So I took a semester and went down to Buenos Aires in Argentina to the Faculdad de Teologia. It was really in the forefront of liberation theology in Latin America. Then for a second semester, with the help of a friend whose cousin was the assistant to a bishop in Rome, I lived in a Polish convent and studied at the Benedictine Seminary in Rome. I audited courses at the Gregorian University in Rome, including one course taught by Avery Dulles. It was an incredible experience.

Finally the institution caught up with Susan, and she began to move toward more traditional credentials.

I became a member of Peninsula-Delaware Conference when I was baptized and joined a church in Wilmington whose pastor my dad had gone to school with. So I applied for Deacon's Orders there. I couldn't go to conference, because that was the summer I was going to Mexico to study at Cuernevaca. So they had a special ordination service for me in December at which I was ordained Deacon and Felton May (now Bishop Felton May) was ordained Elder.

Bishop John Wesley Lord presided at my ordination. He was not in favor of women in ordination. He was very much a leader in the Civil Rights Movement but not much for women's rights. At that ordination service, he gave a sermon on the future of the church as men in ministry. He did it in such a way that it was clear to my parents, who weren't particularly involved in all of this, that he was giving me a message. Well, I wrote him a letter afterwards. Now, it was a nice letter, a concerned letter. And I got a call from my superintendent who said, "You know, he's in the hospital. It was not a very good time." I never met him after that. When I became a bishop, he was no longer coming to council meetings. At my first council meeting, we were given that big certificate that bishops sign for the newly elected bishops. I had the bishop from Florida take mine with him so he could ask Bishop Lord to sign it. I have no idea if Bishop Lord ever made the connection. I just wanted his signature.

I kept thinking that I wanted to go to a larger conference. I had met Bishop Mathews when I was head of the student body at Boston. He was the bishop in Baltimore/Washington. So, I wrote him and asked whether I could be assigned or transferred to the Washington/Baltimore Area, and he agreed. And that's how I started my journey in Baltimore and Washington.

So begins the next step of a most unorthodox journey to episcopacy.

After ordination, I was assigned to a local church pastorate. I stayed there as associate for more than five years and then was on my own in a local church for a year and a half before becoming District Superintendent. Then Bishop Joe Yeakel asked me to be Council Director, which I was for two years. Then, to my surprise, I was elected as a Bishop, though I wasn't even running for it. I spent the night of my election throwing up.

Over and over, finding herself in places she had not been before, Susan made the transition, but not without effort.

All of my life, when I've been put into situations and positions before I was ready for them, I've had to find ways to cope and to give me time to catch up.

A divergent journey leaves Susan with a yearning of sorts and an affirmation of what is most important to her—community.

When I heard people talk about their childhood pastor or their camp counselor, I longed for that kind of history and heritage in connection with the Church. Then when I became a member of an Annual Conference, I thought that I might develop such a heritage of my own. Surely these were the people with whom I would travel life's journey. But then I became a bishop, and the community is different when you are in the Episcopacy. It is a wider community that has been built for me over these years. What sustains me is the knowledge that this larger community will always be there through whatever my life brings.

Networking, community-building, other-empowering—all of those words stay with me as I try to summarize what I learned of Susan and how I have experienced her myself. Her unusual story, in terms of relationship to the church in early childhood, is filled with "connections" to family and friends. Her passion for justice never wanes from the first pushes from the college chaplain to the strong witness she makes in her Episcopal leadership. She may think of herself as one who stands on the sidelines in many institutional settings, but her influence is far reaching and she leaves her mark by touching lives for good.

Sharon Zimmerman Rader

Three blocks in from the Michigan shore of Lake Michigan, in the village of Pentwater, is a stately house, with a columned front porch marking the entry to its two-storied hospitality. There Sharon Rader and her family enjoy relaxation and refreshment. Pentwater has been a haven of rest since Sharon vacationed there as a child. Sharon has been returning ever since, and now her children bring their children.

It was there I spent time with Sharon. In the quiet of a small back-yard guesthouse, we enjoyed the view of grass and trees and the quiet of the village. Though the main street bustles "in season," now there is a serenity that matches Sharon's ease of conversation and a restfulness that mirrors her hospitality. The story starts with her grandparents.

My grandfather used to hunt and fish with Ernest Hemingway in northern Michigan. Named Koteskey, he was an immigrant from Bohemia. He came to northern Michigan with his family, about whom I know very little. He was raised there and became a lumberjack. He was rough and tumble, pretty raw around the edges sometimes. He fell in love with my grandmother, Reda Mae White, who lived up in the Horton Bay area. She married him, as they would put it, "unconverted." He had a religious experience through living with her and going to church with her. He left his lumberjacking, but not his fishing, and became kind of a local preacher type.

So Sharon's familiarity with ministry and itinerancy was almost genetic through her mother's parents. The Koteskeys moved around the northern part of the lower peninsula of Michigan with their nine children, the third of whom would become Sharon's mother.

The piety of her maternal grandparents and the presence of them in her life is a natural background for Sharon's almost seamless story of family and faith.

My grandmother was the warm, caring, compassionate one. And my memories of her are just wonderful ones. I always knew Grandma loved me. Grandfather got quite crippled with disintegrating cartilage in his hips. Today, he would have hip replacement and do fine. But it was prior to that time. So, they began living with their children. They lived with us one whole winter. I must have been in the fifth grade, maybe. I have wonderful memories of my grandmother teaching me to crochet and make this wonderful coffee cake called *kolache*. So I have good memories of them. But we all knew not to cross Grandpa. They were deeply religious. Every morning at their house, or if they were at our house, there was a family devotion time that could go as long as an hour. My grandfather would read from the Bible and make some commentary on it, and then everybody would get on their knees by their chairs as he prayed long prayers.

The family devotion time around the breakfast table was something that my mom and dad continued. There's a letter in my boxes of stuff that Blaine, my husband, wrote to my folks when we got engaged. He said that our family devotional time was one of the things he most admired about my family. So while I struggled against it as a child, I think it was very formative.

Sharon, born in 1939, speaks of being her parents' second child.

Their first child was born breech and died a couple of days after being born. My father took that baby, whose name was Richard, by himself, in a small casket in the back of the car to be buried because my mother was hospitalized for two and a half weeks after Richard was born. So she was anxious when she got pregnant with me. When I was born, my father was in the tuberculosis sanatorium, so my mother was anxious about my birth. I was born breech also, which my mother didn't know until she got to the hospital.

So I was raised as the oldest child and was, in fact, the oldest living child. My brother was born three and a half years after me. We lived in Battle Creek during all of those growing-up years. Until I was nearly five years old, we lived about two blocks from what is now the Washington Heights United Methodist Church. Then we moved to a rented house near the airport in Battle Creek. We were right on the flight path for the runway. At that time, there was an Army Air Force base in Battle Creek, Fort Custer, which was the induction center for the Army during those years. I grew up with airplanes flying over my head all of the time.

We lived in that house until I was in the fifth grade, when my parents were more financially established. They had gone through some pretty rough financial times during and after my father's hospitalization. We built a house just down the hill and over a block from the house we had been renting, and I lived there until I graduated from high school. My father worked for Clark Equipment Company as a sales engineer. My mother had been a teacher before I was born, and she went back to teaching when I was in the first grade.

Their home carried on the connection with church that had resided in the Koteskey and Zimmerman homes. Sunday was a traditional church-centered day.

Our family was quite traditional—maybe that is the way to put it—about Sundays, although my grandparents thought we were pretty loose because we would go out to eat on Sundays. They didn't think you should do that. When they would come to visit, they would scorn that a bit.

But the tradition was, we would go to Sunday school and church on Sunday morning. We'd often go out for Sunday dinner, we would go home, and my parents would take a nap while my brother and I were to be quiet. And so nearly every Sunday from the time I was in middle elementary school until some time in high school, I would go to the extensive church library in this old Evangelical church, take out these sort of religious novels, and read a book on Sunday afternoon. That was our Sunday. On Sunday evenings we'd have popcorn and apples, and there frequently were lots of people around the house.

Elementary school had its interesting realities, with a brother who was excelling and a teacher-mother with high expectations.

My brother went to a preschool, and because of that he was precocious when he started to school. He skipped kindergarten and a few other grades.

My mother taught at the same school I attended, and, in fact, I had her as my teacher in third and fourth grades. I was to call her Mrs. Zimmerman, even though everybody knew she was my mother. Sometimes when we would go home from school, I would forget, probably because she was still acting like my teacher rather than my mother, and I would call her Mrs. Zimmerman. That was hurtful to her. She wanted to be my mother when we were at home. I think we did pretty well with that, although she would sometimes apologize to me and say that she had used me for an example in the class so it wouldn't look like favoritism. I had to learn how to adjust to that. She was a fine, fine teacher and very much respected in the school system.

I was bright and did well in school all of the way through, culminating in being the valedictorian of my twenty-eight-member high school graduating class. That was a big deal. There was lots of academic affirmation.

Sister and brother are good friends as adults. In childhood, there was the usual sibling rivalry.

There was traditional sibling stuff that went on, but I think in a lot of ways we were pretty dependent on each other. We're different in some ways. He was a year too young for his grade, and so he was always running to catch up, particularly through high school and, in fact, even in college. He graduated from high school when he was barely sixteen. And he stayed at home and went to community college and then transferred to the University of Michigan. He graduated from Michigan at, I think, nineteen, but he was still just a kid and nobody wanted to hire somebody at that age. So he went in the Navy, which became very important to him. He was in the Vietnam War and even extended his tour of duty for a year. He went to Officer's Candidate School and extended for a year after that and came back grown up. Then he earned a master's degree. But there's never been any big rift between us. We don't talk a lot about day-to-day kind of stuff, but I think family is very important to both of us.

I worried about him in Vietnam and was angry when he extended because he was running those little PT boats up and down the river.

Church was always there. They were active members of First Evangelical United Brethren. She learned to exercise what would now be called leadership through her activities in that church. The church organist was her piano teacher, and by the time she was in high school, the piano bench at the church was her place, especially on Sunday evenings.

Her baptism and joining of that church were family events, too. Her grandfather either baptized or dedicated her. She doesn't know. But she does know it was in her grandparents' home with lots of family around. She thinks she was in about the fifth or sixth grade when she joined the church.

It just came to me one day that I wanted to join the church. I told my folks that I wanted to join the church, and they suggested I talk to the minister about it. When I did, he asked if I wanted to join the next Sunday, so I did. No training, no nothing. That's just the way you did it. Probably by that time, I'd been to the altar a couple of times, so he thought I'd had the appropriate religious experiences.

Having a family that was integrally involved in the community and the church and having a mother who taught served to set Sharon apart in some ways.

When I was growing up, my family was more religious than, for the most part, that of anybody else I hung out with at high school. Of my two best girlfriends, one was Catholic and had the freedom of going only occasionally to church, and the other was a marginal Baptist. But our family went to church on Sunday mornings and evenings. It was expected that I go to Youth Fellowship and then to Sunday evening services while my friends were out having fun on Sunday nights. I tried not going a couple of times but was told that my name is Zimmerman and that the Zimmermans lived life a certain way. That was an actual conversation with my father. It was expected that I would be with the family on Sunday evenings at church.

Sharon did not see herself as the girl everyone would want to date and was surprised when the great date invitation came.

I worked at J. C. Penney from the time I was a sophomore. When I was a senior, I was working one Monday night and got a phone call at the store. It was from a guy who was in my senior class. I had

had an occasional date with him. He was the smartest boy in the class and was also the captain of the football team. I can see myself there yet, standing by the cash register and his saying, "I'm sorry to bother you, but I need to do this right now. I want to know if you will go with me to the homecoming dance." And I said, "Uh, are you sure you want to do that? You're the captain of the football team, you know. Don't you think you should take someone else?" And he said, "No, I'm asking you to go with me. I would like to go with the homecoming queen." It was sort of mind-boggling to me. The football team had voted me as homecoming queen. It didn't fit my image of myself. I assumed that my two friends, who I always thought were cuter and more popular, would more likely be voted queen. Although I was a cheerleader all through high school, I spent more time on the floor than leaping in the air because I was so uncoordinated! But I just gutted it out and had fun with it most of the time. But this was such a shock.

Family expectations centered on educational goals. The press on the children was tempered by respect for Sharon's mother.

With my mother, the teacher, there were always high expectations of getting good grades. She obviously knew that I was fairly bright. The first time that I received a grade other than an A was in my senior year when I took chemistry. It was the first semester, the first quarter, and the chemistry teacher gave me a B+. I was just devastated. When I went in to see him, he said to me, "You think because your name is Sharon Zimmerman you're going to get an A, but you're not doing A work. When you want to get down and study and do something more than B work then you'll get an A, but not before." It was a good lesson. If my brother and I didn't get As, we had to answer for it at home. He was much more rebellious than I was and darn near didn't graduate from high school, because he sloughed off an art exam the last semester of his senior year and the art teacher threatened not to sign off on his graduation. I think mother put up high expectations.

Mother was a good teacher. I admired what she put into teaching. She had gone to County Normal, the equivalent of teachers' college, and didn't have a college degree early on. Later she went back to college and graduated the same year I graduated from college. She had taught all of those years with just this County Normal stuff. She always went to continuing education courses but finally wanted that bachelor's degree. I remember when she took a class in astronomy. She'd take my brother and me out on the hill and lay us down and describe the galaxies and the star formations. She loved to teach and loved to have the kids get involved in what they were learning.

Her strong admiration for her mother, and the sense of the times, led Sharon to think of being a teacher. But when she turned from that toward seminary, it was not an easy thing for the family.

It never occurred to me to be anything other than a teacher. And so that's what I trained to do. When I decided to look at seminary training, I initially thought I would be a Christian educator. Later I turned to ordination. But at one point, mother struggled with that. The Koteskey side of the family just didn't get it. Mother had two sisters who were married to preachers and another sister who was a missionary in India for twenty-five years with her husband who was also a minister. But they were always the pastor's wives, and my folks were delighted when I married a pastor. But me being a pastor—this is the early 1970s—was a struggle for her. I can remember one time Blaine teasing her, saying, "You know, she may be a bishop some day and my job will be to carry the bishop's bags." And she said to him, "Blaine, that is not funny. She could be the secretary to a bishop, but she can never be a bishop."

After I was ordained and she experienced me as a pastor, she got much better about it. From the beginning, my dad was interested in my ministry and encouraged me. The first time I wrote an article that was published in *The Interpreter* magazine was during my sort of radical feminist days when I wanted to claim everything I was. I had just begun using Sharon Zimmerman Rader, rather than Sharon Ruth Rader. I sent *The Interpreter* article to my parents, and my dad made some throw-away comment about the article; but he said he wanted me to know how proud he was that I had claimed the name Zimmerman and still claimed that part of the family. I learned something from that.

Other adults were important in Sharon's childhood and youth. She recalls the church organist, who was her piano teacher.

The discipline, the encouragement, the opportunities my piano teacher gave me, bled over into opportunities at high school. I accompanied all of the high school choirs.

Then there was a Sunday school teacher whom I loved. In those days, all of the girls were together in class and all of the boys were together. She was the high school girls' Sunday school teacher. We didn't get much religious education. There were many Sundays when she didn't open the book to teach us anything. We had too much to talk about—what was going on in our lives or in high school. She was there to listen and to make the space for us. She was very important.

Another important adult was a neighbor who lived behind us. When I was struggling with my mother, she was the person to whom I could go, and she'd just listen and be there. She was a young mom, and I baby-sat her kids, so there were many opportunities to be over there. I would go over to her house and sit and tell my stories and deal with what I needed to deal with as an adolescent. She would let me stand in the kitchen and help her cook while I talked. She was just there. My mother knew what was going on and welcomed it.

Sharon's involvement in social justice comes from a long string of influences. It did not start in church, for it was "fairly conservative—not repressively so, but somewhat." It is her mother, again, who opened the door.

The thing I remember is my mother getting involved with her students who were poor. There was a part of my hometown that was called "across the tracks," and many poor kids came from there. I remember when I was in the third and fourth grade, there was one girl in our class who came from a very poor family. She would come to school not smelling good and wearing dirty clothes, the whole nine yards. My mother identified her as a child who had some potential if one could get some supports under her. My mother was concerned that the class was shunning her. In the teacher's lounge, there was a bathroom with a tub, and my mother used to take her into that teacher's lounge and soak her in the tub and clean her up. She would take my old clothes and give them to her so she would be more acceptable in the classroom. I can remember lots of times that my family drove across the tracks, down to where she lived. We would take bags of groceries and other things that the family needed. There were always families like that. There was a trailer park down at the other end of town, and I can remember my mother going there to care for kids. With my mother, there was almost never a religious overlay on it. She just felt that it was the right thing to do.

Growing up was accompanied by the expectations of attending college and having a teaching career. Sharon attended North Central College in Naperville, Illinois. The image of her mother, the master teacher, was always there. But there were also other stirrings.

When I was a freshman in college, the chaplain at North Central College announced to the freshman women that the reason we had come to college was to find a husband. I don't know if he said it point-blank or if that was just what we understood it to mean. We all thought that he said if we were not married—or at least engaged—by the time we were out of college, there was a problem. I remember it infuriated me, but it also planted the notion that I'd better get with it. I was engaged by the time I graduated from college, but not to anybody from North Central College.

Academics got harder!

I had my comeuppance my first semester in college. I had been Miss Smartypants all the way through elementary and high school. I got to college and thought I could sashay through it. The first marking period I got a D in world history, which I hated anyway. I called my dad and said, "I'm coming home. I can't do this, it's too hard. I'm too stupid," and so on. And my father said, "You will not come home." And I said, "I can't do it. I have a D." I had a merit scholarship and was afraid that I would lose the scholarship. And he said, "You will not come home." So I went back and think I ended up with a C in world history. Ugh! I hated that class!

In college during the early years of the Civil Rights Movement, Sharon's racial sensitivity was heightened in a number of ways.

Martin Luther King Jr. came to North Central College. He had to be escorted into Naperville in secret. A group of us were invited to have lunch with him, and it had to be secret. He spoke for chapel, and then the luncheon was in secret, and he was quietly escorted out of town.

There were African American students at North Central College who came from the southside of Chicago, who began to sensitize me to a different kind of perspective on the world. I have a vivid memory of one African American student. We were at a dorm dance one night—no small thing since dancing was allowed for the first time on campus the year I was a freshman. Everybody was just hanging out, and he and I were talking. At one point he addressed me by the wrong name, but I didn't think much of it. I just thought he didn't know me well enough and forgot it. Later on that evening, probably after midnight, I received a phone call from him. He said, "You know, when we were talking, I didn't call you Sharon. I know your name is Sharon. And I want you to know that I know your name is Sharon." And I said, "Forget it. It's one of those things that happened. Don't worry about it." He said, "I need to know if I am forgiven." And I said, "Of course, what is this all about?" And he said, "When you've grown up in a place where nobody knows your name, names are important."

College was great fun for Sharon. She was involved and was learning all of the time. Her mentors included the college chaplain, in spite of his comments about women finding a husband! Under his tutelage, her faith found extension toward new horizons.

I adored the college chaplain because he broke open for me a kind of questioning. I never knew until I got to college that it was all right to question faith and biblical traditions. He broke that open for all of us, but particularly for me. He helped me make the connection between faith and justice and also between faith and mission. When I was a sophomore, he started an organization called Campus Church Community. We used to meet every Tuesday morning for breakfast at his house, and we would plan a Sunday night worship service for the following Sunday night. He would give us a lot of space. Talk about doing leadership development! I didn't understand that's what it was at the time. He gave us guidance, but we ran it.

When Blaine was teaching at Adrian College, he and Sharon became engaged in more civil rights action. Blaine taught with Jim Cone, who was writing his first book on black power and black theology. They were good friends, and their families spent time together. Sharon became involved with some other women at the church who saw that some Hispanic chil-

dren were not doing well in the public school. One difficulty was the inadequacy of their English as they entered public school. A group of young women, Sharon among them, organized. They recruited support from Adrian College service clubs to help them start a preschool for Hispanic children in Adrian. It is still going almost a quarter of a century later.

The thought of being something other than a teacher came after five years of teaching and five years of not teaching while her children were little. Blaine had finished his post-doctoral work in marriage counseling in Philadelphia, having left a teaching position at Adrian College in Michigan. They thought they would not be going back there, but jobs did not materialize and they returned.

We went back to Adrian and built what was, I thought, our dream home. We had to live in some other faculty member's house for the fall semester while the house was being built. We moved into that house the week before Christmas. The day we moved in, good friends came by, brought a Christmas tree, and set it up in the family room. We put the lights on it, and that night before we went to bed, our son Matt sat down in front of the Christmas tree and kind of looked around at it all. He was five, in kindergarten, and he said, "In our next house. . . ." I don't remember what the end of the sentence was, but I remember how it tugged at me to realize that he had moved around a lot in his first five years.

One year and one week later we moved out of that house so Blaine could be on staff at Lutheran General Hospital in Chicago as a pastoral counselor, which he had trained for. That transition was very difficult for me. I had gone back to teaching for a year and a half and loved what I was doing. I was allowed to do creative, experimental stuff with third- and fourth-graders and was having a great time. We were active at Adrian First Church, very enmeshed in that congregation. We were part of a house church in Adrian that met every Thursday night. Since we were young families, from ten to midnight was the only time we were unencumbered. The house church was important to me. It was one of the first places I began to think theologically. I was also writing curriculum for the Evangelical United Brethren Church. I thought we had it all together. Then Blaine made this job change, which was very appropriate for him, but very hard for me.

But that move opened unexpected doors for Sharon.

In the course of that move, I received two phone calls. One was from the associate pastor at Adrian First, who said, "Sharon, have you ever stopped to look at your life? You're really kind of schizophrenic. You're teaching, trying to be a good wife and mother, writing curriculum. Have you ever thought about putting that all together in one thing?" He meant Christian education. And that planted the seed.

The other call came out of being on some conference committee. I was on the Leadership Development Committee and the Conference Board of Education in the Detroit Conference. Those committees were very meaningful for me, and I thought that I should resign from them because we were moving to Chicago. The Conference Council Director suggested that there was no need for me to resign since Blaine would still be a member of the conference on extension ministries to Lutheran General Hospital.

Those two calls were important in pulling me to a different way of being in the church. The idea of becoming a Christian educator made sense to me. I had already decided to work on a master's degree in guidance and counseling to expand my skill. When Blaine and I talked about this idea, he felt that I should get training, even though I might be able to do the job without it. So, we decided that I would go to seminary instead of getting a master's degree in guidance and counseling.

The move was very hard for Sharon. She left a home she loved. She left a teaching job she enjoyed. A compromise for them was to live in Downers Grove, which was familiar territory, located close to North Central College. Evangelical Theological Seminary was in Naperville, so the conversation about Christian education moved comfortably toward enrollment. Not long after Sharon began her theological studies, her boundaries were pushed again.

I think the worship life at the seminary and the times—it was 1972—came together to move me in a different direction. There were only eight women in the seminary when I went. The merger conversations between Garrett and Evangelical seminaries were beginning. There weren't any women faculty members at ETS, but almost immediately I was pulled into the merger stuff. I was on the merger committee and got to know the Garrett people early on. A psycholoist from Michigan who was teaching at Garrett, Kay, called me one day and said to me, "I need to invite you to consider ordination. What I see of you in meetings leads me to think that you ought to be looking at something else." So there was that kind of push. I think that's where the nudging over into ordination came from.

Once she began the move toward ordination, Sharon felt her life come together.

When I began to push through ordination, it felt like all of the pieces of my life came together—the nurturer, the teacher, the religious seeker—were all right there embodied in who I was supposed to be as a pastor. All of the bits and pieces got put together. It wasn't dramatic, like God spoke to me one day. It just seemed to fit.

Sharon recites many strong influences in her life and is unabashedly grateful for them. Blaine, her husband, is chief among her supporters and mentors.

First and foremost, Blaine and I have unconditional love for each other. But there were also some conscious reasons in my decision to marry him. He was interested in learning and in the church and wanted to teach. My decision to go to seminary was not always greeted with great joy. Blaine supported me through that, even while I was in seminary and he was working at Lutheran General Hospital where he took some ridicule from his colleagues about a wife who was out of control. When I was in seminary and reading Mary Daly and anybody else I could get my hands on who seemed fairly radical, he read right alongside me, and we engaged in conversation about them. He's also been willing to share the parenting responsibilities. I would be very different without him.

Part of what fit for Sharon was her experience of strong women in the past and now in the present. A memory of her mother with other women is not insignificant.

When mother went back to teaching, she was older than many of the teachers around. She became a kind of mother figure for many of them. There were always lots of women at our house—teachers she taught with or people whom she mentored or mothered. They would frequently need, or just want, somebody to ride along with them to a ballgame or something and would often take me along. They also became mentors for me. I saw what fun a lot of them had teaching, and it confirmed for me my desire to be a teacher. But as I think about it, I never thought that we were a particularly gregarious family; there were just a lot of people around, including some male teachers whom my parents befriended and who would stop in regularly. My mother loved to cook, so she would plan dinners. At one point, there was a group of women teachers who would come every Thursday afternoon. They would have tea and sandwiches and talk. That began a process for me of seeing strong, professional women. A community of women has always been important for me as a source of nurture and common life journeys.

Kay Wilcox, the psychologist who taught at Garrett, was certainly an important mentor for Sharon. Sharon is indebted to this iconoclastic woman who "ran around in her tennis shoes" and opened doors that had never been opened as one of the first female faculty members at Garrett. But she was also responsible for encouraging Sharon toward ordination.

Following the seminary merger and moving to Evanston, Sharon worked for the General Commission on the Status and Role of Women while she was still in school.

Nan Self, General Secretary of COSROW, was very much a mentor. She saw things in me and gave me opportunities to walk alongside the newly emerging women's movement in the Church.

Talking about mentors, Sharon says:

I would have to say, Judy, that you were also one of those people who influenced me and gave me many ministry opportunities. You opened the door for me to gain leadership experience that reassured people that I might have the ability to be a bishop.

Another woman who was instrumental was Jeanne Audrey Powers. She was Associate General Secretary of the General Commission on Christian Unity and Interreligious Concerns and decided that she would mentor me along also. I was not unlike many other women who were in awe of her. And at one point, she challenged me about that. I said to her, "You scare me, the way you can comprehend things and articulate them and push on the system." She got really angry with me and said, "I have tried to be transparent with you so that you could see who I am and learn. Don't ignore me by telling me that you're holding me at arm's length." She didn't care how mad you got or how much you disappointed her; she wouldn't let you go.

Then there was a woman on the Northern Illinois Annual Conference staff.

When I was in seminary, I still was not thinking about pastoral ministry, even though I was looking toward ordination. I thought I wanted to do something such as conference staff work. I wanted to be an associate, but never a lead pastor. So I asked the Northern Illinois Conference if I could do my field education work with their conference staff. A woman staff person was assigned to work with me. She let me trail around behind her and learn. This experience gave me the opportunity to learn how church people make decisions. She modeled a strong, committed laywoman and a good teacher for me. She also opened up the field of mission to me, and the whole arena of United Methodist Women.

By this time, Sharon had demonstrated leadership over and over. She muses over how that all came to be.

It was probably being developed earlier than that. But I would say that some of the work that I did with the General Commission on the Status and Role of Women taught me leadership skills.

Helping establish the Hispanic preschool in Adrian also taught me a great deal about leading. I don't know how we knew what to do. We just kind of gutted it out. We'd brazenly go and tell these service clubs that this needed to happen and that we wanted it to happen. It was where I began to learn things that are important now. We learned that we needed to include mothers on the planning committee, to find out what they wanted for their children's preschool. Also, we had always met on the west side of Adrian near the church. One day, one of the mothers said to us, "We're not going over here any more. You come to our neighborhood." That kind of stuff I learned early on from them.

I learned about leadership in college, too, because of the opportunities provided by the chaplain and the organization he started, Campus Church Community. He nurtured us and shoved us out there and told us to go for it.

It all seems a seamless fabric for me. I had this opportunity and then this one. I'm not a particularly reflective person, so I don't often stop to say, "Now, what did I learn from this?" But I often ask the people I work with this question and am trying to be more reflective myself.

A lifelong learner, Sharon points to seminary as the greatest place of change.

I think seminary was probably the most radical place of learning. There weren't many women at Garrett Evangelical at that time. Those were the days when women ragged on faculty about their use of language, about being inclusive. Merlyn Northfelt was a wonderful, wonderful seminary president and wonderful friend. He also gave me lots of opportunities. But people used to joke that when Merlyn saw me coming down the hall, he'd go in his office and cower, wondering what I was coming to beat up on him about!

Emerging as a radical, a feminist, and a theological thinker was not easy for Sharon. There were major role shifts through which she had to struggle.

In some ways, those days were confusing for me. On one hand, I was a respectable wife and mother, with a husband who had a very good job and who was an expert in his field. And on the other, I was saying some of the same things that the radical feminists were saying. But it was coming out of the mouth of this person who looked like she was probably safer, or not as extreme, or something. My analysis is that sometimes I was confusing to people. I was into the middle of it before they realized they were going to get it from me, too. Dorothy Jean (D. J.) Furnish, professor of Christian education, and a group of four or five women students would go in to the president's office to talk with him about issues. He would ask four or five women what women wanted. There'd be a long pause, and I'd charge in and I'd say, "Well, here's what I think we want." Afterward, D. J. would say, "I would never presume to think that I know what the women want. And, Sharon, you just talk right back to him." It was a gentle nudging, but a strong reminder to acknowledge my own shortcomings and fallibilities.

I am not sure where I learned how to confront people such as Merlyn. I think I learned early on that issues and people were not the same. One can disagree strongly on the issue and still heartily enjoy the person. I wasn't trying to beat up on people, though that's sometimes what people experienced. But I think Merlyn would take it from me because he also knew I cared about him. Bishop Paul Washburn was the same way.

During my last quarter in seminary, I was able to opt out of polity since I was part of a class attending General Conference and would see firsthand how the book is written. As a member of the first graduating class after the merger and as a woman, I was asked to speak at a Garrett luncheon at General Conference. We had been through a lot that year. So I stood up in that packed room and gave this speech about the merger of the seminaries and how we were trying to incorporate people. When I finished, the crowd immediately stood up and gave me a standing ovation. Merlyn said, "Nobody gets a standing ovation for a little speech at the Garrett luncheon." I didn't know what to make of that, but the first question that came to me was, "In this incorporating of all people at Garrett Evangelical, what about gays and lesbians?"

Relationships. It is always about relationships for Sharon.

I have been gifted with friendships that just don't let me go and hold me accountable. I have been challenged by many who say, "All right, you're in a place in which some of the rest of us can't be. You need to be our voice. You need to speak on our behalf. You need to challenge the Church."

Sharon has not experienced direct rejection much in her life, but she does recall the first appointment to a church.

I felt powerless about the whole situation. The hard thing about the rejection was that there was nothing I could do about it, because the issue was who I was. I couldn't change being a woman. And they were not going to have a woman. It didn't matter whether I was smart enough or good looking enough or a nice person. It didn't matter. I was a woman and there was nothing that would change that.

When all is said and done, it goes back to Sharon's family.

Mother's oldest sister, Frieda, is still alive in her nineties. When my mother died, Aunt Frieda came to me and said, "Sharon, you don't have anybody to pray for you anymore, and my commitment to you is I will pray for you every day." I saw her three or four years ago, and she said, "Remember the promise I made to you when your mother died?" And I said, "Yes Ma'am, I do." And she said, "I'm keeping it." It's not earth shaking, but it's clear in my memory. It's sort of like you're never left alone, you're never without resource. I hadn't claimed that as clearly and as fully as I have since I've been a bishop.

It may have been from the day I was born that I knew women could do what they had to do. My mother was alone. My dad was in the sanatorium, and she had to cope. She had this baby and no source of money and needed to rely on a community that was not her own—Seventh-day Adventists. My dad had been working, selling insurance for the Seventh-day Adventists. They gave her food and helped take care of me. When she was finally able to get back on her feet and went back to work at J. C. Penney, a Seventh-day Adventist couple took care of me while she worked. From the womb, I knew a woman who had to pull it all together. So, from out of the chute, there was a presence around me. Women can do what they need to do. Women have always done what they needed to do. Perhaps my mother wasn't any more unique than any other mother, but she instilled in me a confidence that there is nothing I cannot accomplish.

That confidence is carried by Sharon with dignity and a kind of quiet ability to do whatever is required of her without much "fuss or bother." Sharon is gently strong, very adept at building and maintaining relationships across all kinds of social barriers, and carries in her being the never-questioning sense of faith that has been her bedrock. She has exceptional organizational skill and "savvy." She has made history by being twice elected to a four-year term as Secretary of the Council of Bishops, the officer who most keeps track of the work and agenda of the Council. Never flinching from the hard work, she has provided excellent leadership and modeled a way to use "power" that is selfless and gracious. Her story reflects the assurance I have always experienced—an assurance of the gracious love of God that accompanies her in all circumstances.

Beverly Shamana

California has been home for Beverly all of her life. She speaks fondly of her nuclear family.

My family is made up of Mom, Dad, two sisters, a brother, and me. I am number one, my two sisters are next, and my brother is the baby. We were just recalling the other night how firstborns know how to organize, take charge and monitor everything and everybody, and enjoy doing it.

The story of her birth in 1939 is poignant though she tells it with a smile.

I was born in Los Angeles. It's a story with a sting and reflects the racism of the times. My mom and dad had been making deposits on hospital costs for my birth in Pasadena, where we lived, at Huntington Hospital—a kind of layaway plan. Mom said they had one more payment left when it came time for me to come. Because they hadn't made that last payment, they had to leave Huntington Hospital and were sent to L.A. County Hospital. They didn't get their money back.

Race was an issue from the start. But an early experience with her father indicates that it did not always stifle outrage.

Pasadena at that time was still in the throes of the pre–Civil Rights days, of course. There was the heavy pressure of racism. Mom tells the story of a restaurant at which she and Dad were ignored. They asked for service and were told by the waitress that she was not allowed to serve Negroes. They moved to the counter seats and, after a long time, were served plates of spaghetti. After a few minutes, Dad took his plate and slammed it face down on the counter, and they walked out. It was a downtown restaurant. There was a strong black community in Pasadena. My grandparents were part of it. But Pasadena had restrictive laws and expected certain behavior of its black folks. My dad's expectation of receiving a certain kind of treatment and not getting it was a violation of his integrity, and the restaurant wasn't going to get away with it. What stands out in my mind is that he was not going to take any guff.

Her forebears had migrated west.

My dad was born in Oklahoma. My mother was born in Texas. I knew my grandparents. Not my mom's dad. He died when she was fourteen years old. But I knew two step-grandparents. My grandmother outlived two husbands and married again each time. They were great people.

We spent time with grandparents on both sides. I remember it was my paternal grandmother who bought me my first pair of what I called fancy shoes as a junior high girl. We went to a downtown store, and she let me pick out the shoes. I walked on air because of those shoes. My grandmother on Mom's side lived in L.A. She came over every week on what was then the streetcar, the old rapid transit line.

The family's four children came in a period of eight years. The baby brother got special treatment, according to Beverly.

I think Charles got a lot of favored treatment. After all, he was a boy after three girls. A boy finally arrived, not to mention that he was the baby. I remember him as a kid doing these special tricks of flipping himself over a broom. We would hold a broom handle on both sides and amazed all of us by doing chinups and flips and all sorts of things. Whenever anybody would come over, we would show him off.

Her parents provided a stable home. Her father worked as a plastering contractor.

There are lots of places still standing in and around L.A. and Pasadena that my father plastered. Mother was mostly home but did work part time for the Department of Recreation in Pasadena. She was in charge of crafts and games and trips and competitions and all sorts of things that happened at the parks and recreation center.

My family was active in church. But at first it was not a Methodist church, although my mom had grown up in The African Methodist Episcopal Church before she was married. My dad's folks were Baptist, so Mom joined their church—a rather large Baptist church in Pasadena I attended the first ten years of my life. My grandmother was president of the missionary society, and my grandfather was the treasurer at the church. I remember Baptist camp for kids, Sunday school, altar calls, and seeing people slain in the spirit. I remember playing piano for the Sunday school. That's when I first learned how to play for a group. I remember Mom saying, "No matter what happens, don't stop playing. Keep going. If you make a mistake, keep going." It was good advice then, and it sure helps now.

Music is a theme throughout Beverly's life. She was a pianist, choral director, and a teacher of music.

I started playing when I was about five years old. Mom taught me my scales earlier than that. But I started with a music teacher when I was five or six. My mother was a pianist.

Beverly's mother started thinking about becoming a Methodist because of a neighbor.

She said she wasn't really getting the kind of nurturing and discipleship that she wanted, though she was very involved and the superintendent of Sunday school. But something was missing for her.

There was a couple who lived behind us—a Hispanic woman and a Caucasian man. They had two boys and a girl. We used to play with them a lot. They went to the Methodist church three blocks down the street. Mom was good friends with them, and they told her about the Methodist church and brought home a weekly card that explained the scripture of the day. Mom got one every Sunday. Something about that was intriguing to my mom. She liked things made plain. She is an artist and likes visual stimulation.

She wanted to leave the Baptist church, but she couldn't. When I was nine, I remember waking up one night and finding myself on the floor. I didn't know what to make of that. So I got up and got back in the bed. After sleeping for a while, I woke up on the floor again and got back in bed. I found myself on the floor next to the bed a third time. I got up and crept into Mom and Dad's bedroom, woke my mother up, and, in tears, told her, "God said you should pray more." Oh yeah, a nine-year-old telling her mother how to conduct her spiritual life. You can imagine how afraid I was to say those words to my mother. But it seemed like a message from God that I was supposed to say to her. I didn't know what that was about at the time, and it was recently—when I was writing my book, *Seeing in the Dark*—that I asked Mom about it. She said, "You know, I was in a dilemma trying to choose what to do at the time. I wanted to leave the Baptist church but didn't think I should. There was such a history. We had Baptist ministers going way, way, way back. And I didn't think I could do it and not be ostracized by your dad's family or by the church. Now here I was the Sunday School Superintendent and I am going to leave and be a Methodist with no good reason? But your message to me helped me reach a decision. I did pray more about it and decided that it was okay for us to leave the Baptist church and go to the Methodist church."

It's pretty amazing to me. Makes me think about the spiritual influences that are in our early lives. Somehow in the early years there was some experience with the mystery of God. I don't know what I would have called it at that time. I probably forgot about it and went on being and doing whatever girls be and do at that age. But something happened to me when I was nine.

They moved to the Methodist church, but not before Beverly had been baptized by immersion.

I was immersed and baptized in the Baptist church. I remember my immersion. I remember putting on the white robe. I remember the steps down to the baptismal pool, behind the choir loft. I remember walking the steps down into the pool while the choir was singing. I remember how big the minister's hand was over my face. I don't remember the words, but I remember going under the water and coming up drenched and sputtering—and knowing that I was baptized.

From the beginning, Beverly lived in racially integrated settings. School and church were both racially mixed. Elementary school is a pleasant memory.

It was a racially mixed school. There were Spanish-speaking kids as well as black and white kids. In fact, our neighborhood was mixed. A Japanese family lived at the corner, and a German family near by. I can look back on my grade school pictures and see that they were very mixed classes. Nevertheless, there was only one black teacher in the school.

There was artistic bent in much of the family.

Every year we spent several days at the Pasadena Art Show at the civic center where Mom's art was on display. We kids would weave our way through easels filled with oils, watercolors, and charcoals of all kinds of subjects. As a kid, my sister was a great artist. She still is and has her own business now. She would draw on sheets of butcher paper saved from the meat wrappings. Her work was published in the *Pasadena Star News,* and she won lots of awards for her art. Music was my outlet in grade school and church, and my piano lessons continued all the way through college when I got my degree in music.

Living comfortably was not without some sacrifice on the part of her parents.

My dad did not always have steady work. There was a time when we were separated as a family. At one point, when he could not find plastering work in Southern California, he went to Las Vegas with a crew and worked in a parts factory. On weekends, we would troop to Las Vegas and stay with several families because of costs. We would rent a house and combine the cooking and accommodations, with only a curtain between families. I remember my dad's being away. I know it was difficult then for a black man to get steady work, so they had to go where the work was. I remember seeing him at the union building and guys standing around waiting to be called for work. Lack of work for a black man in the 1940s is a vivid image in my childhood mind.

So secure was home life, that Beverly did not have a sense of being deprived.

I never thought of us as poor. But I remember putting cardboard in our shoes when they had holes in them. I was careful not to lift the soles of my shoes because the cardboard might show. We had homemade clothes and hand-me-downs. We didn't always have a full lunch pail, but I never remember being hungry. Other girls had more expensive clothes than I had. I knew they had paid more money than we did. That's why that pair of fancy shoes from my grandmother was so important.

Though living on the West Coast during World War II, Beverly has few childhood memories of it at five years old. Her father was not drafted for a medical reason. She has faint memories of rationing stamps and white oleo. Her location on the coast did not bring with it any sense of being in danger or of being threatened. Though others may have been worried, those around her gave her a sense of safety, and life went on at her home.

Beverly's teens were enhanced by her musical gifts.

In junior high, I got recognition right away because of music. I played for the boys' and the girls' glee clubs. That made me the only girl in the boys' glee class. I became more proficient, more aware of different kinds of music, because of the glee club teacher. I thought she was a great teacher, and all of the students dearly loved her. She took me to her house, and we became more like friends. School talent shows were another outlet for my music, which brought recognition from students as well, not just from teachers. Some of those kids in the talent shows have gone on to great careers.

Public presence was already forming her, not only in music, but also in other settings.

In tenth grade, I was elected class president, which gave me the opportunity to speak at the graduation ceremonies for all of the area Pasadena schools and City College. I spoke on the theme of the importance of religion.

But that wasn't my first time speaking. In the black Baptist church and in my maternal grandmother's AME church, there were lots of opportunities for kids to speak. The expectation was that you would give a speech on Easter and Christmas and Children's Sunday and other special days. The older you were, the longer your speech. You had to memorize and practice your speech. You had to do well, to stand and deliver. We did a lot of that.

Beverly's comfort with, and leadership in, integrated settings increased through her church experiences.

The Methodist church in Pasadena was mainly a white church. But it was as racially mixed as the neighborhood. That was one of the hallmarks of this particular church. In the mid- to late 1940s, several churches sent members to ensure that it grew as a mixed church. It was kind of an agreement. I'd love to know now how the bishop and leadership put it together. It was early for such experimental thinking, and it was a progressive place to be. It helped having two African American pastors sent to us. There was an active youth ministry. One minister at the time would truck us around from church to church. "These people need to see you and see what it is like to be part of a mixed group, to be in a mixed situation," he said. "So we're just going to help them see what this church is about." Every other Sunday, we would meet with another white youth group and talk with them.

I went to church camp every summer. I remember going forward to commit my life to Christ. I remember doing that in the Baptist church, too—the altar call kind of thing. I remember it at camp and I remember it at church.

Beverly's early thoughts about her vocation:

We made "vocational notebooks" in junior high. Every student had to choose three vocations, research them, and put together a notebook about them. I remember that Mom, who was an artist, made the cover for mine. She didn't have fancy paper or anything like that. It was cardboard. But she drew beautiful figures on it. I remember one vocation was a teacher and one was a lawyer. To this day, I can't remember exactly what the third one was, but I want to say minister, though I'm not sure.

I had also dreamed of being a concert pianist. I practiced a lot and thought I was going to be one for the longest time—well into college. It was only after I realized that practicing was an eight-hour job like any other that I gave it up.

I went to Pasadena City College for two years and did choral work there. That's where I decided I wanted to be a choral music major—because of the director. He was such a fine man. I accompanied the choir most of the time. He always praised my accompaniment. He was such a great conductor. I went to Occidental College (Oxy) on his recommendation. I had tried to get into Occidental after high school and was not accepted but got in later as a transfer student. I felt sort of second class because I hadn't been there the full four years, but I wouldn't trade PCC for anything. It's where my dad graduated. I was the first in my family to graduate from a four-year college.

Traveling with the glee club was a major part of her time at Occidental College.

One weekend, the glee club left campus for a concert. I set my overnight case on the bench, but when the bus came and we all rushed aboard, I forgot it. We performed in formals and tuxedos, and halfway there I discovered that I had left my suitcase. I'll never forget what happened next. The women took pieces of their formals and constructed a dress for me on the spot. I got one woman's slip and another woman's shawl. Someone else gave me her sash and another her stole. They cut and tied and tucked until I finally had a dress. Then they squeezed and shielded me so that my face and voice were all that people saw and heard. I felt so cared about and supported. I was the only African American woman in the glee club. They took care of me and put their arms and their netting around me. It was really something. I will never forget it.

At another concert, I was to perform during the break between the first and second half of the concert. I was going to play a fancy number—by Mendelssohn—but my fingers all became thumbs. I was never so embarrassed in my life. I got hung up in one part of the piece and couldn't get out of it. I forgot. It became a trap. I kept playing the same part, hoping that if I did it just one more time I'd get the second ending, which would then take me to the next part. I was just stuck in this one first ending. I don't know what I finally did, but whatever it was I got to the end and slunk off of the stage. And the director said, "How could you?" I wanted to run out and say, "I'm sorry everybody. I couldn't find the second ending."

People didn't talk about race at Oxy in those days, but there was a huge sense of being a minority, of never quite belonging.

I was one of five black students. My roommate was from Kenya. I'd never known anyone from Africa, and we had little in common. She knew nothing about American culture, and I knew nothing about African culture. People kept trying to put us together because we were the same color, but it didn't work. We were courteous as roommates and did things together. I also took her home for family time. But there was such a gulf between us. I know now that she was as lonely as I was. There's something of yourself that goes underground when you are separated from your people and your roots so that you're not your full self. You can certainly function, but you aren't free to flourish in the same way as when your support group is with you.

I went home every weekend and during the week when I didn't like the food in the cafeteria. So I never made the full transition to Occidental's campus culture. Although I had been in mixed schools all along and felt thoroughly comfortable, there seemed to be such a gulf between me and the other students at Occidental. I didn't feel involved and still don't feel much of an affinity for my time there.

The Civil Rights Movement was inescapable. Beverly may not have been very active in the movement early on, but she traces her growing awareness.

The Civil Rights Movement erupted on the West Coast with the Watts uprising in the mid-1960s. We went to see Martin Luther King Jr. when he came to Pasadena. And there were marches and other protests in Pasadena. I was in my early twenties and not a part of the movement yet. There were pockets of political activity, but it did not sweep over the whole black community. The church that I was in was still a mixed church, and we did work for change. We put on programs, brought speakers, and talked about the Civil Rights Movement.

My awareness and personal involvement for racial equality grew over time with the understanding of systems, although it really came home to me in a personal way. When I got engaged and put my picture in the paper, I got a nasty letter that said, "You have no right to be in a white paper. Monkeys like you belong in the zoo." Later, there was a cross burned on our lawn. This would have been before I got married, sometime between 1961 and 1962, because I had put my black face in a white newspaper. We were outraged. We had been there all of our lives, but suddenly I wasn't good enough.

After college, Beverly began a teaching career.

I married in 1962 and began teaching music in an all-black junior high school in Compton, which was about an hour away from Pasadena. Later, I taught music at the high school in Compton for five years. It was a special time for the students and me.

I was finally able to get into the Pasadena school system by doing long-term substituting. The music teacher was sick and never came back. I think that's the only way I got in. It was hard to get into Pasadena when I graduated. I had to come through the substitute route to get in and get accepted.

Beverly's call to ministry came through her work as a layperson, specifically with the Ecumenical Institute of Chicago.

When I was in my twenties, the mixed church I had attended merged with a white church and moved to a new site. And that's when we got a new minister who got us involved with the Ecumenical Institute, a movement of lay and clergy in the 1960s and 1970s concerned with societal issues. That planted the seed for ministry. We went to the E.I. "mother house" in Los Angeles and met with other churches. We took a religious studies course. Before this I had never heard of Tillich or Bultmann or Bonhoeffer. Suddenly, it was as if some other part of me came alive. I told E.I. to sign me up. I went to Chicago and stayed a summer. I lived in those crowded, cramped quarters and was glad to be there. I was so excited. And then I trained. I said, "Yes I'll go this weekend and teach." I taught the course in Ridgecrest, Nevada, a little tiny place, and also in Las Vegas. We recruited the classes, set up the room, taught the classes, made the pitch for the institute, and did the follow up. It was a lot of work. I jumped in feet first. The religious studies course opened me up to the larger world of the church and community renewal. A cadre met every night and many weekends at the church. We did community surveys, celebrations, and political dialogues.

It took a while, but the call finally took form.

I taught for ten years but finally decided that I didn't want to be sixty-five and a high school counselor in the public school system. I didn't want to do that all of my life. So I decided that if I was going to stop, I needed to stop then. I also learned that I couldn't have kids and that adoption was not an option. That's when I became a substitute and got back on the long-term teaching track.

The journey continued, with Beverly ducking all of the way.

I retired and drew down my money. That Christmas, my husband gave me a knitting machine. In three years, I'd opened up a store, R. J. Knits, in Pasadena and sustained myself and three employees for over four years with clients, home shows, fashion shows, and hotel shows.

During this period, my husband and I divorced after ten years of marriage. When I tried to rent an apartment in Pasadena, I had to call the Fair Housing Council to help me because racism popped up again. It just wouldn't go away. More than once, a vacant unit was suddenly filled when I showed up at the door. I joined the Council later. Then Pasadena Redevelopment demolished buildings on Green Street for a new mall. One of those buildings was my business.

I still had my job directing the church choir, and between interviews, I joined the steering committee to elect a local woman to the California Assembly. It was good experience, but she lost. Still, the money I was earning wasn't enough. I borrowed from everybody I knew—even my pastor. I was embarrassed and even tried to get food stamps, but after several appointments and long lines, I was denied. That was a horrible experience—so demeaning. I know something about the despair of unemployment because of that time in my life.

With so much time on my hands, I joined the inner-city task force and the Mayor's Committee for a Neighborhood Congress and led a committee on world hunger and aging. Then a job opening for Executive Director for the Annual Conference Commission on the Status and Role of Women was announced in the conference paper. I had gotten involved in district things at that point, too, and my pastor suggested I apply for the job. At the time, I had a girlfriend whose feminist consciousness had been raised. She kept saying to me, "Beverly, don't you understand what's happening? Don't you get it?" I said, "That's a white woman thing. I don't need it. I'm fine." She was white and a very good friend who just kept hassling me. She was so adamant, but I was so content with my life and role. Yet, things were changing fast.

The pastor kept at me, but I didn't know if I was feminist enough. He told me, "This job is yours and you need to make them know that they need to hire you. And you need a job." So I applied and went to the interview. And they offered me the job. It was a part-time job, and I kept it for a year and a half, from 1975 to 1977.

Then financial difficulties hit Pacific Homes and took out many conference jobs and programs, including mine.

While the job with COSROW lasted, it was an experience of molding.

My job was to go out to churches and talk about the equal involvement of women in all phases of church life. I learned. And in that itineration, I met women clergy. I remember going to a conference at Claremont where the Reverend Faith Conklin served communion. I was so moved. All these years, I had never received communion from a woman or seen a woman preach.

I was elected to General Conference and on the way back home went to Glide Community Church. I was blown away. When I got home, I tried to duplicate Glide worship. My pastor turned me loose with a new night service. It was great fun to try my hand at it, and we had some success. I became a member of the General Commission on the Status and Role of Women. In that eight-year term, I met even more clergy women and became more radicalized about the issues.

Sometimes the call finally just wears a person down ...

I woke up one morning, and it was like someone had jerked me up by a yo-yo string. I said, "I'm going to seminary." I didn't know what seminary was about. I didn't even know how the words came out of my mouth. All I knew was that women who were preachers went to seminary, and I was going to do it, too. It was totally unexpected, but I knew I had to go.

I originally intended to get a Ph.D. in organizational development, a field of sociology concerning the way organizations grow and react. I had heard Julius Del Pino, who preached at our church one Sunday, talk about graduating from Garrett with a Ph.D. in organizational development. I asked him about it and started visiting seminaries. Garrett-Evangelical had the best plan and program for my needs, and they seemed to like me. I was one year into a joint program with Northwestern when the Garrett professor retired. We had to have one person on the faculty at Northwestern, so I couldn't continue in that program. Then I decided to pursue pastoral ministry.

Shamana is not Beverly's family name. It is a name she created for her ordination in 1979. In her first year of seminary, she heard about people changing their names and taking one of meaning to them. And so she chose Shamana—from two words, shaman (wise one) and mana (a pacific islander term for spirit).

When we were finished talking, I asked Beverly to name the significant moments that she thinks made all of the difference.

Becoming involved in the Ecumenical Institute and teaching the religious studies course. Working with the Commission on the Status and Role of Women. Being nine years old, on the floor of my bedroom, and telling my mother to pray more. Speaking in the Rose Bowl, and being trained for public speaking in the black Baptist church. Teaching music to kids. Having a faithful mother and dad who became active with me in the same church. Though he had dropped out of church for a while, Dad became a lay leader and did all kinds of things in that church. And when I went to seminary in Evanston, everyone was so proud and excited—the church, Dad and Mom, the whole family.

Bishop Shamana is an exciting person. This woman of so many talents, and such a variety of life experiences, comes to Episcopacy with easy laughter and generously offers her gifts of music, needlework, and simple delight of life. Though her journey to ordained ministry was convoluted, I finished this conversation with a feeling that she had been in ministry from the beginning of her several careers, which is, of course, what we wish all could see in their lives. I think Beverly had an unconscious, but evident, sense of the sacredness of all of life and has lived according to that understanding.

Ann Brookshire Sherer

Ann Brookshire Sherer is a child of the North Carolina mountains. Family heritage is in her heart, and, in a sense, her home is the family archive. From room to room there is the story of this forebear and now that. Family heirlooms—knit goods, bedspreads, quilts, and even her mother's wedding dress—adorn the residence. Different rooms are dedicated to different people and places. Visiting Ann's home is truly a walk through her history.

Her home also harbors memories of many people coming and going, including two daughters of an African bishop who were living there when I visited in August of 2001.

Tall, gracious, and loquacious, Ann welcomed me—and those whom she hoped would some day be readers—into memories of her early life. The story starts in North Carolina.

I was born in Wilkes County, North Carolina, on September 24, 1942. My mother is Annie Jo Haigwood Brookshire, and my father is Homer Woodrow Brookshire Sr. Three and a half years later, my younger brother, Homer Woodrow Brookshire Jr., was born.

Like two other women bishops (Sharon Rader and Susan Hassinger), there is a story of an earlier child who did not survive.

Before either of our births, our mother had a child born in the midst of the 1940 flood. He died, and this remained a powerful part of our lives. We went to the cemetery every year on his birthday. He was perfectly healthy, but the cord was wrapped around his neck and there was not good medical care. If they had done a C-section, he would have been fine. So my brother and I were born by C-section. I know that he was precious to my parents and that my brother and I were as well.

Wilkesboro was the setting for both sets of grandparents and their fore-bears for several generations. One part of her heritage resides in her name, Amelia Ann, which was taken from her paternal grandmother. Her maternal grandmother's name was Ethel Octavia Haigwood.

My grandmother Amelia married when she was fourteen. She ran away with her high school teacher, causing a scandal in the little rural community. They farmed poor mountain land. She had four living children by the time she was twenty and eight by the time she was forty. Her husband, who was fourteen years older than her, died in 1931. Yet her spirit was always hopeful, gentle. My father deferred marriage for a number of years to help care for the family. His younger brother managed the farm during the week under my father's direction, while my father went to the WPA.[1] When I was growing up, we had pictures of both Jesus and Franklin Delano Roosevelt, and we were never clear who was the savior of the world! There was a co-Redemptorist and it was not Mary.

Her mother's family also suffered the effects of the Depression. Grandfather Haigwood was a farm manager for the county judge. When the judge lost all of his property, the only job available to Thomas Haigwood was school custodian.

Having my grandfather as the custodian at school and then later in life at the church shaped how we saw ourselves.

My grandmother Haigwood was partly an invalid, partly a drug addict, and partly just broken by life. She suffered from severe depression and stayed in bed sedated as long as I could remember. She was addicted to prescription drugs. Her three-year-old child became ill but was not taken to the doctor. The child died, and it was a defining experience for my grandmother. My mother said they spent the rest of their lives going to the doctor every time they sneezed.

Ann felt close to her mother's siblings, an aunt and two uncles. Her Aunt Marie continued to be part of their lives for all of Ann's childhood. All three aunts and uncles managed to earn master's degrees.

My Uncle Tom describes a whole wall covered with leather bound books in his grandparents' little cabin. Where they came from was uncertain. This branch of the family had enormous respect for learning, and several of the cousins determinedly pursued an education. Despite growing up in modest circumstances, many of them went on to become physicians, dentists, educators, and businesspersons. This branch of the family had a strong achievement drive and a deep commitment to learning.

The drive for learning, hard work, and success was modeled for Ann by her mother's sister, Marie, as well as by her mother.

My Aunt Marie encouraged learning. She was a teacher, a principal, and later Director of Elementary Education for the State of North Carolina. Unmarried, she was an intimate member of our nuclear family, spending many weekends and every holiday with us after her parents' deaths. In many ways, I had two mothers, Marie and my mother. My former husband once said that I was tired all of the time because I tried to keep house like my mother and perform professionally like Marie; they both spent twenty hours a day working. There was always an expectation to keep learning and to do everything well.

There was never any doubt that Ann and her brother would go to college. Her parents saved every day for their college education. She never had to work while in school, but she was expected to do well.

My parents did without luxuries so there would be opportunities for my brother and me. They started an education fund soon after my birth and talked about me going to college all of my life. My mother was always a little uneasy about her lack of higher education. Her brothers and sister went on to college while she went to business school. Her dream had been to be a nurse, maybe even a physician, but money was scarce and she took a job as a bookkeeper. She soon met and married my father and shifted her emphasis to helping him succeed. She understood marriage to mean that she should focus on helping her husband excel. She encouraged him, and he held many positions of leadership: civic club president, Scout leader, church deacon, and town commissioner. Mother wrote every speech my father gave and helped him practice it. She wrote every report for his work. Her own activities were in Eastern Star and the church. But Daddy's activities always came first.

Politics was a natural part of family life.

Daddy was a professional Democrat. He had a variety of patronage jobs that went back to the WPA days and the friendships he made there. When I was a little girl, if something broke, he would say, "Dern thing's gone Republican." That was his cuss word. My father was quite conservative. I remember when George McGovern was running, my brother said, "Daddy, surely you didn't vote for George McGovern." He said, "Well, I go to meet my Maker with one thing clear on my conscience: I have never voted for a Republican." It left a huge imprint on me.

When I was growing up, we talked about a lot of political figures. My father especially admired Harry Truman and Adlai Stevenson. He thought Stevenson was defeated for president because he was too intellectual and that idea irritated my dad. Governors Umstead and Sanford were also heroes of the family.

Politics were not merely a subject for debate, but a call to action.

There were only 2500 people in the whole town. We knew practically everyone. But everybody had a place. It had been the aspiration of my parents and my mother's brothers and sister that they would move out of their place into a broader education, a different kind of service to the world and community. In our family, in my high school, in my church, everybody was expected to contribute. We were to make a difference in the world. My teachers said that, my church said that, my parents said that. There was a strong impetus toward service and giving to others. In all of those places, we were supposed to work hard and do our best. Sloughing off and being lazy were not allowed. There was a sense that the family counted on us to do that. We were expected to bring honor to the family. I don't suppose I ever achieved anything without calling my father first thing and letting him know.

Ann's sense of self was mostly negative.

I didn't believe that I was a pretty child. I looked like my mother's sister-in-law, my father's sister, whom my mother did not like. I was as tall as I am now by the time I was twelve years old and was skinny and awkward. My mother wanted a beautiful little girl with curls. She told me I didn't have any hair until I was almost three. She would tape a little bow to the top of my head. I looked just like my father who is as bald as a ping-pong ball. I looked like that side of the family. Mom adored my father, but I wasn't exactly what she wanted. The message was always, "You'd better learn because you probably won't succeed as a woman." As an adult, I am surprised to look back at pictures and realize that I was an attractive child.

Ann's relationship with her mother was problematic. The effect of being told she was not attractive lingered a long while. Ann found herself drawing closer to her dad than to her mother.

Most of Ann's elementary teachers had taught her mother and remembered her as poor. There are stories about her mother having to wear her brother's shoes to school because that was all they had. No wonder there was a drive to fit in. And so Ann found herself always wanting approval that never came. When she ponders about when she might have won her mother's approval, she sighs.

Probably never. I came to know that I was good enough, valuable, in God's eyes. I knew I was valuable to Mother, but I was never quite good enough. She gave me all that she could—clothes, lessons, opportunities. I came to know that as the love she could give. I was good enough in Daddy's eyes. He loved and accepted me in ways easier to experience as a child. This probably explains why my first years of preaching were deeply rooted in what Paul Tillich called "accepting your acceptance." God's acceptance was good news indeed.

Public, graceful, and able, this woman remembers her young life as quite different.

In the midst of all of the activity, I was often a lonely child. I did not have social skills valued by elementary school children. I often felt on the outside. I loved to read and would retreat into reading. I still read three or four recreational books a month instead of watching TV. I made very good grades and was a bit cocky about that.

I was also a Brownie Scout and a Girl Scout and stayed with it through high school. I liked to compete and worked to get as many merit badges as I could.

I had moments of joy and fun in the family, but I was always enormously insecure. I felt my parents also lived with general unease. There was not much experience of grace. I grew up with a Calvinist theology, experienced through Southern Baptist eyes, even though our pastors were generally well educated. Even so, church was the bright spot of my life.

There were occasional outings to a concert or movie, but frugality and a strong work ethic were the main virtues instilled in Ann.

Mother and I went to the community concerts. I took piano because my mom liked the piano and could not play. I loved the music and still do, though I do not like to play for others. We went to the movies occasionally, but not often. Money was scarce in our family, and frugality was an art form. We were careful with money. We did not squander money, and we did not squander time.

Mother believed that God expected her to work, and work she did. She thought that she must be home to be with her children after school. Thus she did laundry and prepared food early in the morning. She worked until 2:30 as a bookkeeper and then hurried home to be there for us, clean, fix supper, and help Dad preserve the garden produce. She worked eighteen hours a day. As I got older, I realized Mama was always tired. She expected more of herself than any human being could do.

My mother never understood reading as working. If you were reading, you weren't working. She loved to read, but she didn't like us to read in the daytime. Getting work done was the focus of our lives. I still consider studying and reading a luxury. I think I am working when I am answering letters, going somewhere, or doing administrative detail. Valuing reflection and just being comes hard for me.

That didn't keep Ann from reading then or now. She especially remembers how Aunt Marie fostered her idea about women, and how she struggled to get it right.

I was in college when I learned about Eleanor Roosevelt, whom I still admire. My Aunt Marie tried to introduce me to great people, especially great women, through biographies. I remember her giving me a biography of Helen Kim—the first president of Ewha Woman's University in Seoul, Korea—before we traveled to Korea. I admired my aunt, and she nurtured me with stories of great women. As a little girl, I was particularly intrigued with Amelia Earhart whose name I share. I also loved the Louisa May Alcott books and read all of them when I was thirteen and fourteen, though I sometimes didn't get the point. I was so surprised when someone told me that Jo was the heroine of *Little Women*. I thought it was Beth. The weaker one. The sweet one. I was like Jo, but I could not see her as the heroine. When I read the book again in college as part of a children's literature course, I was startled. It shows you the lens through which I saw the world. Little sweet Beth is the ideal, not Jo. Not Ann. I have a loud voice. I am tall, I am assertive, I have strong opinions. I like to get out there and mix it up in conversation. But Beth was the ideal. Jo and I were all wrong.

Church was the place she felt most safe.

I loved the church. We went to North Wilkesboro First Baptist Church from the time I was on the cradle roll. I felt at home there, happy and at peace, and the most secure sitting between my parents in worship. The old hymns still make me smell my daddy's aftershave lotion, feel my mom's dress. I liked worship and Sunday school.

Many of the adults took time with me, encouraged me, and loved me. These people loved me, and they convinced me that God loved me, even if God was displeased a good portion of the time. In this community and in the quiet of the sanctuary where I often just sat, I had some profound religious formation and experiences.

Ann remembers a sense of having said yes to God. But that didn't settle it for her.

I just could not figure out what you were supposed to do after you said yes. I walked down the aisle, down the "sawdust trail," for weeks after joining the church because the pastor kept asking if we had sinned and needed to repent. I kept going to the front at the close of every evening service until my mom said I was embarrassing the family. So I stopped. When I later found my way into more traditionally liturgical services, it was good news to discover not only a prayer of confession, but also a prayer of absolution. The concepts of grace, "growing in grace," and the "means of grace" were also glorious good news to me.

I was seven years old when I was baptized. I remember walking into the baptismal pool with the minister. He was a very kind man whose informal theology was better than his formal theology. Right before I went in, he said, "Ann, honey, when I put you under the water, you're going into God's loving arms and coming out to see God's great big smile. God loves you." So that's what baptism was. I had an understanding of grace that really was not the focus in the Southern Baptist church. I think the SBC focuses on "my choice, my decision." Baptism is more about the self and making a decision than about what God is doing. That understanding of God's love got me through the "you-are-worth-no-more-than-an-old-dirty-rag" sermons at revivals and church camp.

The religious emphasis came from her mother; her father was largely silent about his faith.

My mother always taught Sunday school. Every Saturday night as long as she was functioning, she sat propped up with pillows and studied her lesson and read her Bible. She taught her Sunday school class and went to her Circle and to the women's organizations with great commitment. She sang hymns, and it was obvious that her faith meant a great deal to her. However, when she sang "This World Is Not My Home" it was a good idea to scatter. Her large Bible was always open to "Abhor what is evil; cling to what is good." My father never talked of his faith and left Mama to ask the blessing and tell us the stories. But he always went to church and was pleased to serve on the Board of Deacons.

Her brother was a strong athlete. They lived what Ann calls parallel lives. Seldom did they participate in each other's events. They did not even attend graduation ceremonies for each other. She does remember going home from college to see a state high school championship football game in which he played. They had played together as children to some degree. But even as they shared in family events, there was not a great deal of interaction.

We went to my Grandmother Haigwood's every Saturday night and to my Grandmother Brookshire's every Sunday afternoon for the first thirteen years of my life. My brother and I would be in the backseat, but we interacted very little. I really don't know why. He said I was bossy. Of course, I don't remember it that way. We excelled in different things. I was a really good student, so he figured out how to excel in other things. He played golf and tennis and went to the country club and was invited to many social events, which pleased Mother.

My mother and brother were closest. He remembers her reading to him: He said that she read him all of *Gone with the Wind*. I don't remember my mother ever reading me a story. She may very well have, but I don't remember that. That was not a part of the family routine. I just remember her being busy. The first little house we lived in didn't have hot water, and she had to heat the water on the stove and use a wringer washing machine, those kinds of things.

If childhood was melancholy, adolescence was vigorous and active.

High school was a new world, a joy. I found a way to relate to others. I found my leadership gifts valued. I found close friends. Nine of us formed a group and did lots of things together. These women encouraged me to try things, and they were there for me. I dated and had fun. I kept doing good academic work and graduated near the top of my class. My brother teased me about the senior yearbook, calling it the "Ann Brookshire memorial." I had participated in cheerleading, the yearbook staff, several clubs, the homecoming court, Girls' State, student government. I was elected "Most Likely to Succeed." I had almost come to believe I could make a difference. I liked all of those activities, and I liked my life. I liked hanging out with friends. I liked dating. I enjoyed Asian history and other history courses. I liked English and all kinds of literature. I did struggle with math and science but discovered I could do them when I had to.

Important adults began to notice Ann. Through them, she gained confidence and was given opportunities to lead and express herself.

The church hired a fabulous young youth director, Andy, who was there through most of my high school years. He lived in the apartment building right across from my home, and he and his young wife—they were just married—took me in. They talked with me for hours and helped me believe that I was valuable. He listened to my woes and helped me dream about my future. Andy was a good youth director. He knew the boundaries and helped me find my sense of self-worth. He invited me into community, into his family. It was good for me. He tapped me for leadership at the church and made me proud to do it.

Through this amazing transformation, Ann experienced encouragement from many sources. Her father was on her side. Her Aunt Marie cheered her on. She had a friend Diana, whose mother had confidence in Ann. Several teachers saw potential and provided special opportunities, including a class for seven students in Asian history.

I would sit and talk with Ree, my Aunt Marie, and my friend Diana's mother. I leaned on Mom's friend Sina. Mother and I just could not communicate, but there were other people to listen and help.

Political and social consciousness had always been part of home life from the beginning. Her professional Democrat father read the paper with her, listened to the news, and discussed what was going on. They had opinions on current political figures. Ann organized Young Democrats in high school.

My mother and father had deep compassion for the poor, and both—especially my father—expected us to treat all persons as persons of worth. I once made a snide remark about what somebody was wearing, and he took my allowance away for two months. They expected their children to be kind and good. We were to care about what happened to all kinds of people. Yet, there was still a deep racism. Our county had a small African American population, but in my world it was clear they were different. Not quite like us. I got to know the African Americans that lived as sharecroppers on my grandmother's farm. I was not allowed in their little dirt floor home. But we were taught to be kind, if patronizing.

I never went to an integrated school. There were very few persons of color in college. My dad wanted kindness but separation. During my college and seminary years, we had our most harsh words around the subject of race. When the church would not open its doors to people of color, I was furious; that began my stepping away from the institutional church.

Ann first attended Mars Hill Junior College, a small liberal arts junior college supported by the Southern Baptist Convention, in the mountains of North Carolina.

College began to form me. The women in the dorm were wonderful. Several classes helped me learn to think and grow. But, oh the rules! For example, there was the six-inch rule, which is as close as boys and girls were allowed to get to one another. It was crazy,

crazy stuff. We could not date after 7 P.M., but we could go walking with our prayer partner early in the morning. We discovered that necking at dawn is just as much fun as necking at dusk. It was a strange legalistic world, and I knew instinctively that rebelling against such a system was healthy. I started to think for myself. My closest friends did the same, and we gave one another permission to name things that were stupid and purposeless.

A professor of political science at Mars Hill fueled my interest in political systems that had begun in my family. He would begin with, "You can't believe what I read last night." Then he would begin to lecture with an enthusiasm that was contagious. I have been reading history and political science ever since.

Probably the most important teacher in my life taught Bible survey at Mars Hill. His method was impeccable. He walked into class, held the Bible in his hands, and told us what his faith meant to him. Then, after bearing witness, he told us that everything he had learned had given the Bible a deeper meaning for him. Then he started on critical theories such as JEDP (Old Testament names for different strains of writing), and we all wrote furiously. He helped us understand that he was trying to deepen, not destroy, our faith, and we would have followed him anywhere. Class began at 2:30 in the afternoon, and he often stayed and talked with us until time to walk to dinner.

College was a time of coming into my own, discovering gifts that I could use, developing an adult faith, and getting deeply drawn into biblical studies.

Ann's formation really was toward being a homemaker, that wife and mother role. She had strong models for that. To walk around her house and look at what's in it reveals how fully she has invested herself in that. Though she has now claimed her vocation, homemaking is her heritage.

My high school boyfriend proposed marriage in my freshman year. I loved him, but I had to finish college. There was never a question in my mind that I must complete college before I married, so we moved in different directions even though it was painful. However, it was clear from my parents that I needed a major that would fit well with marriage and a family. I could be a nurse or a teacher. I majored in elementary education because it was a good security system if I ever needed to work. There was never a sense that my vocation would be primary. It was only through the pain of divorce many years later that I came to realize that my vocations in teaching and ministry had never been primary. I had carried them lightly. My calling as wife and mother had been primary even though ministry had been my great joy and had called forth my best gifts. All of us—my former husband, my parents, and me—were conflicted about how all of those roles should be balanced.

After junior college, Ann went to the University of North Carolina in Greensboro. She struggled to find her place in the significantly larger academic setting. She became involved in the Baptist Student Union and became president of the campus chapter.

The BSU was a wonderful place to continue to grow. The sit-ins had begun in Greensboro a year or two before, and we began to grapple with the Civil Rights Movement and to talk about how we could be part of the change. I caught a glimpse of a different world.

Then the SBC sent me on a mission trip to South Korea when I graduated, and I discovered a new world. Before this, I had never been more than 250 miles from home. Now we traveled to San Francisco, Hawaii, Tokyo. We stayed for two months in South Korea, building a school and living in tri-racial community in which we tried one another's foods and learned how one another saw the world. We came back through Hong Kong, Taiwan, and the Philippines. We stayed with Southern Baptist missionaries who did not fit the stereotype and who introduced us to new types of people and new ways of thinking about the world and church. They thought for themselves, lived an indigenized gospel, and were deeply concerned about racial justice. When we flew across the international dateline, they even urged us to try champagne. It was my first drink. It was another step beyond a faith of rules.

That interaction with other students, and subsequently having roommates from other cultures, pulled Ann deeper and deeper into world citizenship and a drive for justice. She found herself a social change agent.

God was calling me to be part of working toward the creation of one community of people who would dwell in peace and justice on the face of the whole earth. This began a nudge toward seminary and theological education and opened me to the idea of going to Boston and meeting Harvey Cox at Blue Hill Christian Center in Roxbury/North Dorchester. That led to my living with a wonderful, compassionate African American woman, Valerie Russell. Once I began the journey, doors opened and life-changing experiences kept coming. But it was not a pain-free, easy road.

Most women growing up in the 1950s and 1960s experienced the lingering norms of what women could, or should, do. Some occupations were suitable. Marriage was always to be desired, and homemaking was the highest calling. The edges had been pushed across time, of course, but the women's movement and its cultural effect was still in its infancy for our set. There were a host of ways that Ann continued to experience not being good enough—in social skills, in scholastic work. There were mixed signals from many directions.

The cultural expectations around what women do set some limits on me. Individually, persons would tell me that I could do anything that I really wanted to do. I scored well on tests. I had good grades in high school and college. I had been a leader in high school and college. All of these things told me that I could do many things and had options. But I still had scars from being the outsider in childhood, though I had learned how to make friends. Some of me felt not good enough, but another part of me was growing. I wanted to move beyond my self-imposed limits.

I taught for a year and a half in a Chapel Hill elementary school. I discovered that I did not do this especially well, and I didn't like that feeling. I wasn't particularly good at helping fourth- and fifth-graders learn how to read and think. That long time of teaching school between seminary and college was an experience of doing something not very well and having the sense that I'm not good at this. I didn't like that feeling.

Years later when Robert and I had moved to Florida, it was a joy to teach adults at Stetson and to discover that I was good at it. I could even teach education courses and enjoy it. It was the experience that author Parker Palmer describes in *Let Your Life Speak* (San Francisco: Jossey Bass, 2000): "The things that you don't do well are God's way of saying 'This isn't right for you.'"

In 1965, Ann decided to go to Boston to attend Andover Newton Theological Seminary, an American Baptist seminary. At the time, there were only six women students at the seminary and little women's movement activity.

I didn't know why I was going to seminary. My vocational goals were foggy at best. My parents thought I'd lost my mind and was wasting money. But I got a free ride—a full scholarship—and me and the guys with the high draft numbers went to school. Most of us did not know what came next. I went to seminary partly because I thought this was the right venue to figure out what I was called to do. I thought the kind of people and love and nurture I'd experienced at BSU, the kind of community I enjoyed, would continue there. I had trained for a vocation I didn't want to do. I knew that I wanted to serve, wanted to make a difference in the world, and was deeply concerned about racial justice. I thought this would be a place where I could keep growing. Part of me wanted to explore my gifts, part of me wanted to find a life partner, and part of me was on a walk with God. The answers did not come easily. I still was unclear as I neared graduation.

Her parents were quite upset. Ann now sees that as mostly fear.

That was the time of the riots, in the late 1960s. I lived in Roxbury/North Dorchester, the roughest section of the black community. There was a kids' program upstairs and an alcoholic men's program downstairs. I was twenty-two years old. Those kids taught me how much I didn't know about the world, how really hard it was to work among the poor, how sheltered I had been, and how much I had to learn before I could be effective. I found out that I would have to learn to be more comfortable in my own skin to be able to accept their radical difference. One or two of my professors at seminary didn't think I was serious about theological education. In three years at Andover Newton, no one asked me if I was considering ordination.

I was in a clinical experience that was devastating while I was at Andover Newton. The clinical supervisor, who was a Greek Orthodox priest, was a horrible man. One day during clinical group session, he said to me, "There's nothing wrong with you that getting screwed wouldn't cure. Just figure out you're a woman." That set me back several years. I am so fortunate that there were enough inhibitions in me that I didn't turn into a promiscuous idiot in that time because he made me think that I was a freak.

When I first went to Massachusetts, I worked for a short while in an American Baptist church in Fall River. That was a depressed community, terribly poor. The pastor could not talk to me directly. He would say, "Let us pray," and tell God what was the matter with me. I did that for six weeks before quitting and going back to seminary. That was the Southern Baptist world I wanted to escape. Then I went to work for the Blue Hill Christian Center, started by Harvey Cox. An African American man who actually ran the center taught me how to live respectfully in another culture.

After finishing seminary, Ann pursued ministry in avenues other than ordination. Married, raising children, and following her husband around, she found work wherever Robert's job took them. It was a patchwork quilt of experience. Much of her work had to do with integration issues, and that only cemented her already sharp consciousness of the ills and divisiveness of racism.

She had known Robert in Chapel Hill, and when he proposed she said yes.

I was still a southern woman, and it was time to get married. It was not a very good reason to marry Robert. We shared values. He was from southeast Alabama and was doing a Ph.D. in black history. We were into saving the world together. He worked in black colleges for a long time.

So started several years of pilgrimage from black college to black college. These years netted a fist full of opportunities to work in interracial settings and for integration. She had some work in a church as youth director. Then she joined the North Carolina Good Neighbor Council where she worked on school desegregation. Authorship of a school constitution was part of her portfolio.

I had a real sense of success in my first job after seminary and gained a lot of confidence in myself and my ability. I convinced the man in charge of the North Carolina Good Neighbor Council in Raleigh to let me work for him. He created the job Information and Communication Specialist. I wrote the newsletter and other information items. I had developed a strong sense of self that would allow me to do that.

There was always a sense that if I really wanted to do something, I could. Sometimes I didn't try really hard, because I didn't want to find out that I couldn't do everything. But what would have happened if more people had pressed me when I graduated from seminary and had asked me what I was planning to do with my degree? Or what if a group of persons in one of the congregations I attended in Massachusetts or North Carolina had said, "We see the gifts for ordination in you"? But those questions were never asked, or those affirmations given. At that juncture, in the late sixties, I might have pursued ordination sooner.

From North Carolina, Robert's work took them to Deland, Florida, for two years to teach at Stetson University and then to Lorman, Mississippi, where Robert taught at Alcorn A&M.

When we were at Alcorn (the black A&M School for Mississippi) we lived on campus because there was no place else to live. I thought it was wonderful. Robert hated it. There were people from India and Pakistan and several African countries.

Church hunting became interesting for these former Baptists.

In Deland, we finally joined the Presbyterian Church and had our young son baptized. Most of the faculty members in Rob's department attended there, and we enjoyed the fellowship. It was not a theological decision. Then we moved to Mississippi where we visited most of the black and white congregations in the area. We went to the Presbyterian church in Port Gibson first. It was 1971, and social change was everywhere. Eighty-five percent of the community was persons of color. When a young white couple with a child walked in, they were delighted. Then they discovered we worked and lived at Alcorn. They just walked away and left us. No one followed up on our visit. They were so afraid and uncertain, they wanted nothing to do with people who wanted a different cultural pattern. The next weekend we were returning from Jackson and saw a finger pointing toward heaven atop that Presbyterian church. Rob grinned: "It is a little hard to tell which finger is pointing, isn't it?" It was one way to deal with rejection.

We visited other churches and often attended church on the campus. Near the end of our time in Mississippi, Rob went to the United Methodist church in Port Gibson. The next day, the pastor came out to the campus and played tennis with Rob. Then he stayed for a glass of iced tea. He told us about United Methodist polity. He said that his people were not all that different from folks in other churches in Port Gibson, but because of the polity, he couldn't be dismissed for coming to Alcorn. Both the bishop and district superintendent supported him. He also told us about the social principles. We were open to find out more.

Soon afterward, we moved to Marshall, Texas, for Robert to work at Wiley College. We immediately found a United Methodist church, attended, explored the theology and polity, and joined. I was asked to begin employment as a part-time youth director. I had a lot to learn, but Gene Steger and Bryan Brown, the pastor who followed him within a year, were willing to teach me. For the first time, I was with clergy who began to encourage me toward ordination. They invited me to conference and introduced me to clergywomen and others.

Meanwhile, I had been talking with other women in places such as the League of Women Voters and a small reading group. The feminist message was finally getting through to me. These experiences merged with the invitations of Gene Steger and Bryan Brown, and I began the candidacy process. I was ordained a deacon in 1976 and an elder in 1978.

It had all pointed to this. When she began her first appointment as "pastor in charge," Ann knew she had found her calling.

I had liked youth work, but when I came to my own church, I experienced a joy in vocation that I had never known. I liked to preach, to teach, to visit, to plan, and to dream. There was a sense of "rightness" I had never known. That this was my true calling was affirmed during that first year—in spite of some difficulties.

The church to which I had been assigned, White Oak United Methodist Church, was a new church with very little grounding in United Methodist polity. Just the year before, they had considered becoming a Congregational Methodist church. They were deeply troubled that a woman had been sent to be their pastor. Some refused to take communion, others wanted to take back gifts they had given the church, and eventually about forty people left. Those who stayed were loyal and gracious. Those who wanted to be United Methodist began to attend. In the next three years, we gained almost one hundred new members and a new congregation was born.

We built a parsonage, and our family moved into the community. We resettled a Vietnamese family and began to focus on mission. We developed a program for children and youth. The Sunday school and worship attendance grew. In spite of some painful times, I had found my place to serve among those incredibly fine folk.

I will never forget a member of my congregation. He and his wife had me to lunch almost every Tuesday and Thursday when I was in town that first year. We would eat and then pray that I could go visit the people who didn't want me there and stay gentle no matter what they said or did. Those lunches and visits changed me by giving me patience and courage.

Only once did I lose my cool completely. It was after we had moved into the community. The Missionary Baptist pastor began underlining passages of Scripture for his congregation's children to take to school and taunt my fourth-grade son. The kids were running him in circles. I tried talking to the teacher. When he came home crying yet another day, I called the Missionary Baptist pastor and said, "If you were any kind of a man you would deal with me directly and not through children." He hung up. By grace, I was gentler with my own folks, and they tried hard to make things good for me and my family.

Relationships with other clergy began to grow and those friendships and affirmations continued to build a platform of confidence under Ann.

My District Superintendent was uneasy with a clergywoman and always brought his wife with him when we needed to talk. But when people began to attack me, he stood with me. He invited me to mimeograph the church bulletin in his office, which meant a weekly visit. We became colleagues.

From the beginning, the other pastors in the district were mostly kind and went out of their way to be supportive. I will never forget their "Hey, gal, come sit by me" welcome. When I moved to Texarkana, the pastors of the three other churches told their boards about this neat woman who was coming to town. That word was spread, so my new church was not so afraid of me. This congregation feared I would be a Pentecostal—these were the only women in ministry they had known. They told me later that they relaxed when the head usher told them I used a manuscript for preaching!

When I was ordained Elder, I was ordained with two other women. We were the fourth, fifth, and sixth women members of our annual conference. After my ordination, the other women clergy invited me to a retreat, and we continued to meet at least twice a year. That community of women sustained me, and many of them remain my closest friends.

But her parents were still skeptical and held back.

My parents didn't come to my Deacon's ordination in 1976, but Daddy came to my Elder's ordination. All of this bewildered them. Then they came to White Oak and shared in worship. My congregation, by this time, was used to me and made my parents feel welcome. This made them relax, and they were glad to see me happy.

Ann thinks her mother may have seen this as a bit of success, since she was married, rearing children, and had a career—in other words, doing it all just like her mother did.

Perhaps the most meaningful gesture my father made for me came a few years later. My father was on the Board of Deacons in our home church, as he had been for thirty-plus years. A family friend recounted the story to me. A young woman from Appalachian State Teacher's College and a seminary graduate worked at the church for a summer. She wanted to be a chaplain and asked the church to ordain her. My father stood with tears in his eyes and said, "If we had done this earlier, maybe Ann would be working for us now. I move we do it. Let's ordain her." They voted to ordain her without a dissenting vote. Dad was wrong, though. I needed to be United Methodist. Still, his love and the radical step by that Southern Baptist church moved me deeply.

Although Ann has moved away from the cultural and religious conservatism that nurtured her, she still has a deep appreciation for that heritage.

I'm sure it was God's prevenient grace that I was well nurtured in the North Wilkesboro First Baptist Church. Despite the large doses of judgment, I did learn about God's grace and love through that congregation. The Southern Baptists communicated the global nature of the faith in their emphasis on mission and paid for me to go halfway around the world to serve for those three months after college. It was a Southern Baptist chaplain who opened my world in college. When I tried to live out what they taught me, many were annoyed, but I am indebted for the gifts they shared.

It has been a journey of grace. I have been especially grateful for the knowledge and experience of sanctifying grace that I longed for even as a child. As I studied Wesley theology, I knew that this is the grace I was seeking so long ago when I walked the aisle of the church again and again. United Methodism is my chosen spiritual home, and I am grateful for the tradition into which I am now grafted.

Ann reflects upon authority, both her own and that of others.

I grew up in a legalistic culture and learned early to push the boundaries early. Mars Hill taught me that to live with senseless rules is harmful. Dealing with sexual misconduct in these last fifteen years has taught me that boundaries are essential. We live with law and grace, boundaries and choices.

Growing up southern, I learned there are better ways to create change than to charge in directly. Subtlety and tact are virtues if they are undergirded by principles. That was even true in dealing with my parents and my school.

My own sense of authority has come slowly. As I have learned to accept my own worth as a gift, and live as a self-differentiated person, I have begun to understand my own authority as a gift of God. It is not a way to dominate others, but a way to stand alongside and offer gifts of grace. The Church has granted me authority in my ordination and consecrations. I have learned to build a team and to work with others to lead it. I have learned to make difficult decisions and to live in community with the consequences.

Through God's grace and forgiveness, I am continually learning from my mistakes, and discovering how to keep offering myself and my leadership. I have authority because of my worth as a human being, who is rooted and grounded in God and community. I have struggled with many self-doubts, which still occasionally rear their heads, but I have found a way to walk that strengthens me and lets the gifts that I feared as a child now be used. I am confident enough that I can listen to others and learn. I can also make hard decisions and move on. By God's grace, I will keep growing in self-awareness and in my capacity for connection so that I can lead with gentle and confident authority.

And, indeed, she does! Ann's love of life bubbles up through her laughter and her ability to see the humor in situations without demeaning other persons. She best laughs at herself and keeps an even sense of self in the midst of difficult moments. I found the story of her life to be coherent with the woman I have come to know as a world citizen and committed to spending herself on behalf of others. Her patience in waiting for the time to become ordained is a sign of her confidence that God will work things out. She still functions that way—trusting God to work things out in the long run, and doing the best she can in the meantime. The best she can is sufficient.

NOTE

1. In 1935 Congress created the Works Progress Administration (WPA), President Roosevelt's program to employ 3.5 million workers at a "security wage" during the Depression.

Mary Ann Swenson

The Episcopal residence of the Southern California Area is cool and pleasant inside. Set amidst the lush growth of Southern California, its interior shows the sparse living style of its occupants. One front room is empty save for a draftsman's table, a life-size cutout of Dale Evans and John Wayne, and a pile of rolled-up rugs and needlework hangings that have come as gifts from the various cultures of that area. The guest room is furnished with family heirlooms about which Mary Ann speaks with deep feeling. Small wonder, then, that she begins her memories with her grandmother without being prompted.

Grandmother Elizabeth Cox Stevens, my maternal grandmother, was known as Mama Hutke, meaning "white mother" in the language of the Native Americans of Oklahoma. Having been widowed, Betsy, as she was called, took up missionary work for the Baptist Women's Missionary Union, educating and camping with Indian tribes across Oklahoma. Never having had a driver's license, she traveled by bus.

This legendary story about Mary Ann's grandmother so impressed her that, as a little girl, she would tell people:

I can hardly wait to grow up and be a widow because then I can do what I want to do, which is be in missions and serve the church. That's what my picture was as a child in the South in the early 1950s—that girls looked after their husbands, and then, after their husbands were gone, they could do what they wanted to do.

Mary Ann believes the southern culture of her childhood played many significant roles in her sense of self and personal formation. She maintains a healthy balance of the gifts and scars of that culture.

I was blessed to be in the presence of profound thinkers in a South that was both alive and yet deeply racist.

The contradictions of life came early to her.

When I was a young child and my dad worked at the butane company for my uncle, we would visit my uncle, and right down by their house were the houses of black families. There was a little girl around my age whose mother worked for my aunt. We became friends. I remember her as one of my first black girlfriends. I'd play at her house when we'd visit my aunt and uncle. We also had black women at my grandmother's house who helped raise us. But our schools were segregated, and relationships with people of color in my childhood in Mississippi were that they had the serving jobs and were not the served. Then I became troubled because when I would go to church, we would go through a black ghetto to get to church. I went to this wonderful, outstanding church downtown. It was huge and fine and preached the gospel and had revivals. We would get right with God and be saved again and be going on to perfection. Yet, we would go through this black ghetto to get there, and I couldn't reconcile that. When I asked questions about why those people lived that way, I couldn't believe the answers that came back to me: "Oh, they're lazy. They just want to live that way. They don't try or care for themselves." Well, I just knew that wasn't right. I began to learn about systemic racism and the powers that oppress.

That culture had other influences on Mary Ann.

In the South, you learn that you must be gracious and show hospitality to the other person at all costs. So you totally deny yourself. What I became enraged about was that you couldn't find a stronghold for truth. Always showing a face of hospitality and graciousness to other persons, no matter what, means you don't always tell the truth. So I don't trust people telling the truth in the South in the same way. I don't mean to blanket people in the South, but it's that particular cultural dynamic.

Her parents met at Northeastern Teachers' College in Tahlequah, Oklahoma. Her father won a scholarship to college to play the saxophone.

But when he entered school, his talent for math and science took him into the department as a tutor. He eventually majored in physics and chemistry.

Though she never heard him play the saxophone, he helped her on the clarinet and piano and taught her to dance.

He would dance with me, and we would do the Arkansas Stomp and other things. Music was everywhere in the house. Daddy couldn't carry a tune, but he saw to it that music surrounded us. He wired the house for speakers in every room. I would wake up in the morning to songs coming out of my bedpost.

Mary Ann was born in Pine Bluff, Arkansas, in 1947. When she was two years old, they moved to Jackson, Mississippi, where an uncle gave her father a job as bookkeeper and treasurer for his butane company.

They joined Capitol Street Methodist Church where Roy Clark (now a retired bishop) was pastor, an influence that would linger for a lifetime.

Roy Clark was a hero in the struggle for equality because he preached the gospel and stood up for its being inclusive and protested against the White Citizens' Council. He tried to encourage the South to be more open and not closed. The fact of the matter is, every Sunday from the time I was five years old until I was fifteen, I listened to Roy Clark's preaching. As an adult, when I listen to cassette tapes of his sermons, I realize how much his theology, and how he communicated it, shaped my thinking. He'd been educated at Yale and there he was in Mississippi, a thinker.

Mary Ann's parents invested their lives in providing her with a safe and happy childhood.

I was a happy kid. I was lavished with radical generosity and radical hospitality. My parents and my family did that for me. And so, when I preach that concept, that's really real. In times of suffering and difficulties as an adult, I've often wondered whether I'm being punished for having a happy childhood. Then in gratitude, I realize that I can suffer because I really have been blessed in ways in which many have not.

I had such a sense of safety. So I felt safe to take risks and to do adventuresome things and to have a world of fantasy and to test out and to experiment and to try new things.

Mary Ann says she is a good mixture of both of her parents. She was very close to her father, though he died while she was in college. She has tended her mother the rest of her life, loyally and lovingly.

My family says that I'm more like my father's brother and that my father's brother's son is more like my father. That's what they used to say when we were kids.

I got my sense of duty and responsibility from Daddy. When he died, I was internally in touch with my obligations and responsibilities to care for my mother in what would be a shifting role in my life. I just knew the mantle was there and what that meant.

It included some months of intensive caring for her mother in Mississippi and then experiencing her death as this book was being formed.

She has more to say about family characteristics coming alive in her.

I guess in some ways I'm like my father's mother. His mother was an extrovert, and I was always afraid that I'd be like her, and I am. I project negative aspects about that, though there are positive ones. She was really our family matriarch, and she threw big parties to which everybody came. They thought she would manipulate the family to do what she wanted. So I have my negative impression, and I try to manipulate in legitimate ways. I watched my grandmother. I know how to do this. But I try to do it in ways that are healthy in our society and in our time.

She ponders about her grandmothers.

Even though both women were so important to me, I realize now how little I really know about either one.

Family nurture is deep and unending.

So I was an only child, growing up in Jackson, Mississippi, and I attended a fine Methodist church with fine theological leaders who made an incredible witness in that community. I had a sense in my childhood of really being called in the womb and of being close and loved and never had a sense of anything other than the love of God in my life. I learned later that my parents had continued to try to have children, but my mother had five miscarriages. One little sister lived long enough for me to visit the hospital when she was born. I knew my dad had been out to the cemetery to bury her and that they had given her a name. I realized later that with each one that did not come, what they invested in me was more and more important. That's part of my story.

It was not always pleasant between mother and daughter.

She was a dominant, confident mom. But she didn't give herself credit, and I didn't realize that as a kid. I thought she very bright, but she didn't think of herself as being smart.

Those elementary friendships and behaviors were full of life and verve.

I was part of the baby boom generation, and new elementary schools and junior high schools and senior high schools were constantly being built to accommodate all of the kids. We moved, and in the sixth grade, I went to a new school and made new friends who stayed with me through high school. Two of them later told me that when I first came to class, they didn't like me because they thought I was the teacher's pet. But once they got to know me, they discovered I wasn't so bad after all. I had no clue that I was seen as the teacher's pet. I was just a really good student who was performing and overachieving, so the teacher encouraged me. But they saw it as being the teacher's pet.

She lists her elementary teachers, saying of each "good teacher."

I feel a hunger and grasp for knowledge and just soak it up. So if there's a teacher from whom I have a sense of being able to learn something, I just soak it up. My father was also that way. Learning was always important to him.

Girl Scouts was a steady influence and shaper. Her mother was a troop leader from the time Mary Ann was in Brownies until she graduated from high school.

One leadership experience in Girl Scouts was especially significant. But this experience was not without its downside.

In 1964, I was selected to go to a national Girl Scout event in Cassanovia, New York, called "Quest for Quality." There was one other girl from Mississippi going. She was black and I was white, and we knew each other because her mother had taught in our nursery at Sunday school when I was a child. She and I were the same age, so we got to know each other. But to prepare for the trip, we had to meet in secret at the Girl Scout office. We were at risk for having crosses burned in our yards for being a biracial couple of girls going on a trip together. That was the cultural air of hostility surrounding us. During that summer, Medgar Evers and three girls in Philadelphia were murdered.

Once we arrived, there were a hundred girls from all over the world, and no one knew anyone else. My friend and I were in separate events, so I made some friends, but I was lonely. In those two weeks, I learned leadership skills that have shaped my whole life and that have helped me push to the edges and push to the depths. That wouldn't have happened if I hadn't had the privilege of that experience.

Was she ambitious?

I don't know now. Our lives are so full that it all gets cloudy. But as a young person, I was very driven. It wasn't about success or stardom, but rather about achievement and making a contribution. And it was about saving the world and offering the gospel. I really believed we could transform planet Earth into the kingdom of heaven in our lifetime. Foolish girl!

Mary Ann's dad was an avid game player and taught her how to play all sorts of games.

When I was in the sixth grade, I was the neighborhood tetherball champion. No one could beat me until the boys became so tall that they could play over my head. But I was still able to beat kids that were taller than me through strategy. I learned strategy by playing tetherball.

Being so active in games, and competitive, one would wonder if Mary Ann was ever taught that boys ought to win. It seemed so much a part of the culture.

I had two insightful and significant conversations with my father around this subject. The first one took place at a sixth-grade dance at which my parents were chaperones. Of course, my dad took pictures and danced with me. And he said, "Now, Mary Ann, you're a very good dancer. But you have to learn to let the boys lead." That's metaphorical for our lives.

The second was when I was a teenager in high school, and my dad and I were playing tennis together. He was helping me and coaching me in my tennis game. And I said to him, "Daddy, what do I do if I'm playing tennis, and I'm a better tennis player than the boy I'm playing with? Am I supposed to let the boy win?" And he said, "You just play your best, you always play your best." Those were great lessons in grace and in honoring other people and yet doing the best I could.

In high school, Mary Ann shone, always in the lead, always a groupie, always doing those things that gained her special credit. She does not believe she was so much popular as given a mantle of leadership.

I had boyfriends all the way through. I was smart, was a Girl Scout, had lots of friends. I was really active and an overachiever. I had so many credits and awards that you couldn't keep up with it all. But I don't know that I was exactly popular. Although I was elected a cheerleader and to the homecoming court in the ninth grade, I also received a Danforth Foundation award, which was a leadership award. So, I guess my mantle was a mantle of leadership, not a mantle of popularity. And that was different, definitely different.

Of Mary Ann's childhood heroes, one set were missionaries from her home church to Africa. They sent pictures from the Congo, and it engendered in Mary Ann a desire to be like them.

They went to far-off places, lived God's love, and developed community where they were. That became a picture of how I could live anywhere on the planet and still be part of the community of faith and be in relationship with whomever mattered to me wherever I was on the planet.

In fact, that sense of creating community is a part of how Mary Ann functions. She creates family wherever she goes and is very good at keeping in touch across the years.

Because I am an only child, I make family. It's a way of building a world for myself, of having both mirror and window through which I can see my own reflection and also see out to what lies ahead. I really didn't have a sense of being alone or afraid of being alone when I was a child. Yet being able to be connected with other people and to be in relationship with other people gives me a sense that we are all God's family. Staying connected matters.

Also among her heroes are the two women who taught debate.

Those debaters were assertive. They "got in your face" and "took charge." They were adventuresome. They encouraged me to develop myself. I do think they also thought the boys were better—people just play to the boys in the South. But even so, they didn't shortchange me in any way.

They began to expose me to what a closed society Mississippi was and to the fear and innuendos being used nationally—creating a culture of fear, fostering mistrust of communists and everything that could be labeled. I also saw how that was used to perpetuate racism in the South. Southern culture is like ancient Hebrew culture, in the sense that there is mainstream patriarchy, there is also an underbelly, a counterculture.

Mary Ann talks of always being in love with the gospel, deeply immersed in the church, and never thinking it should be any other way. But the first formalization of that came in her teen years.

In 1961 or 1962, when I was fourteen, I went to Camp Wesley Pines during the summer. One night during worship, I went forward to rededicate my life to Jesus Christ and pledge myself to full-time church-related vocations. When I got back home, my pastor gave me a copy of the vocational book that the Board of Higher Education Ministry put out, which told about the kinds of ministry that girls can do: play the piano, marry a minister, become a missionary, be a director of Christian education, be a deaconess. So those were the options available. But I knew my call was a call to preach. I was clear about that. But girls didn't do that, and I didn't have any images or pictures of girls getting to do that.

She told her parents about the call to preach. While they did not negate it, she remembers her mother saying on the way home from camp, "Now, Mary Ann, everybody doesn't get to go to Africa." She comments that when she later moved to Washington State, it might as well have been Africa.

Still, everyone affirmed her having a religious vocation. It was a good thing for girls to do. But, of course, that meant getting married and taking care of some man.

You were expected to get married and have a lot of children, teach Sunday school, and raise the next generation. You would have to wait until you are a widow to do anything. That was the cultural piece.

With the experience of growing up in that culture in her heart, and with the counsel about what a girl could do, Mary Ann went to Millsaps College in Jackson, Mississippi, on a debate scholarship. Though she enrolled in pre-ministerial courses, all of the boys were given student appointments, but none was offered to her. Girls didn't do that!

This distinction between what boys and girls do had begun to emerge in junior high. In fact, although the childhood years were always described with delicious happiness, there was a shift in the sense of joy and well-being as this gender gap came into view.

I encountered the belief that boys and girls were different, not equal. There was sexism as well as racism in that Southern society. I couldn't do everything boys could do even though I might be equal with boys in some ways. There was a double standard.

As Mary Ann began to prepare for college, the differences were really pointed out.

One dramatic instance happened during the process of applying to colleges. My only rejection came from Vanderbilt. I'd been a straight-A student and, though my test scores weren't brilliant, they weren't bad. In the rejection letter, it was clear that when it came to out-of-state students, there was a different standard for boys than for girls. They would let in out-of-state boys who had certain level SAT scores. But girls had to have higher scores to be admitted. It was unbelievable. That was a learning experience.

She did receive a scholarship to a Presbyterian school in Memphis and went for a tour.

The football jock giving me the tour of the campus said, "Well, certainly you know you've been accepted here at the school. But I don't know about scholarships. We like to reserve our scholarships for boys because we like to give our scholarships to people who are going on to graduate school. And girls don't." Those were a couple of examples of sexism. There were lots of other examples of how girls were encouraged to act or not to act.

Millsaps was a wonderful choice. She received a scholarship in debating and forensics. Her father sold his business and went to work for the state of Mississippi to fund college. She went through his savings in the first year or so.

At first I couldn't decide what to major in—religion or English or mathematics or speech and theatre. I ended up double-majoring in religion and speech and theater because I had wonderful religion professors who were heroes for me.

I really had some fine teachers there and a good education, and I am very grateful. Millsaps opened its doors to people of color and was called the most courageous little school in the South at one time for pushing to be open when the rest of the South was closed.

Washington State is the scene of a major turning point in Mary Ann's life.

After my freshman year of college, I had my first summer job in Washington State. The phone call came out of the blue. The associate pastor at my church when I was in junior high was now a pastor in Washington and offered me a job as a summer youth worker. It might as well have been God on the other end of the phone. He was an instrument of God at work in my life during that time. I was struggling and feeling lost at school. I accepted the job and had a wonderful summer. I've always said that the coldest winter of my life was my first summer in Washington State.

After my sophomore year in college, I was asked to come back to Washington for the summer to work. My old high school boyfriend, a relationship that had been off again, wanted me to stay home so we could get married. He was Baptist, but pretty agnostic and cynical at that time in his life. I told him that I planned to go to Washington and that we could get married when I came back.

When I got to Washington, members of the church arranged for me to meet the older brother of some of the kids in my youth group. He had just gotten home from the Navy. His mother decided to have the youth group out to the family farm for a hot-dog cookout and marshmallow roast. That way, the youth director and her son got to meet each other. The youth and I went out to a little island in the river in a small boat. I was standing in the water with a pair of blue shorts on, in water up to my knees, and I looked over on the shore and here was this handsome guy. It was love at first sight. And it's been that way ever since.

We got acquainted that night. It did take him a couple of weeks to ask me for a date. But he did. On our first date, we went with his whole family to get his younger brother at 4-H camp, and then we visited his cousin and went on a walk on the beach. It was just a whirlwind romance. By the second or third date, he had proposed two or three times. I extended my stay for a few days at the end of my tour of duty as the youth director. When I returned to Mississippi, I thought, "He was wonderful, but I'll never see him again." Even with the proposals, I didn't believe I'd see him again because Washington was so far away.

But he called my dad and said, "I'd like to come to Mississippi and marry your daughter." And my dad didn't tell me right away that he had said that. My dad said, "Mary Ann, tell me more about this young man you met in Washington." I did. He came at Christmastime and lived with my parents that spring. I was living on campus at college, and he rented a room from my parents and stayed at their home.

So, he came to Mississippi at Christmas, courted me, got a job at Delta Airlines; and we were married in Mississippi that summer. My mother has a version of his sitting and having a talk with my dad asking for my hand in marriage. All of the questions she thought my dad should ask him about being proper suitor for their daughter weren't asked. Instead, they bonded with each other and told old war stories.

We stayed in Mississippi until I finished school, and then we went back to Washington. He had been in Vietnam, so he hadn't finished college. We went back to Washington in 1969 and I got a job at Mason Church in Tacoma and he went to the University of Puget Sound.

I was at Mason Church from 1969 to 1972, an influential and important time in my life. I was a part of a staff, a team. I was the full-time youth minister and worked with the senior pastor, the associate pastor, and the director of Christian education. Even though I was the youngest in the group, they included me and valued me as a member of the team. It was a wonderful learning opportunity early in my life to be so received, and it shaped my leadership style. It was a wonderful two years. That community nurtured me with their leadership and their gifts. I threw myself into being part of and loving that community.

I wasn't quite ready to go to seminary, even though I completed my local preacher's license. I'd spoken at church, and had also done some guest preaching at small rural parishes out from Tacoma. So I'd been affirmed in preaching and moving forward with ordination. I loved youth ministry; yet I was called to preach.

Her husband finally raised the question of going to seminary.

I came home from work one day, after my husband had graduated, and he said, "Well, isn't it about time we went to seminary? Does The Methodist Church have a school in California? I sure liked California when I was there in the Navy." I said, "Well, yeah. Claremont's there." One of my professors at Millsaps really thought the world of Claremont, and I knew it had a good academic program. I even began thinking about getting a Doctor of Ministry: "Nobody's going to take a young woman seriously, anyway. I might as well get a doctorate. I'll at least have credentials." And so, I did. But I cried and cried when we left that church and that town because it was like leaving home for the first time. I didn't want to leave. I had felt very fulfilled there, so it was difficult to leave.

Finding a way to pay for seminary proved to be a challenge.

When we got to Claremont, my husband got a job. We had some scary moments at first, trying to find a place to live and putting food on the table. He actually got his first job washing dishes at Howard Johnson, and we found an apartment because the dorms at school were full.

I had gotten some help from scholarship money, but I also asked for help from the Board of Ordained Ministry. The response I got back from the Board in Washington was something like, "Thanks for your application, but we really like to save our seminary scholarships for our men students who have families. We're sure your husband can get work, and maybe if you curtail your spending, you'll be okay." I saved the letter. Years later, when I was elected head of the General Conference delegation at the annual conference, I discovered that one of the people on the delegation was the man who had written that letter. When I showed it to him, he just about died. It was twenty years later, and he didn't remember it. He was so embarrassed. That was all the justice I needed, you know. I received him well in the delegation. He's a wonderful person, and we're good friends.

So, my husband worked. We didn't have a cent. We were really beggars, trying to pay for an education. But we paid for it all as we went. We didn't have any debt. We scraped and worked and paid semester by semester. He worked at the cafeteria at the school. He would cook and clean up, and we got free meals. He would clean up while I'd schmooze with the other students. That's the pattern for our lives. He works in the kitchen, and I schmooze with the people around the table!

When asked if she would change anything about her childhood, Mary Ann thought a long time.

I really would have preferred not to have been an only child. But I would not be who I am if that had been the case. And I would change the social culture, the social context of the South in which I lived. It was a closed society and hierarchical and racist. There was gripping poverty, and yet the church turned a blind eye to that. The church was one of the perpetuators of the racist system rather than an agent of change.

It is an amazing struggle to overcome that kind of feeling. She has a long story about when it became a crisis of faith in the 1980s.

That became a real crisis of faith for me at more than one point in my life. It hit me particularly hard during the 1980s when I was District Superintendent in Washington. I was attending a meeting in New York. A Bible study leader was talking about the witness of Paul in Ephesus when what Paul really wanted to do was destroy all goddesses and gods of the surrounding culture. Paul was driven by his missionary zeal to promote Christianity.

During this discussion about Paul, a lightbulb came on for me. I'd known about racism and fought against it and identified myself as a minority person in a majority culture. I felt as if those who supported solidarity with the poor, with racial minorities, and with women were the minority culture in some feudal way. I had a zeal to be a missionary, to save the world, and to offer Christ's love to the world. But at that moment during that Bible study, I felt a profound sense of betrayal. I realized that the church I had served with my whole life had also been the oppressor of people since right after Jesus' crucifixion.

Mary Ann was stunned, suddenly reviewing in her mind early instances of violence against people in the name of Jesus. She began to see the cross as a symbol of violence and destruction.

That symbol has been manipulated to perpetuate horrible, horrible acts against human beings in the South, where I grew up. But now I realize it was the same all over the world: slavery, oppression of people, atrocities against humans, domestic violence. It was crisis enough for me in the 1980s that I went home and told my husband that we might need to quit.

She felt unable to be prophetic because she was dependent on satisfying congregations. It was tumultuous for her, and she says it may not be fully resolved yet.

But in the midst of this, she found another hero, Carlyle Marney.

I never met him face-to-face, but he was one of my heroes. I got hooked on him when my father, who taped sermons at Capitol Street Church, sent me tapes of a series of sermons that Marney had preached there. I absorbed everything I could read or learn from his thinking and about who he was.

Roy Clark, her childhood pastor, reported to her that in a conversation with Marney about the church, Clark suggested leaving the institution that was so rife with racism. Marney is said to have replied: "Leave the church? There is nowhere else to go." For Mary Ann that was a way to live with the tension. She agrees with Marney that there is nowhere else to go. Staying in the house and claiming its redeeming and nurturing characteristics have become her way of holding fast.

When it is all said and done, how does she feel about her growth from happy child to mature and bold adult?

When I look back on the little girl and the young woman I was, I wonder where she went. She was playful, happy, adventuresome, undaunted, zealous, driven, eager, curious, self-confident. Now I often seem cautious, not really fearful, but exhausted. Counting the cost, weighing and measuring. I'm not nearly as free to act, because I know the price. I've lived through the cost. I don't feel safe and am very aware of the risk. But that happy child does come out now and then. She will not be done in.

I have been really clear through all of the detours in my journey, that it was the clarity of the call to preach the gospel and God's unconditional love that kept me going. It was about becoming more perfect in love of God and neighbor, following Jesus as a way to life. I was confident that Jesus offers us abundant life and that we are called to live and join with the community of others to make it possible for there to be abundant life for every child born on this planet. That's what it's all about. No matter what job I have, I'll do that task. To express the love of Christ and to love the world as Christ loves the world is what we're about. My vision for my life is about love—living love, offering love, and seeing the world through the lenses of God's love. I am called to help a community of people become and embody love in who they are and in the way in which they live their lives.

I have a sense of being on the same course throughout my entire lifetime wherever it has taken me. Knowing and never doubting or questioning that course stays with me. Churches or institutions or organizations or denominations can rise or fall, or civilizations or nations or flags may come and go. The reality of Christ is real for my life. I believe that our world has outlived the reason for nation states and political governments and organizations. We shouldn't have to have green cards and wars at borders and immigration policies. There should be a free flow of people across the land that is planted. People should welcome one another with hospitality. We should receive strangers and be people of care and friendship. As Gandhi used to say, "The earth has enough for everyone's need, but not for everyone's greed."

When I finished listening to Mary Ann's story, I found myself smiling and realizing how pleasant and provocative she is. Her small stature is no indication of a lack of authority or appropriate power. In fact, her intense self-presentation and her ready laugh invite people to "make merry." I believe all of this rises out of her deep internal grounding in the grace of God. It is from that confidence in God that her authority comes, and her leadership is full of grace and openness and generosity of self and the gifts God offers through her.

CONVERSATION IN NASHVILLE

In January 2003, eleven of the thirteen women bishops met in Nashville for a day of conversation and reflection. Although I proposed an opening question, the circle determined its own direction for most of the day. We ranged through emotions, history, questions. There are some very vulnerable and intimate stories in what follows. Here is a glimpse, not just of the past out of which we came, but also of the feelings that accompany us today. There are twists and turns in the conversation because now and again someone would circle back to an earlier point in the conversation. The record is that of the day. The flavor is conversational.

I believe this to be the most important part of what this project offers. Here we are, largely unmasked, and trusting one another and the public who will "listen in." Over and over, I marvel at the strength, depth, and faithfulness of these women. My appreciation for them has grown as I have worked with their stories, and it has stretched greatly in working with this conversation time.

I began the conversation with an attempt to tie us back to the times of their telling their individual stories to me. My question was: Can you find an incident or learning experience in your childhood, teen years, or young adult years that directly affects the way you do your ministry now? I offered the first comment as illustration. From there the conversation is reported as it unfolded, without further intrusion of commentary.

CRAIG: When I was about fourteen or fifteen, I opened my first bank account in Liberty, Missouri. Probably had twenty bucks in it. One day the bank president met my dad on the street, and he said, "Ray, Judy's overdrawn her bank account. What do you want me to do about it?" He said, "Call her in." That desk was an acre of mahogany in the bank president's office. And I had to climb up on that leather chair. He lectured me on the responsibility of caring for money, how irresponsible I had been, and how important managing my money is. I'm telling you, I have not overdrawn my account since. I balance my checkbook on the day the statement comes. And one of the things that irked me as a bishop was fiscal irresponsibility. It just drives me crazy when pastors get in over their heads or the church's books aren't in order. I really think that can be traced back to that encounter with that bank president. I learned fiduciary responsibility in the bank president's office.

KAMMERER: I feel like I literally grew up under the hands and feet of United Methodist women. My grandmother was the founding president and member of WSCS in her church. The women of her circle would always come to the house. My sister and I would listen as we sat on the floor, wearing little matching dresses and shoes and socks. We heard about missions. We learned about their lives and heard their Bible study. That was a powerful influence on me. And we participated in thank offerings and missions sponsored by WSCS with our allowance. I am convinced that my love for The United Methodist Church and my sense of mission and what is possible for a small group of people came to me when I sat on the floor as a little girl at grandmother's knee and at the knees of all these women.

RADER: My dad was a traveling salesperson for an insurance company and traveled all over Michigan selling insurance. He loved to go down back roads to find this, that, or the other thing. By the time I was born, he worked in the office of a manufacturing firm. But he loved to pile everybody in the car on a Sunday afternoon or on a vacation and take off down whatever road led out of Battle Creek and drive an hour or two to some place. My brother and I didn't always appreciate that, because, since we didn't know where we were going, there seemed no end to the trip. My dad just loved to look at whatever we encountered along the way. My mother would watch for bittersweet growing in the hedgerows or for a weed called pixel and make Dad stop so she could pick it. I've often thought that part of the reason it never bothered me to get in the car and start out for one of those little rural churches—the ones with directions such as go past the big tree on the corner to where the red barn used to be. I find those drives interesting enjoyable. I think those times that we shared together as a family, just going out for those Sunday afternoon or Saturday drives, were a kind of training.

HASSINGER: Sharon, that's helpful. I never made the connection. I had some similar things happen. Since both of my parents were in education, they had summers free. But even during the school year, Sunday afternoons Dad would often say, "We're going to do thus and so." For years my grandmother lived with us, so it would be my parents, my grandmother, my brother, and me in the car. We didn't know where we were going, but it almost always involved stopping some place to eat, which was a rarity in the family. Sometimes he did have in mind a destination. I also love just driving around. That sense of exploring, of learning about, of discussing things—I hadn't thought how that informs my ministry now.

CHRISTOPHER: There's another dimension of that for me. And I would identify learning—not just head-learning, but growing and discovering—to be key elements in my childhood. My parents were always helping us learn new things and have new, growing experiences. I think my theology has been radically shaped by that. I believe the Christian faith is a journey and that we are continually being shaped and learning new things. I think my ability to embrace and welcome change was formed by that learning and discovering and growing as a child.

SHERER: Our Sunday afternoons were more likely spent with family. So we would visit family up in the Appalachian mountains and spend time listening to stories. My father and uncles were storytellers. So we would sit for hours and tell family stories and stories about farming. I still love stories and am shaped by THE story. Even dinners in our home were three hours long because after the meal, the adults got a cup of coffee and stayed at the table and talked and talked. Each one's story built on the next one and triggered another memory. And so story is really important.

When I came home from college, we would eat dinner together every Saturday night. My dad and brother would go do something, and Mom and I would sit there and empty two or three coffee pots just talking. And that's how she reconnected to me. That front porch in North Wilkesboro was the place where the whole neighborhood gathered. There were four big rocking chairs. And again it was story after story. People who walked by would come up, stand on the walk, talk, then continue on their walk.

FISHER: When you asked the question, this jumped out right away. I think of the depth of my spirituality around the discipline of prayer. It cost a lot to heat a church building for prayer meetings, so we had a lot of cottage meetings. And our house was where cottage meetings happened. It was not unusual on Tuesday evenings for the saints to gather downstairs. The children were sent up to bed while they were down there having a prayer meeting right in our house. That was a real big part of our journey. I've continued to appreciate that spiritual discipline of prayer, and it's a key piece of who I am. Every blessed Sunday morning, the family had to get on our knees. And we had family prayer. It was not always Daddy and Mother praying. We had to take turns and pray, and you never knew when you would be called on. Praying has really been a foundation for me, I know, in my journey. It started at the knees of my grandmother and my daddy and my mother.

MORRISON: Growing up, I experienced the church not with my own family, but with my grandmother. Her church was a Wesleyan Methodist in a small town in western New York State. There was a man in the town called Crazy Joe. The word was that he had been shell-shocked in the war, but others said he was that way before the war. He couldn't step on cracks. I can still picture him taking a long time to walk to the post office because he had to jump over all of the cracks in the sidewalk. Well, he was a member of my grandmother's church and would always come bursting into the church with his arms out because he had always wanted to be a preacher (that was the other thing they always told about him). But no one would bat an eye. There was a place for him in the church. His intrusion was not an intrusion. That image has stayed with me. There was a place for "crazy Joes" in that church, and I think that experience has informed my ministry.

251

CHRISTOPHER: I think it was a congregation that formed me as a child and as a youth around that very same issue. I was extremely shy. For me to get up and lead a Methodist Youth Fellowship program was more than I thought I could ever do. Yet that congregation and that youth group helped me get up and do it. So I discovered a sense of power, of my ability to contribute.

SHERER: The church was the place where I always felt safe, warm, and cared for. When I was an awkward teenager, I viewed myself as terribly inept. The church was the place where I didn't feel that way, where no matter what happened they loved me and took care of me. Even when I had a lover's quarrel with the church, I still had this sense. And those experiences still shape how I want to build community, to create a sense of warmth and security and acceptance every time we gather.

MORRISON: You know, as I sit here and listen to you tell the stories of how the church nurtured, I feel a sense of longing because in a way I never had that kind of nurturing. I have a strong appreciation for the church, but I sometimes fall more on the side of being frustrated for what it isn't. Maybe that's because for a long time the church wasn't for me. I didn't have that as a basis. Perhaps I push for my ideal vision of what the church should be rather than settling for what it is.

FISHER: I think one of the pieces where you, Susan, have really blessed me is your ability not only to build community, but also to play within that community. Seeing a bishop play is such an oddity. You've taken your cabinet to skating rinks, gone sledding on cardboard boxes during appointment-making. I wondered what kind of bishop would do that. I was so straight-laced. But I have learned how to play.

HUIE: As I heard Ann talk about the way her family told stories, I thought how that is certainly descriptive of my family as well. And I really get it from both sides of my family. I used to love to spend the night with my maternal grandmother, and she would tell stories, not only family stories, but all kinds of stories. On my father's side of the family, every one of his siblings is a storyteller. When we have family gatherings, one story after another is told, largely around the family table. I grew up listening and absorbing lots of different kinds of stories as well as family stories.

When I was thinking about going to seminary, I struggled with history of Christian doctrine and with the philosophy of religion. I just couldn't get there from here. And yet when I read the stories in the Gospels and in the Old Testament, I was just there. It all came alive for me. When I was working on my D.Min. and I read the desert mothers and fathers for the first time, I understood, for the first time, that I was a theologian. Although I couldn't get my mind around the conceptual parts, I understood the story. My life is shaped by this story. And my preaching is shaped by the story. I think it all dates back to hearing my grandmother, my mother, my father, and my aunts and uncles telling stories. That's who we are—the people of the story.

The other thing that I was reflecting on is the issue of relationship. The summer before my junior year in high school, my grandfather died. My grandmother and grandfather lived just about 300 yards from our house. My grandmother was eighty-seven years old and had never spent a night by herself. And so when my grandfather died, the girl grandchildren took turns spending the night with her to help bridge the first summer. She couldn't drive, so somebody had to take her to the grocery store, and that became my way of helping her. She had to go on Thursdays because that was double stamp day. I cannot tell you how long it took to buy groceries, because all of the farmwomen came on double-stamp day. Going to the grocery store was less about buying food than it was about seeing people. How are you, and how's your grandchild? These encounters took place up and down the grocery aisles. And, of course, she would have to tell me how I was in relationship with this person or that person and how they were all related to one another. It would take us all morning to shop!

CHRISTOPHER: Like the contemporary women at the well.

HUIE: As I reflected on that later, I thought what an incredible gift that was to me to learn how important those relationships are. Not only relationships with God, because this is my grandmother who had such deep personal piety, but also the relationships that showed the love of God and love of people. Every time you move into a new place, you don't know anybody so you start trying to figure out the relationships and how they relate to you and you to them. Peoples' lives are a web of relationships. I think The United Methodist Church is fundamentally relational. I think grace is relational. The real connection is relationship.

SHERER: Being a part of this community of women, it occurs to me what a gift it is to know this community and to be known by this community. It is a great gift.

KELLY: I think we've been very open with one another, and why we feel the need for times when we can just come together.

CRAIG: Now I think that spills over into the influence we have on the church and on the Council of Bishops. I think everyone of us could sit here and tell a story about relationships and how we've come to value those. And we are very self-conscious about that. I'm not sure that males in this culture are encouraged to be self-conscious about relationships in the same way. So when you get a critical mass of women in an organization or in a body or community, like a council of bishops, who live out of this value, it also begins to permeate the way that organization, that community, lives out its life. Areas that we serve talk about how different it is when we're there. I think it has to do a lot with this valuing of relationships.

FISHER: It's humanizing.

MORRISON: I think there's another way we have affected the Council of Bishops, though. Most of us were elected bishop at an earlier age than has traditionally been the case. In terms of my own adjustment, most of the other bishops are from a very different generation, and have a very different way of seeing things, of relating and functioning.

KELLY: My mother always told us, "Knock on any door, open any door that's closed, and walk through any door that's open." She sent us off to school with the words, "Go get 'em." My parents believed that everyone has a purpose, and so as children we were not allowed to join any club or any group that was not oriented to doing good. You couldn't just belong to a card club or a dance club. Everything had to have a purpose. It was this sense of community. There was the sense that if a black man did something, it included all of us—all black people. If a white man did something, it was just another man. Well, the thing about it is, you had to create the opportunity for yourself.

RADER: We've had a number of stories in which people have said, "I was shy. I was bashful. I was awkward. I didn't believe I could do." I can remember in college, saying to somebody that my story is the story of an ugly duckling. I always feel like I don't really fit. Maybe someday I'll grow up to be a swan, but I'm really the ugly duckling. I don't know how many of the others who haven't spoken it still felt that. And I don't know if that's just the phenomena of girls in adolescence and it's everybody's story, or if there is a commonality about that. I don't know what, short of God's grace, helped me emerge from that. It was an extremely painful period for me.

CRAIG: I was a tomboy who felt absolutely out of sync as a teenager. I was not at home in my teenage years. I was highly successful: I made good grades and was popular. But I didn't date much. The boys were my buddies and told me their love troubles, but they didn't ask me to the prom. In many ways I really was miserable as a teenager. And yet, I suddenly emerged in all kinds of leadership roles. Don't know how that happens. Strange.

HASSINGER: I was terribly shy in elementary school and high school. I only began to emerge, to be able to speak in public, in college. Though I had never applied the term "ugly duckling" to myself, I think I also felt that way. Even though I did have some leadership roles both at the church and in school during those years, I was never part of the "in" crowd, nor did I want to be. And I still consider myself shy.

FISHER: I remember when I was about six and my older sister Clem was about eight, we sang our first duet at church. In the middle of it, I started crying. But guess what? The people in that little church started clapping and clapping and clapping. There I was scared to death, and trying to sing it. So they picked it up and began singing. They did not let me experience that as a failure. I was always shy, but we were thrust out there. When you made a mistake, it wasn't a mistake, because folks embraced you.

RADER: But one of the words you used, Violet, and a number of others have used, is that you were thrust into ministry either by the community or by your family or whatever. So somebody nurtured you into it somehow. I think that part of what women bring to the mix is the reliance on community and the hope for building a community that will continue to identify and nurture other people. I think men are acculturated to do it alone, and there's always the expectation that you're good enough, that you're going to be just fine. But it's been different for women.

MORRISON: I wonder, though, if in the black community it is both the men and the women in the community who nurtured you? As white women, we mainly talk about UMW or about our grandmothers. I wonder if in our tradition it wasn't mostly the women who nurtured, whereas in the black tradition it seems to have involved the whole community.

FISHER: Can you imagine your pastor asking you at sixteen years old to bring the sermon for youth day? I was scared to death, but I preached about the prodigal son. I'll never forget it.

CRAIG: As I've heard your stories, I have noticed that there have also been significant men in our lives because we're the first generation and didn't really have women to say it for us. In most of our stories, there has been an influential man. The college chaplain comes up in these stories over and over again. It's the significant man who finally says, "Here's an opportunity for you." Now the trick is, you know, are we doing that for other women? We are the offspring of men who saw something in us; who believed in the church being open to us; and who helped us see it, name it, and claim it. Did you grow into your call, or was there somebody who finally named it? I think about myself. I don't know if I would finally have understood that I needed to move from Christian education to ordained ministry, or how long it would have taken me to understand that if Bill McCartney hadn't walked into the office and said, "Why aren't you ordained?"

SHERER: I had been out of seminary for seven years and was a youth director. The senior pastor walked in and said, "Ann, why aren't you ordained?" And you have all the reasons. I always felt like an outsider. Perhaps being the outsider is as much our story as being shy. I didn't think that I could ever be accepted in the Church or that I belonged or would fit in. Unlike Susan, I wanted to be a part of the popular set, but it didn't fit me. It wasn't who I was. I couldn't do that. And that gave me a sense of being outside the gate. I think this made me much more willing to change and take risks because I wouldn't be let in anyway. I knew the pain of the people on the outside, and as I participated in the racial movements in the 1960s, I understood that experience partly out of my own experience of feeling like an outsider.

KAMMERER: I don't think we ever responded to Judy's last question. In terms of identifying experiences that helped shape us in prophetic presence and leadership. Again, my grandmother was influential. She had for decades, as a teacher in the county, been involved in racial reconciliation that I knew about later in my adult life, and she always modeled and witnessed for us the value and equality of all people. My college, my Deep South women's college in Macon, Georgia, was Wesleyan. It integrated for the first time my junior year. I was a dorm resident for the three women students who came in, and I was the only one willing to do it. Then in my senior year, the Poor People's March came through Georgia, and I joined the protest for the first time in my life. I'm aware of the deep, deep sense that's in me that when I, as a Christian in The United

Methodist Church, discovered that all people were not welcome in our congregation, I knew from the very beginning that that was wrong and was not Christian. And it has been formative for me to do anything and everything to help change that reality.

SHERER: I left the church for several years because they stood at the back door of the First Baptist Church and blocked African Americans. I had been taught all of this stuff about telling the story, about "there's a story to tell to the nations," and I believed it. But I was furious at them when they didn't do it, when they betrayed it after they told me it was the truth.

For me it was class. My grandfather was the custodian at school. And part of what pushed and motivated me and told me that I could walk through those doors was that my daddy always told me, "You're as good as anybody else. You can do anything you want to do. You can be part of anything. You can be anybody you want to be." And that message was told to me over and over and over. In that small town, it's hard to break out of the class you live in.

RADER: I was reflecting on Teenie's comment that when one black person messed up, it was the whole; it reflected on every black person. I think as women entered ministry, they felt that too. When one of us messed up, it was like, see, now we know women can't do this. But if one woman did something well, it was that woman who did it. It never worked in the reverse: See, now we know everybody can. The comments were always, "Well, if everybody was like that woman, then it would be different." So you became isolated, or that kind of comparison was a way of putting you down or pitting you against other women. I think for women there's less of that now than there once was.

CHRISTOPHER: I've often felt it was a burden carrying what I'm doing on behalf of all women. The image I use sometime is wearing Wonder Woman bracelets. Wonder Woman defends the world against injustice and all that is evil, and in the sense of defending women and having to play that role I put on the bracelets. But I've decided not to play that role. It's called for a conscious decision not to because it's ungraceful, literally. It is out of grace to take that position. But I think realizing I had to decide not to play the role of Wonder Woman has spiritually formed me.

KAMMERER: Another place on that spectrum is Violet's comment about her experience of when she felt a failure, that the community picked her up and encouraged her and helped her to move through that. That's what I appreciate about the circle of sisters and others in the Council of Bishops who do that for me daily. When things are really tough, I value that rich community of people who know me well and love me and care for me and help lift me up when I don't feel like I'm able to stand or to do it well.

MORRISON: I'm just wondering if in the book you are pushing some of those tough things. I think other folk can identify with them also. I mean, folk here have gone through the belief that "divorce is wrong" and the pain of that, especially women. We all are survivors in our own ways thanks partly to the Church. But we've had to be survivors because of the Church in other ways.

CRAIG: Let's not be naive. The circle has supported us, but we've all been hurt by the circle, too. There've been times when we've all experienced the horizontal violence somewhere along the line in the journey.

MORRISON: We support one another, but we've also heard the pain that some of us, all of us, have been through. But it really needs to be named because I think there's a whole lot of people out there who can connect with that.

FISHER: When you look at the stories we've just told around the race issues, the conversation was very safe. I learned through songs, such as "Jesus Loves the Little Children." I demonstrated or was in a march. But in your journey beyond those nice things, what else happened? I'm serious. What has happened? Where has your voice been? Where has your voice been around these same issues in your ministry as pastors, as superintendents, whatever? How

259

have you made a difference? How have you taken "Jesus loves the little children, all the children of the world" and moved with that?

MORRISON: There's another dimension. I don't want us to lose sight of the fact that a lot of us have had cancer. I believe there's a correlation between our journeys and our health. I believe there's a correlation with the cancer we've had with the journey we've taken.

CRAIG: Where do we feel we've been prophetic and made a difference? Where have you made a difference in your ministries in some prophetic way? What price did you pay to do that?

RADER: Well, I was just looking at you as you were asking the question, and it got real personal and hurtful for me. I can remember an annual conference in Albion, Michigan, that was about to split over whether or not they could support me for the episcopacy. And it was about stances I had taken about the inclusiveness of the Church around issues of sexuality *(tears up)*. Boy, isn't that interesting? That just bubbles right up hard. I can remember you inviting me to come to the front, and I was sitting in the back.

My belief that one's sexuality is given to you was formed through an experience with a wonderful couple in our church who were the youth leaders. They were in their middle thirties, when the man came to understand or to claim his sexuality as a gay man. The couple divorced, and he was asked to leave the church. I cried with my parents about how that was not right. They were both wonderful youth leaders. His sexuality didn't change who he was or how he had been with us or how he had supported and nurtured us. There had been no claims of inappropriate behavior while he was working with the youth group or with anybody else in the church. I think that was one of those moments in my life that couldn't be left. I think there are stances that I take, that I have taken, about inclusiveness when it never occurs to me to think about them first. The gospel story was told and it became my story, and now I've got to live it. It was only after the fact that somebody told me the Church didn't accept that or that those weren't the right rules.

Peter Miano, one of our missionaries in the Middle East, says that Jesus was shaped by Galilee, not by Jerusalem. He was outside of the rules of Jerusalem and the Galilee region formed him in a way that allowed more freedom to give expression to ministry. In some ways I think we ought to be creating more Galilees than Jerusalems or figuring out whether we belong with Jesus in Galilee. Perhaps the dilemma is that as a bishop you're asked to be part of Jerusalem, part of the establishment, rather than part of Galilee. And you live in that tension.

MORRISON: Well, I think the rubber hit the road when we became bishops. I can go back to the whole Sophia controversy and feeling that I had no support whatsoever. I thought it was theological discussion and didn't understand what the big deal was. And I've been labeled ever since then as a radical feminist. Early on, I felt little support in the college. I watched my colleagues pooh-pooh charges brought about others because it shouldn't go any further. But when the charges were against me, they believed the charges should be investigated to avoid looking like they were being supportive of one their colleagues and not dealing with the issues.

I felt little support, just hanging out there, except for some of you who stood up for me. And I'm just saying, it seems to me that the rubber hit the road—whether we could be who we are and stand for what we are—when we became bishops. There's a way in which we've been pushed ahead because we were the first, and if you were somewhat safe you got ahead. But the issue is, now that you're there, what are you doing now? Where are you standing and how vocal are you and how present are you? And that's my struggle. I'm not saying it to you; I'm saying that to me. And that's been my battle all along, and I don't think I've come through it well. That's where the cancer comes in and a whole bunch of other things—wondering how much am I doing, who am I, and how to live with integrity.

KELLY: It's the journey. You have to be ready. It came to me the other day: we cut down our agendas to size. We want God to fit what we can easily be comfortable with. But God has already cut

God's self down to size in Jesus Christ. And that's the greatest thing that's known. That's the greatest story. We're to fit the larger story.

SHERER: Extremely formative for me was my first church splitting. Forty of them left just because I was there, and that was literally the only social issue the church could deal with. So the myth my friends and I operated out of as clergywomen in the Texas Conference was that we could probably do our ministry and have one other social issue, but no more. And that was the context out of which I did my early ministry. You know, people have said the same things to me as they said to the rest of you in the interview. "Oh, you can come be on my staff since you have adoptive children and won't have babies." You know, terrible, awful things like that.

Before being appointed, I had been very socially active in the Civil Rights Movement. But I suddenly pulled back. Coming into ordained ministry changed me. I began to think that all I could do was nurture my people and be present and that I was the only social issue that they could take. Because my husband, Rob, worked at Wiley College, a historically black institution, I could speak on race. In White Oak, they were angry because persons of color came to their church, came to my house. We brought the first persons of color into the Texarkana church. But there was a part of being in that environment and feeling so on the front line that made us timid on other issues. I don't know if anyone else had that experience or whether it was just being in the Deep South.

CHRISTOPHER: I never thought about being timid, because people couldn't take on more issues. But I do remember being at a pastors' school in Wisconsin where a pastor/counselor stood up and talked about how pastors enter a congregation. He said that you shouldn't tamper with the symbol system of the congregation in the first year. You don't tamper with those symbols until you get to know the congregation. And I remember angrily standing up and saying, "There's a basic assumption here. That's a white, male, privileged assumption because I am a threat to a symbol system just by showing up." I called into question all kinds of symbol systems. That's the first part of what you were talking about, Ann, in terms of the role that we play in the life of the congregation—we shatter symbol systems and paradigms just by virtue of who we are. This also means that we invite people into a whole new way of life, which is the redemptive side. But there's the unsettledness and the invitation to change that sometimes breeds resistance and anger and fear and violence.

SHERER: And just feeling like if only you could build a relationship, then maybe together you could move into a different future. But I walked into the White Oak Church with the two back rows of people sitting with their arms folded. They would not take communion or participate at all. And they ultimately left. It was my husband's job on Sunday morning to keep my children from hearing the ugly things being said about my family. I didn't want them to know what some of these people thought about their mama because I didn't want them to feel badly about the church.

CRAIG: It's 2003, and we're still appointing women to churches where people walk out. Yikes!

KAMMERER: I'm finding Vi's question and your question just so painful, I think, because of what serving as an episcopal leader has cost me. The first system I needed to address as the new bishop in my conference was an informal system of appointment-making in which the large-membership churches call the shots and slip a list of preferred pastors to the bishop. Against generations of that system, I communicated to each district how we were going to do appointment-making and consultation. My cabinet and I have lived into that for six years now. Some of that has been at great cost as we treated churches and pastors equitably, bringing women up to senior pastorates, creating more opportunities for pastors of color in our conference, and working hard to create multicultural settings for people to serve in ministry. During the second year I was bishop, the Vieques situation unfolded. Our son was in the military, but I found myself supporting the people of Vieques against the presence of the U.S. Navy. It was a powerful crucible in my Episcopal life. How do you stand as a leader, and as a Christian mother, so that you're connected firmly to your family, yet against the position of your government? At first I felt very little support or even understanding in my college. It seemed to me that there was little leadership building there. It just absolutely killed my soul and chipped away at it year by year. That has changed some, but it sometimes still continues to the point of my questioning how long I want to do this actively or whether I should look for another way to express my leadership in the Church. Actually, my call, not my leadership, but my call. Then there's the continued need in our jurisdiction for the clergywomen, whoever we all are, to organize, prepare, and contend against the systems of election. I have run into a lot of brick walls but I keep running at them. Sometimes full force, but sometimes being stopped by them on behalf of my people, my conference, and my sisters. But I am living the story. I've been faithful.

CRAIG: A wonderful woman in west Ohio, who was a staff member, died last summer at fifty-two. About two weeks before she died, she called a circle of women together around her. She had a passion for addressing systemic evil. We thought we were going to say good-bye to her. Oh, no! She had an agenda. She asked us: Where are you seeing systemic oppression and what are you doing about it? I think that's the question we're pursuing. As bishops who also happen to be women, how are we addressing the particular kind of systemic oppression that we uniquely face?

KELLY: There's another part of my upbringing that I'm so grateful for—the whole sense of calling the church to accountability if it's going to call itself a Christian institution. We have to. We felt we could make a difference, not just in the Council, but also in the church and in the world.

SHERER: But we talk ourselves out of it in a variety of ways. There was this enormous sense that if you did anything that caused persons not to value your leadership, then no woman would ever be able to serve. Breaking that myth in my life has taken enormous energy and work because of the huge sense of responsibility that comes with it.

KELLY: It's the same responsibility that you have in terms of race and being a woman, too. I think that we have done a great deal simply by being and doing and working in new ways. When you're alone in a situation and are part of a whole system that devalues you, it is just debilitating.

CRAIG: But it does remind us that a woman alone in a room is still a woman at risk. And a woman alone in a room full of power—systemic power that does not value women—is really at risk. And it's 2003!

RADER: I think that's true. I also think that if we're going to tell the truth, we will sometimes deny our power in the room—even when we're alone. And sometimes, when we're alone, we have more power simply because we are alone. There is this other layer of not just gender or sexuality or race or whatever. It's a layer of feeling like I have to carry the whole church somehow. So if I speak prophetically or make a radical decision of some sort, then the apportionments might fall off and the conference ends up in turmoil. I've brought that on. Or I've hurt the larger community. It's not only about our own self-protection, but also about protecting the whole that, in some ways, doesn't deserve to be protected.

MORRISON: Or, we're getting ready to be assigned to a new area. This is now. I mean, go back to Denver Fifteen statement.[1] We would ask members of the Council to sign, but they would say, "Well, I can't this time, I'm up for a move." I'm talking about the way the system pushes in on us or compromises us. Us—I'm saying us.

CRAIG: I really do believe that Denver was a genesis of whatever negative energy entered my body that set the cancer free. You can't look at General Conference in May of 1996 and all of the stuff that happened that summer and not see that. A depression. Me depressed? Never! But I suffered a bout of depression in the fall and cancer in April. Now true, the cancer took a while to get active. But I'm never going to be able to separate those things in my mind and body.

265

And what happened to me was that I got trapped by that very thing you mentioned, Sharon. When the West Ohio Conference began to rattle around and lose money because of me, I took that whole thing on myself. I forgot that I wasn't responsible for how people reacted. I was responsible for my own faithful living. But I lost that altogether. Administratively, we worked on a way to respond to that crisis in the life of the West Ohio Annual Conference. But a whole body of people worked on that. And I had to deal with all of this mail and stuff. It took a while for me to get my self-differentiation back in place and remember that those people who were saying those things about me didn't have a clue about who Judy Craig is. They hadn't a clue.

KELLY: They didn't have a clue who Jesus Christ is!

CRAIG: Well, they didn't—you're right. But why is that such a trap for us? Is it because we're raised to be nurturers and caregivers? And so we have this overactive need to make sure that everything around us is okay and when it isn't, it's our fault.

RADER: It's a trap for some men bishops, too.

CRAIG: It's a trap for any leader. There's always the seductive side to authority, isn't there? It's so easy to begin to believe that we're more than we are.

MORRISON: We get to have our own room.

RADER: We've talked a lot about community, but the reality is that we've not always been community. I don't know how much we just checked in with one another, whether we agreed with one another. We haven't always taken the time to say to one another, "You're going through a tough time. How are you doing with it?" Let me take my own story. Everybody knew last summer that the Institute for Religion and Democracy (IRD) took me on for what happened at Kaioros Kommotion, a gathering of people who call themselves Progressive Christians, for a conference in the fall of 2002 in Madison, Wisconsin. The number of my episcopal colleagues who spoke to me at all about that could be counted on less than a hand. It wasn't that they needed to agree with me. But I needed for them to ask whether I was okay in the midst of what I thought I needed to do. One of the best signs of hope I've had in a long time was when IRD stopped making me the poster child and made Joe Sprague it. In our college, somebody finally said, "Joe, can we talk about this?" It was clear that not everybody saw it the way Joe saw it. But there was the sense that we could deal with it differently if we could all just tell the truth. I don't think we can act until we reflect on what we are doing, and until we ask ourselves: What is the truth about all of this? Where is the pain?

HASSINGER: I was reflecting on how my style of being prophetic is seldom through the spoken word. It has more often been expressed in action or in community.

In terms of race, I have brought in required anti-racism training, as I know others of you have. I've been getting a lot of flack about that in the last several months. I've heard some say that it isn't the conference's issue, but rather the bishops' issue. But racism is growing in our country, and it's the right thing to do. So you go on. You try to build a critical mass for change in the climate. There were charges filed with the Religion and Race Commission, accusing me of racism, and charges filed with the college. Our cabinet will be six persons of color and four white. As that number of persons of color has grown—so that there is less white privilege within the cabinet itself—there have been cries among the clergy (primarily from white males) about being overlooked. Then there are cries about the appointment process because we have placed persons of color, men and women, in churches previously reserved for whites. So, you know, you talk about power. There is power and it can be used. At the last annual conference, we held a repentance service, and I chose to use that as an opportunity to make a statement in which I described white privilege, acknowledged my white privilege, and then led the conference in confession. In every district, I am doing diversity presentations and getting various reactions to that—some greatly appreciative and others saying this is not our issue, particularly in northern Maine and northern New

Hampshire. That area is 97 or 98 percent white. So the reactions are subtle.

In another instance, a resolution came at the last annual conference to revitalize a congregation as open to gays, lesbians, bisexual and transgendered persons. Every month I get a variety of letters saying that that is wrong for me to have allowed the resolution to come on the floor, and threatening to take the matter to the judicial council. And that church is growing—it's not huge—but it's clearly targeting a particular audience. I have not made any statements about where I am on that issue. But my job is to create a climate where those kinds of directions can happen, maintain that climate, and hope to stay self-differentiated enough not to break down in the face of reactivity.

CRAIG: That's a wonderful model of another way to be prophetic—a very powerful way to be prophetic. And it's important to me for us to embrace all of the different ways of doing that. There was a time in the early women's movement when we really tried to force one another to be alike. I remember getting chastised for not playing the political game the way I was supposed to play it, according to some of the women. Part of the beauty of having enough of us in the episcopacy is that we don't have to be alone. When there were just three of us, we kind of hung onto one another.

CHRISTOPHER: I see it in working to unite conferences. The challenge I've had set before me is how do I help the conference create a whole new system based on an understanding of the New Testament church that is an inclusive, multicultural church. We are asking how every process we put in place reflects what it means to be New Testament church. We've been six years at doing that, putting together a New Testament conference with processes and values rooted in the Gospels and Acts.

CRAIG: As I look back over my sixteen years as Bishop, I was one of the early ones and have had a wonderful time when it's all said and done. I've had experiences, gained important life understandings that would never have come any other way. I don't know that

I made as much difference as I would like to have made. It's time to sit back and assess and ask: So what did it matter? One of the things I'd like to think that mattered was that I simply was—that there were three women bishops and the Church still hadn't collapsed entirely before we could add others. I feel as if part of my role (and you may want to think this way, too, Teenie) was to continue to push against the absence of history, save for Marjorie. And that very pushing against the absence of history, with some modicum of joy and effect, contributed to the future. I had some other wonderful high moments. The episcopal address was probably one of the highest moments of my life and three days later was probably one of the lowest moments of my life. I mean, it's not often you get to be the darling of the church and the goat of the church in the span of three days. I feel good about being one of the early people to step up to sexual misconduct. But I think the primary contribution was just being willing to be. I feel fine about that. I don't need a big piece of history. One of my delights is watching all of you, particularly from this side of retirement.

HUIE: Ann, I think you should tell your Mozambique story. In the sense of presence making a difference, that's a beautiful story. It's as poignant and hilarious as any story I know about just being there.

SHERER: There are actually two stories, and they both happened in Africa. We were in Harare and a pastor took me to a hospice for women dying of AIDS run by two Irish women, both of whom were Roman Catholic nuns. When we came through the door, one woman yelled in this huge voice to the other one, "Sister, Sister, come quickly. The Lord has sent us a woman bishop before we die." Three years later, we were in northern Mozambique. I was traveling with one of the pastors in our conference, who spoke Portuguese and related well to the Mozambican people. They seated us on the front porch with the men, and we talked for a little while. Then I realized that the women were in the backyard cooking. So I went where they were tending their fires. I don't speak much Portuguese. One of the women and I began to talk about our children with our four or five shared words. I told her that my children were named Anna Maria and Roberto. And she said, "Ah." And she ran to get her daughter who was also Anna Maria. Anna Maria stood there for a moment, looked at me, and then said, *"Obispo! Obispo!"* (Bishop! Bishop!). A little girl in Savannah, Missouri, came up and threw her arms around my neck and said, "Someday I'm going to have your job."

Every one of you has those kinds of stories. I believe that our presence has made a radical difference in the Church. And I think we give other women courage to try things just by our very presence. I try to seek out the little girls in every church I go to, sit down and talk to them, and ask if they're called to ordained ministry.

FISHER: I've lived in east Africa twice as a missionary. But when I went back for The United Methodist Church with Bishop Ndoricimpa, the Sisters were so excited. They had not seen a black female bishop. There was such excitement—they brought gifts and danced. That gave me such a sense of gratitude to God for placing me in this role so I could come back to my own people, to my motherland, and say to my sisters in the motherland that there's a place in the church for them. Maybe not today, but with hope and faith that the day will come for them.

HASSINGER: I think one thing to which we as women contribute is helping the church look at the process by which women bishops make decisions. That's a slow process. But I think that by our styles, we often help raise questions about whether we must make decisions only by parliamentary process and debate. Can we engage one another in theological reflection and storytelling that undergirds the decision-making process? That's not comfortable for a lot of people, but I think it's a contribution many of us are making in the Church.

CRAIG: We're a long way from done. What are we pushing against? How are you doing it? And what is the price tag on it for you?

SHERER: Entitlement. I think the hardest struggle I have had in Missouri is dealing with persons, especially clergy, who think that by staying in a church long enough and not really messing up, that was their place. So as we began to match gifts and pastors with churches, the backlash around entitlement became enormous. And the second place where entitlement crops us is around pension and insurance. There's an enormous amount of money that goes into taking care of us. There were even persons in the conference—middle-aged clergy—who said to me, "I can see no reason for the conference except to take care of clergy."

We're trying to shift the culture to one that focuses on making disciples, helping the Church grow, becoming a transforming agent in the world, being open to the Hispanic community, and starting missions in poor communities—all of the things that we're doing. But it's difficult to do that rather than to focus on what can we do for ourselves that makes us more secure. I've experienced quite a bit of hostility because I've said that this is where we're going as a community and we're moving in this direction. It's not a punishment not to send a person to a particular church. It's a decision about gifts. The anger over those decisions is sometimes hard to live with. But I've really found a way to separate from that in the last year or two. I had to do that or die.

CRAIG: I think some of our brothers are trying to do some of the things we care about, too, but it seems as if we get criticized harder for it.

MORRISON: I think that's been true all along. Like in the Denver Fifteen statement, I think the women who signed it were attacked far more than the men. And that's true of other things that have come along.

HUIE: I agree with that.

CHRISTOPHER: And to express deep feelings more confrontationally. It's not a head disagreement, but an irrational reaction, coming from some place (I'm not sure from where) that sort of vomits the stuff on us.

I've experienced episcopacy as a spiritual discipline, and it can either take our lives from us or give us life, depending on how we choose to relate to it, I think. I found it to be formative in the sense of helping me grow in grace. And specifically one of the agendas given to me is how do I love those folks who seek to diminish, degrade, distort, and take my life from me. Learning what it means to be faithful and to live the gospel has been a real learning lab for me. And so I'm grateful. I'm grateful. Somebody asked me what had prepared me to be a bishop. And you know, I think one of the key things of preparation has been my experience as a woman in the life of the Church, as someone who has been not welcomed or wanted, and has been a target of derision. That has really prepared me singularly to be a bishop, to allow me to lead, to step out and do that which is countercultural, to be self-differentiated because I have learned that from my experience as a woman in the life of the Church. So I can be grateful for that experience because, as a result, I have grown in my own faith and my relationship with God.

HASSINGER: I would echo that to some extent, Sharon. The life and role of a bishop has forced me to be more intentional about spiritual disciplines than I have ever been before and to seek out counsel in relation to those spiritual disciplines in ways that I never did before, with a spiritual director. But if I had not been pushed by some of the issues, some of the relationships, I wouldn't have had to do that.

HUIE: Before I was elected, I went on a silent retreat every year. Now I always go twice. After my first year, I knew twelve months was too, too long to wait. That's a way of echoing in my practice that I have to step up and intensify because the things that draw me away from faithfulness are so much more intense, so much more seductive, so much more difficult than I ever experienced before—and I thought I'd experienced a lot. I thought I had some pretty good experience coming into this, but I've learned. It is an arduous journey. Part of what I've missed in being a bishop, apart from this group sitting around this circle, is the relationships that I had with clergywomen. It is one of the heartaches for me. I still have some relationships with clergywomen back in southwest Texas. But I did not realize what a support the annual conference clergywomen were until I didn't have them anymore. Those people are still there. But I can't have relationships with the clergy-women in Arkansas anything remotely like the set of relationships I had in southwest Texas. For me personally, that's been hard. In my early days, I came in at a time when there were a lot of male clergy who did not want me there and didn't hesitate to say so. Out of that, I developed some relationships with clergywomen who stuck together pretty tightly because it was a tough time. Those relationships were powerful, strong relationships, and they expanded over twenty-something years in southwest Texas. When you go to a new place as the bishop, you can't do that with either males or females. I never had it with the males in the same way that I had it with the clergywomen. But I miss it. I miss it.

KELLY: The job itself isolates you. I think once you leave a local church, you don't have the diversity of people to relate to who enrich and inspire you. That's why cabinets need to be close with one another. When I went to California, they asked me what they should call me. I said, "What do you mean, what shall we call you?" And they said, "Shall we call you Leontine or Teenie?" I told them they could call me "Bishop" because the journey had been too rough to settle for less.

HUIE: I do want to say this. There's something I treasure, some-thing remarkable about this community gathered here and our sis-ters who are missing. I treasure each one of you. But I treasure all of us together even more. I think there is a sense in which each of us, though we may not know the particulars of the others' journey, know enough to know that nobody came here without paying a price, and that everyone continues to pay the price in her own way. There's a connection among us that's grace-filled and unique. I sometimes realize, you know, how quickly I get caught up in my own stuff. It is important to stay connected to one another.

KELLY: I'm glad we take the time to do that because it's good on a personal level as well as on an inspirational level. It's good to have that to hold on to because there are just some things that women do differently. Our thought patterns are different. I think that's part of being a woman and why it's important for women to stay together because the whole culture has shaped us in different ways. We know that we need to relate to people, to know that we're not out there by ourselves, and to make connections somewhere. And for me, the whole connection of The United Methodist Church is the relationships that you build across the Church.

SHERER: I would be surprised if all of us haven't, at some point, had to say to a clergyperson, "You have mistaken my smile and kindness for weakness."

KELLY: Oh, I had some senior ministers at my first pastor school who said, "You know, we are so glad you're here with us, but you smile too easily. And you can't be friends with everybody. And when are you going to move so-and-so?" They said you run your cabinet like a team. I said I do because I believe in teamwork. I think it's as important for the process to have as much equity as the end result. How we get to where we're going is very important. I understand that nobody knows what it is to be a bishop until one is a bishop. No matter what you've done, there is no experience like being completely immersed. From the day you start, you are there. And the expectations and interpretations of what you do are different from every point of view. That's why the little stuff begins to get you (what I call the junky stuff). It's not that you don't have time for it, but you don't have to bear it. We're human beings. And I think that's one of the joys of our being together. We have acknowledged one another, those who have come and those who will come, that we're all together.

CRAIG: One of my yearnings is to live long enough to see a little more matching of "the talk and the walk." I yearn to live long enough to see more of that.

KELLY: And we've got to do it.

CRAIG: I am alternately in despair and in hope.

KELLY: Well the older you get, and the less time you have, you wonder if it will ever happen. But then a lot of things have happened that nobody thought would. I'm grateful as I watch you younger bishops. I am grateful for the hope that you bring.

KAMMERER: I remember in the beginning year or two of my service as a bishop, how incredibly free I finally felt in the journey of my own living out of ministry. I finally had the freedom to be authentically who I was and to share my gifts with the Church, because, through consecration, the church had really blessed me for the first time. I just had this extraordinary sense of freedom. I really thought that once I'd been elected, the Church couldn't do anything to me, but I was very wrong about that. In the first year or two, that sense of joyful freedom to claim fully who I was and my call was just absolutely delicious. And I treasure that. But I think until more changes happen systemically around me, where I live, that it's a freedom that's now cut off for me. I really expect the rest of my life in the episcopacy to be about helping change that by my presence.

I feel wonderful about having the extraordinary privilege of shaping a cabinet and building community life within the cabinet and how, by the grace of God and my own intuition, I've learned to have such a community. By the end of six years now, the word is out in our conference that people respect the cabinet. They say things like, "You all really do care about one another in that group." It's not a trite comment. They know the ways that we're truly present to one another and how we've tried to send in teams rather than one person where there's a problem projecting an appointment. We have literally stood together in a staff-parish meeting or on the floor of the conference around some issues. Our conference had never seen that. I hadn't seen that modeled in the Church. I think the skills for building a cabinet team, a community, and the commitment to do that will be valued. Some people wonder if things will just go back to the way it was after I'm gone. But I know in my head and in my heart that I have been part of something really wonderful and think the conference has begun to glimpse and live into the kingdom of God. I believe that. And we have grown every year. We have the best apportionment record.

MORRISON: I love what I do, most of the time. It's a privilege. The more difficult part for me is feeling silenced a lot. I think that's the toughest thing. And it's not just on social issues. It's partly on who I am. You think Bishop Joe Sprague is out there, well, I'm way out there. In some ways I feel as if I can't express my faith in ways that aren't doublespeak. Remember, I don't come out of a church tradition, so I don't come with some of the traditional language. But I think I'm here for a reason. There's never been a doubt in my mind. I think I am a very good community builder and in my cabinet. I also give a lot of space for people to be in ministry. I protect them and provide for people who are probably as far out there as I am or further. It's okay. But I'm saying that's been the toughest struggle for me—deciding when to speak and when not to speak. I remain silent in the Council. But then that's my style, to work more behind the scenes.

I can get really strong when I think the Council has been silenced. I think we're not providing leadership. We're doing better than we ever have, but we're not providing the kind of leadership the Church needs, because the Church has silenced us. It has created an institutional ethos where people who speak out get beaten down and can't be authentic. I think that's also true with a lot of our clergy who aren't living inside what they're having to talk and be. In the end, I think the compromise helps folk lose the passion that they had at first. My struggle is to keep that passion when I feel as if it gets me in trouble. It may be my problem and how I deal with it. But it's been the biggest battle for me and obviously still is.

CRAIG: I always struggle with the ability to stay in genuine dialogue because of the projection people put on us with the title. Once we open our mouths and speak, that's it. And if we're a processor who makes decisions by talking out loud and the first thing we say is certainly not the last thing we're going to say and once we open our mouths people don't respond, well. Wait a minute. Talk back to me. The inability to stay in honest unfolding dialogue because of images persons put on the office you hold, is always frustrating to me. Talk back. Let's wrestle this out. I don't have any *ex cathedra* pronouncements. Talk to me. That's the other half of the silence. So, I shut up. I stop participating in discussion groups. Even in retirement, there have been a couple of attempts to bring me into small groups where I ought to be content to just sit silent and love the conversations, but they'll push me to speak; yet the minute I speak it's shut down. They've invited me as Judy, but they still treat me like the Bishop.

SHERER: The first year I was in office, people would think that whatever I said was the last word. Then they would say, "But you just changed your mind. You said...." But gradually they would get it. Cabinets can learn this.

CRAIG: Do some of the others of you feel that you guard how you speak on theological and ideological matters and sociological matters because of the office?

HUIE: I think I watch what I say publicly and even privately. Private conversation, even if it's just a side comment, sometimes gets relayed to other people out of context, so being either judged or praised totally out of context is the consequence. I think I tend to be very cautious—not just in public but also in private. There are also so few opportunities for whole conversations, so you end up with sound bites. My theology doesn't fit very well in sound bites. I might point out that Jesus' theology didn't either. He told a lot of stories. We're not in a culture in this point in time that wants to deal with multivalent meanings and symbol-rich conversation. Most people just want flat, linear, and literal. That's more frustrating to me.

CHRISTOPHER: Part of the issue for me is, I'm an educator at heart. So the question that I always carry in my mind is, how do I help the person I'm with be formed and take the next step in his or her journey? That's different from pushing my agenda. I listen to folks based on where I think they are and the possibility of where they can go and then make response. Oftentimes my concern is not how do I get my agenda on the table, but rather how do I listen and help people take their journey. It's a pedagogical thing.

CRAIG: What if there is the crisis moment when there really does have to be a sharp prophetic word?

CHRISTOPHER: Yeah, of course. There's no question about that.

HASSINGER: I'm thinking not just about the role of bishop, but also the role in family relationships is affected. It was painful to know that the whole annual conference was probably talking about what was going on with my marriage, going through separation and divorce. A number of us around this room or this circle are single. But to be in this role without anybody else in the household is very lonely at times. Even though you can't talk about much of it, having someone with whom to share would be nice.

SHERER: I remember our orientation as bishops. I think I told Sharon that I hadn't felt so isolated since I showed up at the junior high prom without a date. Robert was not at that first orientation, because he was in Canada, lecturing. Twelve people walked around the lake holding hands. I have never felt as isolated and not in community anywhere I have ever been.

MORRISON: And my famous story is at my own orientation. They had planned orientation for the spouse of the newly elected bishop. I was the only bishop elected. But they went ahead and gave the orientation for the spouse even though the spouse wasn't there. That's the honest-to-God truth! I got both!

RADER: Ann and I went through orientation for the Council eleven years ago. There's been a lot of change, even in those eleven years. Ann felt like the woman who showed up at the prom without a date. We were at Junaluska, and on the last night, they wanted to take the spouses to do something different. And one of the spouses came to me and asked why I was sitting in my room. She thought I belonged with the spouses. We had been there all week, and she thought Blaine was the bishop and I was the spouse. That's what the expectations were.

KELLY: I just have to quote Mary Ann. I remember when we were at St. Simon's Island and Mary Ann was talking to me and her husband, Jeff, was right behind us. One of the older bishop's wives said to Jeff, "And what do you do?" Before he could answer Mary Ann said, "He does the same thing you do: He takes care of the bishop."

CHRISTOPHER: Charles's line is always that he does the bishop's laundry.

HUIE: Think how different and how wonderful it will be when we have some bishops, especially women, with children. We have created a job and a role here that's just not family-friendly. I know we have Vi who has an adopted son. But the first women elected tended to be single—widowed, divorced, or never married. Then there were several of you elected who had no children for many reasons. I remember wondering if the Council would ever be a place that was friendly with people who have children.

See, that says that this job is created in such a way that it's real hard on families. That's a judgment on the church in my opinion. We say good words about children but are in a system that is so unfriendly to families, including to spouses.

RADER: In our orientation, I can remember Bishop Ed Boulton telling us that he would take his calendar and put the Council of Bishops meetings, the cabinet meetings, and the college meetings on it. Then he would take his calendar home, and have his spouse and family put all of the dates they needed on that calendar. And the rest belongs to the Area. He did it in that order and held to that. He also put days for himself on there as well. I tend to let everything else come in and then I ask where is the time for Blaine and me to do something, to get the family together, whatever it is. And I think if we could train ourselves to set aside time for our families, I think it would help a lot.

HUIE: One of the many things I respect about Mary Ann is how she has cared for her mother in the last year and half of her life. That is just remarkable to me.

RADER: Going to a new area and being so far away from her mother geographically.

HUIE: She's done it. But Mary Ann has paid a big price personally. You can just hear her struggles.

CRAIG: We are an extraordinary company of women. We're all firsts and many times in our lives we've been *the* first. This is the first time a circle of women bishops has ever sat down and tried to discover where we came from. What do you want to say to the readers of the book about what it is to be in a circle of firsts?

MORRISON: I'd take nothing for the journey.

CHRISTOPHER: And in that same vein, step out on the promises.

SHERER: Have you heard that Barbara Brown Taylor story where she talks about going up in the mountains of Vermont or New Hampshire with a partner and getting stranded at the top? The only way they finally reached safety was by holding on tightly to each other, even when they argued about in which direction they should go. That's the other piece—the holding on tightly to each other as you move through the journey.

CRAIG: I want to say there's no way to account for it except for the intervention of the Divine. There's just no other way to account for it.

CHRISTOPHER: And there's no way to be sustained in it other than through the intervention of the Divine.

HUIE: After I was elected, I was asked many times how I got elected. My standard response was, "It was a miracle." I think it was, and I think it is. I think that every day. It is a miracle—not only in my particular election in 1996 in South Central, but also in that of the whole group of us here, for heaven's sake.

CHRISTOPHER: Last time around, three African American women were elected simultaneously! It was a wonderful intervention of the spirit.

KELLY: In the long run, God reigns no matter what happens. When we plug into your own faith perspectives, we know that we couldn't have made it without our own faith, because there's certainly nothing in any of our backgrounds that made us feel we were destined to be bishops. But when God calls and that call is clear to you, then God also sustains. No matter how much the pain, there's somebody there for you in every situation. And we have been there for one another and will be there for anybody who comes in. And we've been there with the men, too. I find that many of the male bishops talk to us very freely about some things that they might not say to the other bishops.

RADER: I'm struggling with the "first" language because I was not first. I was not first. I was not first ordained in the conference. I was not first DS in a conference. I was not the first elected woman from a conference. I was not first woman in Wisconsin as a bishop. If this is a circle of firsts, I don't experience myself in that way.

KELLY: You used early instead of first before.

RADER: And I think it will be fun someday when a woman follows a woman directly. Does that bring greater possibility of continuity of vision-living stuff?

CRAIG: We've seen that in some local congregations that's been the fact. It's been a lot easier for the woman to follow another woman in terms of continuity. So why wouldn't that be true in conferences? It'll depend on the women, I suppose.

And so the conversation went. What appears is only part of a long day's conversation, in which delights and pains, disappointments and hopes were aired frankly. Some are so recent as to make them not "ripe" for publication. Others implicate persons with whom we work, but there is no desire to embarrass or provoke. This offering is intended to provide a brief glimpse of the connection from our childhood stories to our adult reality as bishops of the Church. These quotes do not sum up anything definitively, but do hint at the reality of what it is like to be a woman in leadership in a role still usually imaged as occupied by a male. Perhaps this tension can best be summarized by the response I often give when people ask me what it is like to be a bishop: "It's as bad as I feared, but ever so much better than I imagined it could be!"

NOTE

1. This refers to a statement issued by fifteen bishops at the 1996 General Conference expressing pain over proscriptions in the United Methodist Discipline against the ordination of gay and lesbian persons.

AFTERWORD

When I agreed to put together a book that contained the stories of the thirteen living women bishops, I didn't have a clue about how to begin. Now that I have put it together, I wonder at my audacity. I hope the readers find something of value here, for these are stories of valuable women.

I have been stirred in my soul over and over as I have read the stories. Little girls playing with their dads, learning to play an instrument, reading encyclopedias for entertainment. Teenage girls thinking they are not very attractive, discovering languages other than their own, reading theology, taking posts of leadership. Young women in college, marching in demonstrations, challenging the status quo, making decisions about the investment of their lives. Maturing women, hearing and answering a call against the advice and beyond the comprehension of many, and resisted by others. New pastors facing hostility from some and delighted welcome from others.

Now we are bishops, both middle-aged and claiming senior citizen status, both serving and retired. We have aged—I think gracefully in most cases. Each of us would be quick to say we feel blessed and privileged to be bishops of The United Methodist Church. And each of us quickly confesses the role is bigger and more demanding than anyone can know until the mantle is put on one's shoulders.

Marjorie Matthews was lonely in the Council of Bishops for four years, the only woman bishop there. She spoke of the isolation she felt at mealtimes and in social times. She was single and female. The Council really didn't know what to do with this diminutive powerhouse of a woman. She had to push against so much as a "first" that she chose not to push hard at the Council, and simply endured her isolation.

In 1984, when Leontine and I joined Marjorie, she was very excited. She reached out to us, and we held one another close, literally and in our hearts and prayers. Sadly, Marjorie lost her battle with cancer in 1985. Leontine and I missed her, but we continued to hold onto each other and to encourage each other to make sure the Council knew we were there.

But we were glad, when Sharon Brown Christopher and Susan Murch Morrison showed up for the fall meeting of the Council in 1988. After the opening dinner, we gathered in a circle and said, "Did you just feel the earth move?" Then we giggled like little girls, so great was our delight. Four in the room and Marjorie in the Cloud of Witnesses! We were becoming a critical mass. You could not miss noticing us in the Council. We began to find our voices even more and move into leadership roles in the Council. It was delightful to think of five episcopal Areas under the leadership of women.

And the joy just kept coming. The year 1992 brought Mary Ann Swenson, Ann Sherer, and Sharon Rader into the circle. We had to have a larger table for our annual night out during Council meetings! The sense of empowerment that accompanied our growing numbers was life giving. We began to move even further into the ranks of leadership in the Council. We chaired standing committees, made reports, and represented the Council here and there. And we kept on leading our Areas effectively and to the delight of those with whom we labored. It was no longer such a surprise to see us as bishops, and there was a kind of settling into the reality that the Council of Bishops is a mixed company now. In fact, it became so comfortable that it was hard to remember there was a "before Marjorie" time in some people's minds. Still, the jokes about "caucusing" when we stood together in the hall or sat at the same table indicated a continuing puzzlement about us.

In 1995, two historic elections took place in the Council. Sharon Rader was elected as Secretary of the Council, to begin her work in 1996. It was the first time a woman was an officer of the Council. And I was elected to prepare and deliver the episcopal address to the General Conference of 1996.

The jurisdictional conferences of 1996 brought more sisters to the table: Janice Huie, Susan Hassinger, and Charlene Kammerer. At last, all five jurisdictions had elected at least one woman! We moved into many roles of leadership in the Council and found ourselves beginning to be diverse. It is wonderful when an emerging constituency, such as women in the Council, has such strength in numbers that its members do not have to pretend to think alike! What freedom to become who we really are! Truth be known, we do share many convictions, but not in lockstep. I don't think we ever did, but the freedom to admit that is always greater when the numbers increase.

Then in 2000 came the wonderful breakthrough—three women of color were elected: Linda Lee, Beverly Shamana, and Violet Fisher. I thought Leontine would float away with delight, as would all of us. One of our common commitments is to inclusiveness in every possible way, and we hungered for more women of color in our midst. They have enriched us already and will become significant leaders in the Council, as they already are in their Areas.

In 2002, a vision not seen, and seldom dreamed, appeared before the Council of Bishops when Sharon Brown Christopher became President of the Council, joining Sharon Rader, Secretary, at the officer's table. There would now be two women leading the Council. It was a magnificent moment and worthy of note and celebration. Small wonder the women broke out into song, "Oh, we're steppin' out, steppin' out on the promises"!

But when one reads the record of the 2003 "Conversation in Nashville," it is impossible to ignore the continuing pain and the high cost being paid. Being a member of the episcopacy is hard work, as is being a leader in this culture! There is a kind of readiness to rebel against or denigrate leaders. As women leaders, we seem even more vulnerable to harsh treatment, attempts to make light of our convictions, and outright challenges. We are not the only bishops who have known the sting of charges, incredibly angry mail, people shouting at us, and people leaving because of us (so they say). But we seem to have experienced much of that with a level of intensity and a kind of steady barrage that has something to do with being seen as more vulnerable because of our gender. Well, folks are wrong! We are not more vulnerable, though we may be targets more often. We are strong and faithful and able. And we aren't going away!

I believe we have made a difference in the Council of Bishops, in the areas we have served, and in The United Methodist Church in general. I believe that the gifts of people who have been seen as "different" are more easily seen now because we are more easily seen. I believe that patterns of governance and decision-making are shifting because women tend to be conciliar and consultative and seek consensus. It is a fact of our shaping. Recent research has shown a distinct difference between how men and women react when faced with conflict. Men tend to hunker down or flee, while women gravitate toward other women, seeking to build community. That difference is making its mark through the behavior patterns of women bishops.

We have lived through two decades of significant history in United Methodism in terms of the inclusion of women in the episcopacy. During those same years, the number of women clergy has grown exponentially, from less than two hundred in 1980 to more than seventy-eight hundred in 2000. There are those who express concern about the "feminization" of the clergy. I don't think that is likely, but it is likely that the clergy will continue to be a shared vocation, all to the church's benefit. Any of us who has served on a staff with men can testify to the enhancement of the clergy leadership in such a situation (providing the male of the team is not so threatened as to undermine the contributions of his female colleague). The balance of voice and style, the choice of man or woman for counseling, marriages, funerals, and other privileges of the clergy all open wider the door of mutual ministry between laity and clergy. If women "take over" or become the majority, it will not be in the lifetime of many who are reading these words. And if that is the outcome in the long run, will God not be able still to use the Church as the divine sign in the world?

Listening to these stories, reading them over and over, watching for the places where we have similar backgrounds, and enjoying where someone is entirely unique, is a treasure I shall enjoy for the rest of my life. Likewise, I hope somewhere in this book is a word of encouragement for some young woman, a word of direction for a mentor, a word of hope for a mother, a word of assurance for a father. I hope people find themselves in these stories and through them hear God's word for their own lives—not necessarily for ordained ministry, but for the particular ministry for which their lives and gifts are suited. I hope people find the young faces of now-powerful women in these stories, and enjoy their humanity because they know something of the young years that so often remain hidden.

Each of these stories has many more chapters to reveal. My last hope is that the stories of the ministry of these women before their election as Bishops will be collected. What were the joys and the struggles that wove those tapestries? There will be more women elected to this office in the future. But this company of fourteen— never forget Marjorie—is surely the mothering generation. We span the decades of women's emergence into the ranks of clergy, and signal the future in a unique way.

ELECTION DATES AND AREAS SERVED

Marjorie Matthews, 1980, Wisconsin Area, 1980–1984

Leontine Turpeau Current Kelly, 1984, San Francisco Area, 1984–1988, retired

Judith Craig, 1984, Michigan Area 1984–1992, Ohio West Area, 1992–2000, retired

Susan Murch Morrison, 1988, Eastern Pennsylvania Area, 1988–1996, Albany Area, 1996–

Sharon Brown Christopher, 1988, Wisconsin Area, etc

Ann Brookshire Sherer, 1992, Missouri Area, 1992–

Sharon Zimmerman Rader, 1992, Wisconsin Area, 1992–

Mary Ann Swenson, 1992, Denver Area, 1992–2000, Los Angeles Area, 2000–

Susan Wolfe Hassinger, 1996, Boston Area, 1996–

Charlene Payne Kammerer, 1996, Charlotte Area, 1996–

Janice Riggle Huie, 1996, Arkansas Area, 1996–

Beverly Shamana, 2000, San Francisco Area, 2000–

Violet Fisher, 2000, New York West Area, 2000–

Linda Lee, 2000, Michigan Area, 2000–